PRODUKTE REFLEXIVEN ENTWERFENS
PRODUCTS OF REFLEXIVE DESIGN

PRODUKTE REFLEXIVEN ENTWERFENS
PRODUCTS OF REFLEXIVE DESIGN

Margitta Buchert (ed.)

a_ku jovis

PREFACE

Margitta Buchert

Research-related design and design-related research in architecture, urban design and land-scape architecture support, shape and generate products of a specific figuration and quality. How can the formation, effect and significance of products of reflexive design be characterised? In what contexts and interplays are they produced? Which (trans)disciplinary impulses, as well as rational and creative hybrids have an effect on the manifestations of design and research? What dimensions of high-quality design of the living environment come to the fore and become perceptible, and what impulses are gained for future-ori-entated action and new insights? Based on examples, the contributions in this book explore in a variety of ways diverse, overlapping modes of knowledge and how they are generated in design and research projects, and relates them to reflexive design.

The contributions go back to the DARA Symposium, which was held on 21–23 April 2022. Thanks goes to all the authors for their interest, commitment and friendly cooperation. Cordial thanks to Julius Krüger for the competent design support, as well as for the layout, typesetting and clarification of image rights. Many thanks to Valerie Hoberg for various trans-lations of texts and the precise proofreading of the endnotes. A special thankyou to Lynne Kolar-Thompson for the translations into English and to Tim Vogel and Susanne Rösler at jovis Verlag for the reliable and attentive support for the publication. Finally, thanks to the Faculty of Architecture and Landscape and Leibniz University Hanover for supporting the publication.

VORWORT

Margitta Buchert

Forschendes Entwerfen und entwerfendes Forschen in Architektur, Städtebau und Landschaftsarchitektur befördern, strukturieren und generieren Produkte spezifischer Figuration und Qualität. Wie können Formation, Wirkung und Bedeutung von Produkten Reflexiven Entwerfens charakterisiert werden? In welchen Kontexten und Wechselspielen werden sie hervorgebracht? Welche (trans-)disziplinären Impulse und rational-kreativen Kreuzungen wirken in die Manifestationen des Entwerfens und Forschens ein? Welche Dimensionen qualitätsvoller Gestaltung des Lebensumfelds treten hervor und werden wahrnehmbar, und welche Impulse für zukunftsweisendes Handeln und neue Erkenntnis werden befördert? Die Beiträge dieses Buches loten anhand von Beispielen in vielfältiger Form diverse, ineinander übergehende Modi des Wissens und seiner Hervorbringung im entwurflichen und forschenden Tun erkenntnisreich aus und setzen sie in Relation zum Reflexiven Entwerfen.

Die Beiträge gehen zurück auf das DARA-Symposium, das vom 21. bis 23. April 2022 stattfand. Allen Autor:innen sei für ihr Interesse, ihr Engagement sowie die freundliche Kooperation gedankt. Für die kompetente Unterstützung der Gestaltung sowie für Layout, Satz und Bildrechteklärung geht ein herzlicher Dank an Julius Krüger. Valerie Hoberg sei vielmals gedankt für verschiedene Übersetzungen von Texten und das präzise Korrektorat der Endnoten. Besonderer Dank gilt Lynne Kolar-Thompson für die Übersetzungen ins Englische sowie Tim Vogel und Susanne Rösler vom jovis Verlag für die bewährte und zuvorkommende Begleitung der Publikation. Schließlich geht ein Dank an die Fakultät für Architektur und Landschaft und die Leibniz Universität Hannover für die Unterstützung der Veröffentlichung.

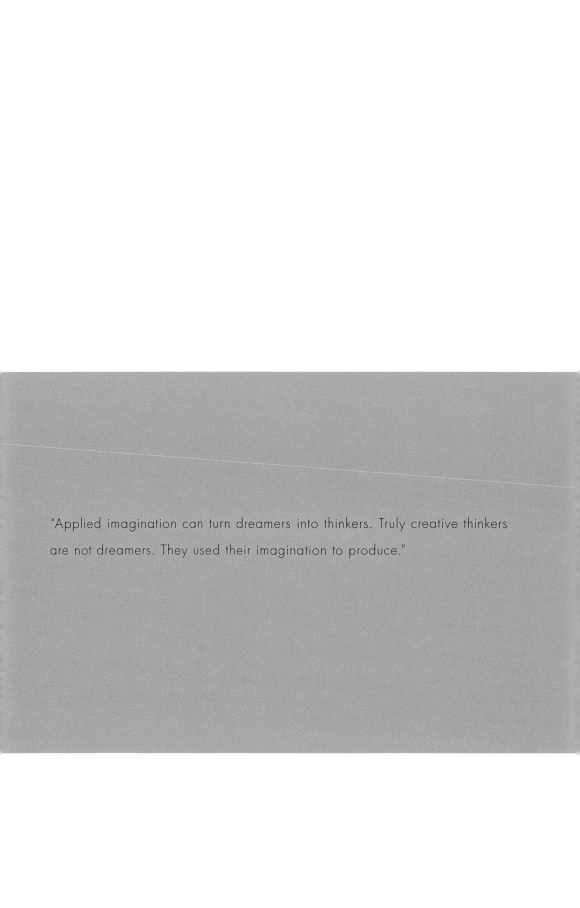

"Applied imagination can turn dreamers into thinkers. Truly creative thinkers are not dreamers. They used their imagination to produce."

„Angewandte Vorstellungskraft kann aus Träumenden Denkende machen. Wirklich kreative Denkende sind keine Träumende. Sie haben ihre Vorstellungskraft in die Tat umgesetzt."

Alex F. Osborn

PRODUCTS AND THE PROJECTIVE

Margitta Buchert

There is a multifaceted spectrum of answers and a plurality of perspectives to the question of products of reflexive design. The intellectual and praxeological roots of such questions are deep and disparate. The following highlights various features in order to characterise this heterogeneity more comprehensively. They illuminate an epistemological interest in the varieties of poietic production of knowledge in the context of reflexive design, thematising possible conventions and modifications of spatial and architectural design cultures and sounding out various creative and projective standpoints, orientations, actions and knowledge practices. This shows the diagnostic, prognostic and stimulating properties of reflexivity. Following that, combinations and integration levels are detailed that are viewed as specific for the open and dynamic field of the practice and knowledge of design in architecture, urban design and landscape architecture and which, in connection with reflexivity, can contribute to the enrichment and evocation of future research-related design and design-related research.

PRODUKTE UND DAS PROJEKTIVE

Margitta Buchert

Auf die Frage nach Produkten Reflexiven Entwerfens gibt es ein facettenreiches Spektrum von Antworten und eine Pluralität von Perspektiven. Die intellektuellen und praxeologischen Wurzeln solcher Fragen sind tief und disparat. Im Folgenden werden einige Eigenschaften herausgehoben, um diese Heterogenität übergreifender zu charakterisieren. Sie beleuchten ein epistemologisches Interesse an den Varietäten der poietischen Produktion von Wissen im Zusammenhang Reflexiven Entwerfens ebenso wie die Thematisierung möglicher Konventionen und Modifikationen räumlicher und architektonischer Entwurfskulturen sowie die Auslotung verschiedener kreativer und projektiver Haltungen, Ausrichtungen, Aktionen und Wissenspraktiken. Reflexivität scheint dabei in ihren diagnostischen, prognostischen und stimulierenden Eigenschaften auf. Abschließend werden Kombinationen und Integrationsebenen aufgezeigt, die als spezifisch für das offene und dynamische Praxis- und Erkenntnisfeld des Entwerfens in Architektur, Städtebau und Landschaftsarchitektur gesehen werden und, mit Reflexivität verbunden, zur Bereicherung und Evokation zukünftigen forschenden Entwerfens und entwerfenden Forschens beitragen können.

PRODUCTS | ARTEFACTS | MANIFESTATIONS   Even if it is to be fundamentally assumed that the meaning of a word lies in its use, sounding out its theoretical leeway at the peripheries and by comparison can show some of its dimensions that drive, provoke and enable its thematisation.[1] All too often, the term 'product' is used to describe instrumental and economised things in the living environment of people, industrialised to a high degree and subjected to economic considerations. Released from such clichés, a product emerges initially as something produced, as a result and outcome, and usually refers to manmade things, structures and systems. With regard to architecture, urban design and landscape architecture, this is associated with buildings and spatial ensembles, as well as with a process of designing as a procedure that contains and can produce knowledge.[2] Practices that interact with media and materials in this process come into play as approaches. And finally, intentions are associated with this that initiate the approach and its manifold contexts. This allows for ideal, immaterial and material products. If the term artefact is used instead of product, the complexity is somewhat reduced. The material production comes to the fore. The human processing or modification is thereby addressed, which proves to be different from a 'natural' object or system.[3] Artefact as a term also often refers to historically passed down, material things of an artificial character, which

PRODUKTE I ARTEFAKTE I MANIFESTATIONEN Wenngleich grundlegend davon auszugehen ist, dass die Bedeutung eines Wortes in seinem Gebrauch liegt, kann das Ausloten seines theoretischen Spielraums an den Rändern und durch Vergleich schon einige der Dimensionen aufzeigen, die seine Thematisierung antreibt, provoziert und ermöglicht.[1] Allzu oft werden mit dem Begriff Produkt instrumentelle und ökonomisierte Dinge im Lebensumfeld des Menschen beschrieben, in hohem Maße industrialisiert und wirtschaftlichen Erwägungen unterworfen. Gelöst von solchen Klischees erweist sich ein Produkt zunächst als etwas Hergestelltes, als Resultat und Ergebnis, und bezieht sich auf meist menschengemachte Dinge, Strukturen und Systeme. Im Blick auf Architektur, Städtebau und Landschaftsarchitektur verbinden sich damit die Bauten und räumlichen Ensembles sowie ein Prozess des Entwerfens als Vorgang, der Wissen enthält und Wissen produzieren kann.[2] Es spielen die Praktiken als Vorgehensweisen hinein, die in diesem Prozess mit Medien und Materialien zusammenwirken. Und schließlich sind Intentionen damit verbunden, die das Vorgehen initiieren sowie deren vielfältige Kontexte. Somit sind ideelle, immaterielle ebenso wie materielle Produkte möglich. Tritt der Begriff Artefakt an die Stelle von Produkt, wird die Komplexität etwas reduziert. Die materielle Hervorbringung rückt in den Vordergrund. Die menschliche Bearbeitung oder Modifikation wird damit gefasst, die sich als unterschieden von einem ‚natürlichen' Objekt oder System erweist.[3] Der Begriff Artefakt bezieht sich vielfach auch auf historisch überlieferte, materielle Dinge artifiziellen Charakters, die auf Fremdeinwirkung zurückgehen und meist durch menschliche Bearbeitung geprägt wurden.[4]

go back to outside influences and have usually been shaped by human modification.[4] A further notional analogy proves to be revealing for design. In the context of design, one can speak of manifestations, in association with the act, the process and the fact of manifesting something. Manifestations can also include representations of abstract qualities.[5] This harbours the potential to go beyond the nature of artefact complexes, for example models, sketches, diagrams, notations and buildings, as material objects.[6] Uncovering previously hidden, invisible and unknown things and phenomena of all kinds and making them perceptible, and the revelation of connections through a perceptible expression, can thereby be shown and illuminated in a more differentiated manner. If notions of products are ultimately associated with notions of productivity, the manifoldness of their facets and their dynamic dimensions come to the fore. Even so, the notion of products appears to contain permanence and therefore an indication of a stabilised condition or interim condition. Possibilities and limits of knowledge and insight production in research also contain comparable products, for example, the research design as a structure, some individual content frameworks as guiding ideas, as well as conceptual and interpretational systematics and ideal and material exemplifications.

Für das Entwerfen aufschlussreich erweist sich eine weitere begriffliche Analogie. Im Entwurfszusammenhang kann von Manifestationen gesprochen werden, verbunden mit dem Akt, dem Prozess und der Instanz, etwas zu manifestieren. Manifestationen können zudem Repräsentationen abstrakter Qualitäten enthalten.[5] Dabei besteht das Potenzial, über die Eigenschaft von Artefaktkomplexen beispielsweise von Modellen, Skizzen, Diagrammen, Notationen und Bauten als dinglichen Objekten noch hinauszugelangen.[6] Das Wahrnehmbarwerden und das Sichzeigen von zuvor verborgenen, unsichtbaren, unbekannten Dingen und Phänomenen aller Art und das Offenbarwerden von Zusammenhängen in einem wahrnehmbaren Ausdruck können damit differenzierter aufgedeckt und beleuchtet werden. Werden Vorstellungen zu Produkten schließlich mit Vorstellungen von Produktivität verknüpft, treten die Mannigfaltigkeit der Facetten und die dynamischen Dimensionen hervor. Dennoch scheint im Begriff der Produkte gerade die Permanenz enthalten zu sein und damit der Hinweis auf einen stabilisierten Zustand oder Zwischenzustand. Möglichkeiten und Grenzen der Wissens- und Erkenntnisproduktion im Forschen enthalten ebenfalls vergleichbare Produkte wie das Forschungsdesign als Struktur, einzelne inhaltliche Rahmungen als Leitideen sowie konzeptuelle und interpretatorische Systematiken und ideelle und materielle Exemplifikationen.

R E F L E X I V I T Y   However, which products can be identified for reflexive design? On what basis and how do they become possible? Products of reflexive design and the network of elements they consist of are like intellectual products, not creations out of nothing. Instead, they are the result of inventive actions and production dependent on external conditions in the context of sociocultural, technical and material production requirements and contexts. The variety of all simultaneous influences is reduced through framing. Orientations then refer to key themes of the basic concept, the direction of the work and adaptation to the status of the specific questions and tasks, as well as to the aims of the project. Restrictive limitation, ascribing complexity to the framing, limiting and reducing variety can lead to models, even if this does not exclude the existence of other options. In design as well as in research, selective framing can act as primary generators.[7] The order in which knowledge components ultimately show themselves depends on the situational constitution and evaluation. After initial vagueness, greater precision and finetuning can be achieved.[8] In this context, reflexive design positions itself with the specific focus of researching knowledge of design for spatial issues by addressing the close relations between design and research and the relevance of reflexivity and reflection as epistemic and creative generators within the context of theory and practice. The reflexive, in the sense of a questioning, distancing attitude and approach, then appears as an important source of perception and understanding, as a specific interaction of conception and production as much as of insight and cognitive content. Reflexive practice offers a forum for trying out, questioning and the production of knowledge.[9] Here we find interfaces with the artistic.[10] This can be associated in the research process, or as a generative action in the basic design concept across projects, with the finding and uncovering of traces of thoughts and actions in other areas of knowledge, such as art, design, literature, philosophy or natural and social sciences, as well as overlapping with these. It can be associated with activities and resonances in which knowledge and ability develop from travelling, drawing, reading books or artistic experimentation, in particular in connection with the questioning of standards and different kinds of experiences. It is about positionings and orientations that all invite designers and researchers to become aware of, experience, articulate, create and balance products from different alternative perspectives.

REFLEXIVITÄT   Doch welche Produkte können für das Reflexive Entwerfen identifiziert werden? Von wo aus und wie werden sie möglich? Produkte Reflexiven Entwerfens und das Netzwerk der Elemente, woraus sie bestehen, sind ebenso wie geistige Produkte nicht Schöpfungen aus dem Nichts. Vielmehr zeigen sie sich als Ergebnis eines von äußeren Bedingungen abhängigen erfinderischen Machens und Hervorbringens im Kontext soziokultureller, technischer und materieller Produktionsbedingungen und -kontexte. Mit Rahmungen wird die Vielfalt aller gleichzeitigen Einflüsse ausgeblendet. Orientierungen beziehen sich dann auf Schlüsselthemen der Grundkonzeption, die Ausrichtung des Schaffens wie auch auf die Anpassung an die Situiertheit der spezifischen Fragen- und Aufgabenstellung sowie die Ziele des Projekts. Die restriktive Begrenzung, das Zurückführen der Komplexität auf die Rahmung, die Beschränkung und Reduktion der Vielfalt können zu Modellen führen, auch wenn dadurch das Vorhandensein anderer Optionen nicht ausgeschlossen wird. Im Entwerfen wie auch im Forschen können selektive Rahmungen als Primärgeneratoren wirken.[7] Nach welchen Ordnungen Wissensanteile sich letztlich zeigen, hängt von ihrer situativen Konstitution und Auswertung ab. Von anfänglicher Vagheit kann dabei zu größerer Präzision und Verfeinerung gelangt werden.[8] In diesem Zusammenhang verortet sich das Reflexive Entwerfen mit dem spezifischen Fokus, das Wissen des Entwerfens für räumliche Fragestellungen über die Thematisierung der dichten Relationen von Entwerfen und Forschen und die Relevanz von Reflexivität und Reflexion als epistemische und kreative Generatoren aus dem Theorie- und Praxiskontext heraus zu erforschen. Das Reflexive im Sinne einer befragenden, distanznehmenden Haltung und Ausrichtung erscheint dann als wichtige Quelle der Wahrnehmung und des Verstehens, als eine spezifische Weise der Wechselwirkung von Konzeption und Produktion ebenso wie der Erkenntnis und des kognitiven Inhalts. Die reflexive Praxis offeriert einen Ort der Erprobung, Infragestellung und Produktion von Wissen.[9] Hierin finden sich Schnittstellen zum Künstlerischen.[10] Dies kann im Forschungsprozess oder auch als generative Aktion in der projektübergreifenden Grundkonzeption zum Entwerfen mit dem Auffinden und Aufdecken von Spuren des Denkens und Schaffens in anderen Wissensbereichen verbunden sein, beispielsweise Kunst, Design, Literatur, Philosophie oder Natur- und Sozialwissenschaften, sowie der Überlagerung mit diesen. Sie kann mit Aktivitäten und Resonanzen verbunden sein, bei denen Erkenntnis und Können aus dem Reisen, Zeichnen, Bücherlesen oder aus künstlerischem Experimentieren erwachsen, insbesondere in Verknüpfung mit der Hinterfragung von Standards und Erfahrungen unterschiedlicher Art. Schließlich kann die Reflexivität auch dezidiert in spekulativer Ausrichtung entfaltet werden. Es handelt sich um Positionierungen und Orientierungen, die allesamt Entwerfende und Forschende dazu einladen, Produkte aus unterschiedlichen alternativen Perspektiven wahrzunehmen, zu erfahren, zu artikulieren, zu kreieren und zu balancieren.

INVENTION I REPETITION AND VARIATION   It is the products of design and research, which with all the incompleteness of knowledge and even of the ability to understand – detached from the conditions and restrictions of production – that can reveal, show and make visible what is specific about it, whether it is as built architectures, urban and landscape spaces, as imaginative ideals, models, concepts and contexts, or as representations and articulations in the sense of results of a process, a future production or as a fiction.[11] Like every cultural production, these products develop in the context of traditions, even if they break with it. References to one's own ideas and projects as well as to those of other designers and other eras are associated with this. With different references, insights can be gained through analogical thinking and actions, from similarity and comparison.[12] Knowledge from experience and knowledge from education come together. The long history and influence of type concepts and typologies, with all their changes and modifications, can act as an example of this. They show how identifications of a series of similar products develop in groupings as the primary mode of building culture transmission. Difference and repetition constantly intertwine in this.[13] Repetition then does not signify mere adoption, re-interpretation or reminding but rather a creative act that generates a difference.[14] It can also be intensified and lead to change, extension, invention.[15] This is interwoven with experiences one can gain and experiences that one has and which one could also conceive as products in the context of design.[16] This shows the dual character of process and product.[17] Experiences form action and perception dispositions. For reflexive processes in relation to practice, sensitisation for one's own repertoire as well as for media and language is of high relevance.[18] Through embodied practices, imparted knowledge and abilities take effect between repetition and variation in doing and producing.[19] All these aspects flow into the iterative productive process and into the restructuring of the available knowledge, even if this leads to a product to be understood as highly innovative and the knowledge itself can only be partially linguistically expressed.

INVENTION I REPETITION UND VARIATION   Es sind die Produkte des Entwerfens und Forschens, die bei aller Unvollkommenheit des Wissens und selbst des Verstehenkönnens – gelöst von den Konditionen und Beschränkungen der Herstellung – das Spezifische daran enthüllen, zeigen und sichtbar machen können, sei es als gebaute Architekturen, Stadt- und Landschaftsräume, als imaginative Ideale, Vorbilder, Konzepte und Kontexte oder als Darstellungen und Artikulationen im Sinne von Resultaten eines Prozesses, einer zukünftigen Herstellung oder als Fiktion.[11] Wie jede kulturelle Produktion entstehen diese Produkte im Kontext von Traditionen, selbst dann, wenn damit gebrochen wird. Referenzen zu eigenen Ideen und Projekten wie zu denen anderer Entwerfender und anderer Zeiten sind damit verbunden. In unterschiedlichen Bezugnahmen kann dabei über analogisches Denken und Handeln Erkenntnis aus Ähnlichkeit und Abgleichung entstehen.[12] Erfahrungswissen und Bildungswissen treffen zusammen. Die lange Geschichte und Wirkmacht von Typuskonzepten und Typologien mit allen Umbrüchen und Modifikationen können dafür als Beispiel stehen. Sie zeigen, wie Identifikationen einer Serie ähnlicher Produkte in Gruppierungen als primärer Modus baukultureller Übertragung entstehen. Differenz und Wiederholung sind darin immer wieder verschränkt.[13] Wiederholung wirkt dann nicht als bloße Übernahme, Re-Interpretation oder Erinnerung, vielmehr als schöpferischer Akt, der Differenz erzeugt.[14] Diese kann zudem zugespitzt werden und zu Veränderung, Erweiterung, Invention führen.[15] Darin verwoben sind Erfahrungen, die man machen kann, und Erfahrungen, die man hat, und die man auch als Produkte im Kontext des Entwerfens bezeichnen könnte.[16] Hier zeigt sich der Doppelcharakter von Prozess und Produkt.[17] Erfahrungen bilden Handlungs- und Wahrnehmungsdispositionen. Für reflexive Prozesse im Praxisbezug sind dabei die Sensibilisierungen für das eigene Repertoire sowie für Medien und Sprache von hoher Relevanz.[18] Durch die verkörperten Praktiken wirken dann zwischen Repetition und Variation im Machen und Herstellen vermitteltes Wissen und Können.[19] Alle diese Aspekte spielen in den iterativen produktiven Prozess und in die Umbildung des vorhandenen Wissens hinein, selbst wenn dieser zu einem als hochgradig innovativ zu verstehenden Produkt führt und das Wissen selbst nur partiell sprachlich erfasst werden kann.

COMPOSITION I SYNTHESES   Products are also to be understood as sediments of ideas and processes by which they have been found. In the design of architecture, urban design and landscape architecture, this can be the compilation, arrangement and structure in a composition that cannot be reduced to types. It is the combinational nature of specifications that brings forth the product in a creative process through the coupling of biological and external resources as organisational modes in design and in research.[20] New and other arrangements that are created through the concentration and shifting of intensities can then also be understood as products of reflexive design, whereby the sharpening of attention and unpredictable circumstances and events have an effect, such as diagnostic and prognostic instinct, coincidences or intuitive leaps.[21] The composition thereby acquires a structure that was not found as such but is rather 'built into a world'.[22] Here one can also find correlations with the artistic.[23] The special capabilities for spatial design that are also adapted for design-related research can be seen in relation to the integration of a wide variety of elements and disciplines, and in the ability to link and combine a range of factors in the composition and to convey them in drawn, modelled or built materialised results.[24] In this way, innovative syntheses arise. They are promoted and strengthened through reflexivity, which includes imagination as a productive asset that is neither purely sensual nor purely intellectual.[25] The unfolding of research of sufficient complexity that corresponds to contemporary conditions, which integrates the levels of practical action, imagination and aesthetics, finds different kinds of generative impulses in this.

KOMPOSITION I SYNTHESEN   Produkte sind auch zu verstehen als Sedimente von Ideen und Prozessen, mit denen zu ihnen gefunden wurde. Im Entwerfen von Architektur, Städtebau und Landschaftsarchitektur kann dies die nicht auf Typen zu reduzierende Zusammenstellung, Anordnung und Gestaltung in der Komposition sein. Es ist die kombinatorische Natur von Setzungen, die durch die Kopplung biologischer und externer Ressourcen als Organisationsmodi im Entwerfen und im Forschen das Produkt schöpferisch hervorbringen.[20] Neue und andere Ordnungen, die entstehen durch Verdichtung und Verschiebung von Intensitäten, können dann auch als Produkte Reflexiven Entwerfens verstanden werden, wobei die Aufmerksamkeitsschärfung und unwägbare Gegebenheiten und Ereignisse hineinwirken, beispielsweise diagnostischer und prognostischer Spürsinn, Zufälle und oder intuitive Sprünge.[21] Die Komposition erhält damit ein Gefüge, das so nicht vorgefunden wurde, vielmehr ‚in eine Welt eingebaut wird'.[22] Auch hierin finden sich Korrespondenzen zum Künstlerischen.[23] Die besonderen Fähigkeiten für das räumliche Entwerfen, die auch für das entwerfende Forschen adaptiert werden, können im Vermögen der Integration der verschiedensten Elemente und Disziplinen gesehen werden und in der Kompetenz, vielfältige Faktoren in der Komposition zu verschränken, zu kombinieren und in zeichnerisch, modelliert oder gebaut materialisierten Resultaten zu vermitteln.[24] So entstehen neuschöpfende Synthesen. Sie werden gefördert und bestärkt durch Reflexivität, die Imagination als produktives, weder rein sinnliches noch rein intellektuelles Vermögen einschließt.[25] Die Entfaltung einer den zeitgenössischen Konditionen entsprechenden komplexitätsadäquaten Forschung, die Ebenen des praktischen Handelns, der Imagination und der Ästhetik integriert, findet darin generative Impulse unterschiedlicher Art.

SPACES OF KNOWLEDGE I TYPES OF TYPES I FUTURE DESIGNS
This also applies to the contributions in this book. They are involved in these complexes of questions and discussions by showing different perspectives on the phenomena through different, even unconventional and undogmatic stances. They are in some cases probing and in some cases very precise approaches that are based on the pragmatic interest in concretion. They were arranged here in groups as spaces of knowledge, types of types and future designs, which describe various dimensions of possible answers to the question of products of reflexive design. SPACES OF KNOWLEDGE can be characterised as those areas that have an effect on the more concrete design and research actions and are also stabilised, modified and extended within them. Various associated dimensions and values of the human experience of the habitat and of personal knowledge constitution, as well as tangible and analogous connections with other artistic and cultural ways of thinking and acting, are sounded out. TYPES OF TYPES indicate research and design dimensions that form elementary and evocative components of architectural, urban design and landscape architecture and assign their respective structures to a historically developed and cultur- ally shaped common ground and to specific knowledge practices of the discipline, even if these are rethought in a new and different way. In FUTURE DESIGNS, fundamental spec- ulative characteristics come together that can be viewed as pragmatic, critical and ideal contributions to conditions and tasks of contemporary design in architecture, urban design and landscape architecture and emphasise the horizon of thinking and researching with social, cultural and ethical implications. With the focus and stance of reflexive design, the sensibilities that bring forth knowledge and abilities in the mentioned fields are sharpened stimulating a wide variety of different products through change and innovation in design.

WISSENSRÄUME I TYPEN VON TYPEN I ZUKUNFTSENTWÜRFE
Dies trifft auch für die Beiträge in diesem Buch zu. Sie beteiligen sich an diesen Fragen-
komplexen und Diskussionen, indem sie verschiedene Perspektiven zu dem Phänomen-
bereich durch unterschiedliche, auch unkonventionelle und undogmatische Positionen
aufzeigen. Es sind teils tastende und teils sehr präzise Annäherungen, die auf dem pragmatischen Interesse an der Konkretion beruhen. Sie wurden hier in Feldern als Wissensräume,
Typen von Typen und Zukunftsentwürfe angeordnet, die unterschiedliche Dimensionen
möglicher Antworten auf die Frage nach Produkten Reflexiven Entwerfens umschreiben.
WISSENSRÄUME können als jene Felder charakterisiert werden, die in die konkreteren
Entwurfs- und Forschungshandlungen hineinwirken und auch in ihnen stabilisiert, modifiziert und erweitert werden. Verschiedene miteinander verbundene Dimensionen und
Wertigkeiten menschlicher Erfahrung des Habitats und der persönlichen Wissenskons-
titution wie auch konkrete und analogische Verbindungen mit anderen künstlerischen
und kulturellen Denkformen und Handlungsweisen werden ausgelotet. TYPEN VON TYPEN
verweisen auf Forschungs- und Entwurfsdimensionen, die elementare und evokative Komponenten architektonischer, städtebaulicher und landschaftsarchitektonischer Entwürfe
bilden und deren jeweilige Anordnungen auf einen historisch gewachsenen und kulturell
geprägten Common Ground und auf spezifische Wissenspraktiken der Disziplin verweisen,
auch wenn diese neu und anders gedacht werden. In ZUKUNFTSENTWÜRFEN verdichten
sich grundlegende spekulative Charakteristiken, die als pragmatische, kritische und ideelle Beiträge zu Konditionen und zu Aufgaben gegenwärtigen Entwerfens in Architektur,
Städtebau und Landschaftsarchitektur gesehen werden können und den Horizont des
Denkens und Forschens mit sozialen, kulturellen und ethischen Implikationen betonen.
Mit dem Fokus und der Haltung des Reflexiven Entwerfens schärfen sich in den benannten
Feldern die Sensibilitäten, die Wissen und Können hervorbringen und durch Verände-
rung und Innovation im Entwerfen eine breite Varietät verschiedener Produkte anregen.

POWER OF THE PROJECTIVE   All the contributions show, with sometimes divergent stances, that products are not to be understood merely as instrumental-material conditions and objects of human action. Nor are products of reflexive design to be seen only in realised buildings and spatial ensembles. They comprise basic attitudes, ideas, intentions, plans, purposes, attempts and various types of media and representations. Here, fields of action refer to the past, present and future and appear in retrospective analyses as much as in attempts from the outset that can also be associated with a utopian impulse.[26] The anticipatory scope ranges from the linking of tradition and breaks with tradition, to direct involvement in the present through perception and action, to a speculative foresight with tangible design and research proposals regarding what might be. An intertwining of multidimensional forms of knowledge is associated with this, with particular emphasis on knowledge generated through performative action and relating to the creation of new conceptual, design and planning competences. In connection with reflexivity and due to the power of the projective, the potential of reflexive design for the refinement of design-related research then emerges as a tool with which different kinds of products can be brought forth, which open up further research questions, as well as discourses and designs as 'concretisations of possibilities' of the future.[27]

KRAFT DES PROJEKTIVEN   Alle Beiträge zeigen in teils auch divergie-renden Positionen, dass Produkte nicht lediglich als instrumentell-materielle Bedingungen und Gegenstände menschlichen Handelns zu verstehen sind. Produkte Reflexiven Entwerfens sind ebenso wenig nur in den realisierten Bauten und räumlichen Ensembles zu sehen. Sie schließen Grundhaltungen, Ideen, Absichten, Pläne, Vorhaben, Versuche und verschiedene Arten von Instrumenten, Medien und Darbietungen ein. Aktionsbereiche sind dabei bezogen auf Vergangenheit, Gegenwart und Zukunft und zeigen sich im rückblickenden Analysieren ebenso wie in Versuchen im Vorhinein, die zudem mit einem utopischen Impuls verbun-den sein können.[26] Die antizipatorische Reichweite spannt sich von der Verknüpfung von Tradition und Traditionsbruch über die unmittelbare Beteiligung an der Gegenwart durch Wahrnehmung und Aktion bis hin zum spekulativen Weitblick mit greifbaren Entwurfs- und Forschungsvorschlägen auf das, was sein könnte. Eine Verschränkung multidimensionaler Wissensformen ist damit verknüpft, wobei insbesondere die Aufmerksamkeit für das Wissen hervortritt, das über das performative Tun generiert wird und sich auf das Entstehen neuer konzeptueller, entwerferischer und planerischer Kompetenzen bezieht. In Verbindung mit Reflexivität und kraft des Projektiven zeigt sich dann das Potenzial des Reflexiven Ent-werfens zur Verfeinerung entwurfsbezogener Forschung als Instrument, mit dem Produkte unterschiedlicher Art hervorgebracht werden können, die weitere Forschungsfragen wie auch Diskurse und Entwürfe als ‚Konkretisationen von Möglichkeiten' der Zukunft eröffnen.[27]

1 Cf. | Vgl. Hans Blumenberg, Theorie der Unbegrifflichkeit, Frankfurt a. M.: Suhrkamp 2007, 7 and | und 12 **2** For more details on this and the following cf. the publications Practices of Reflexive Design, Processes of Reflexive Design and Intentions of Reflexive Design | Vgl. hierzu und zum Folgenden ausführlicher die Veröffentlichungen Praktiken Reflexiven Entwerfens, Prozesse Reflexiven Entwerfens und Intentionen Reflexiven Entwerfens, Berlin: Jovis 2016, 2018, 2020 **3** Cf. on this also | Vgl. hierzu auch Thomas Meier/Christina Tsouparopoulou, Artefakt, in: Thomas Meier/Michael R. Ott/ Rebecca Sauer (eds.), Materiale Textkulturen. Konzepte, Materialien, Praktiken, Berlin et al.: De Gruyter 2015, 47–62, 47–48 **4** Cf. | Vgl. N.N., Artefact/Artifact, in: Merriam Webster, on: | auf: https://www.merriam-webster.com/dictionary/ artifact, 30.9.2022 **5** Cf. | Vgl. N.N., Manifestation, in: Merriam Webster, on: | auf: https://www.merriam-webster.com/ dictionary/manifestation, 30.9.2022 **6** Interpretations that relate in particular to media and materials can be found repeatedly in contemporary design research, cf. e.g. | Interpretationen, die sich insbesondere auf Medien und Materialien beziehen, finden sich wiederholt in zeitgenössischen Entwurfsforschungen vgl. beispielsweise Hannah Groninger/Roger Häußling/Claudia Mareis/Thomas H. Schmitz, Einleitung, in: ids. (eds.), Manifestationen im Entwurf. Design, Architektur, Ingenieurwesen, Bielefeld: Transcript 2016, 9–24, 9 **7** Cf. | Vgl. Bryan Lawson, What designers know, 4. ed., Amsterdam: Elsevier 2006, 91–92; id., How designers think, Amsterdam et al.: Elsevier 2004, 292–293; Frederick Steier, Reflexivity and methodology, in: id. (ed.), Research and reflexivity, London: Sage 1991, 163–185, 174 **8** Cf. | Vgl. Michael Polanyi, Personal knowledge, Chicago, IL: University of Chicago Press 2015, 33–36 **9** Cf. | Vgl. Roland Lippuner, Raum, Systeme, Praktiken. Zum Verhältnis von Alltag, Wissenschaft und Geographie, Stuttgart: Steiner 2005, 215 **10** Cf. | Vgl. Michael Polanyi (2015), op. cit. (note | Anm. 8), 302; Michael Biggs/Henrik Karlsson (eds.), The Routledge Companion of research in the arts, London et al.: Routledge 2011, passim; Silvia Henke/Dieter Mersch/Nicolaj van der Meulen/Thomas Strässle/ Jörg Wiesel, Manifesto of Artistic Research. A defense against its advocates. Zürich: Diaphanes 2020, 18–27 **11** Cf. on this also | Vgl. hierzu auch Marc Pfaff, Poietische Medialität. Entwerfen und Erfinden als Weisen des Hervorbringens, in: Rikke Lyngsø Christensen/Ekkehard Drach/Lidia Gasperoni/Doris Hallama/Anna Hougaard/Ralf Liptau (eds.), Artefakte des Entwerfens. Skizzieren, Zeichnen, Skripten, Modellieren, Berlin: TU 2020, 84–106, 100–101 **12** Cf. | Vgl. Werner Oechslin, Vorwort, in: Eva von Engelberg-Dočkal/Markus Krajewski/Frederike Lausch (eds.), Mimetische Praktiken in der neueren Architektur. Prozesse und Formen der Ähnlichkeitserzeugung, Heidelberg: UB 2017, 6–9, 7 **13** Cf. on this also | Vgl. hierzu auch Chris Abel, The extended self. Architecture, memes and minds, Manchester: Manchester UP 2015, 213–215

14 Cf. on this also | Vgl. hierzu auch Gilles Deleuze, Differenz und Wiederholung, München: Wilhelm Fink 2007, passim; Karen Bard, Verschränkungen, Berlin: Merve 2015, 89, 162 and | und 194   **15** Cf. on this also | Vgl. hierzu auch Enrico Coen, The art of genes. How organisms make themselves, Oxford: Oxford University Press 1999, 19; Dalibor Vesely, Architecture in the age of divided representation, Cambridge, MA et al.: MIT Press 2004, 6   **16** Cf. on this also | Vgl. dazu auch Alfred North Whitehead, Process and reality, New York, NY: Free Press 1979, 3–8   **17** On perception modes cf. | Zu Erfahrungsmodi vgl. Bernhard Waldenfels, Ortsverschiebungen, Zeitverschiebungen.Modi leibhaftiger Erfahrung, Frankfurt a. M.: Suhrkamp 2009, 24; Hans-Jörg Rheinberger, Iterationen, Berlin: Merve 2005, 61   **18** Cf. | Vgl. Donald A. Schön, The reflective practitioner. How professionals think in action (1983), 3. ed., London: Ashgate 2003, 271–272   **19** Cf. on this | Vgl. hierzu Diane Taylor, The archive and the repertoire, Durham: Duke UP 2003, 2 and | und 20   **20** Cf. | Vgl. Rafael Moneo, On typology, in: Emmanuel Christ et al. (eds.), Typology. Paris, Dehli, Sao Paolo, Athens, Zürich: Park Books 2015, 9–26, 12–13; Andreas Tönnesmann, in: id./Peter Märkli, ...Dort sind wir eben wirklich unabhängig (conversation | Gespräch), in: Trans 19(2011), 20–29, 21; Nelson Goodman, Weisen der Welterzeugung, Frankfurt a. M.: Suhrkamp 1991, 20–27   **21** Cf. | Vgl. Hans-Jörg Rheinberger, Papierarchitekturen im Labor, in: Karin Krauthausen/Omar W. Nasim (eds.), Notieren, Skizzieren, Schreiben und Zeichnen als Verfahren des Entwurfs, Zürich: Diaphanes 2010, 139–153, 142; Margitta Buchert, Formen der Relation. Entwerfen und Forschen in der Architektur, in: Helga Blocksdorf/Ute Frank/ Marius Mensing/Anca Timofticiuc (eds.), EKLAT. Entwerfen und Konstruieren in Lehre, Anwendung und Theorie, Berlin: TU 2011, 76–86, 78–81   **22** Cf. | Vgl. Nelson Goodman (1991), op. cit. (note | Anm. 20), 19   **23** Cf. | Vgl. Georg Bertram, Kunst als menschliche Praxis. Eine Ästhetik, Berlin: Suhrkamp 2018, 139–146; Margitta Buchert, Anderswohnen, in: id./Carl Zillich (eds.), Performativ? Architektur und Kunst, Berlin: Jovis 2007, 40–49   **24** Cf. | Vgl. Alvaro Siza, cit. at | zit. bei Kenneth Frampton, Sieben Punkte zur Jahrtausendwende – ein verfrühtes Manifest, in Arch plus 149/150 (2000) 50–54, 50   **25** Cf. on the properties of imagination and its relation to cognition | Vgl. zu den Eigenschaften der Imagination und ihrer Relation zu Erkenntnis Herbert Schnädelbach, Erkenntnistheorie zur Einführung, Hamburg: Junius 2002, 103–104   **26** Cf. | Vgl. Anthony Dunne/Fiona Raby, Speculative everything. Design, fiction and social dreaming, Cambridge, MA: MIT 2013, 142–143 and | und 160; Robin Evans, The projective cast. Architecture and its three geometries, Cambridge, MA: MIT 2000, 363–365   **27** Cf. for understandings of the projective | Vgl. zum Verständnis des Projektiven Vilém Flusser, Vom Subjekt zum Projekt, in: id., Schriften, Bd. 3, Düsseldorf: Bollmann 1994, 9–160, 24

"Science and poetry are equally knowledge."

„Wissenschaft und Poesie sind gleichermaßen Wissen."

Gilles Deleuze

WISSENSRÄUME
SPACES OF KNOWLEDGE

Reflexive design finds one of its articulations in the questioning, evaluation and continuous extension of personal knowledge bases. The traditional corpus of knowledge has been familiar for a long time as a concept for characterising the formation of knowledge bases. In various disourses of the recent decades, aspects of bodies of knowledge and knowledge of bodies or embodied knowledge have been increasingly discussed.[1] Alongside this, with the composite of knowledge spaces introduced here, especially in the spatial design disciplines of architecture, urban and landscape design, it is possible to describe easily understandable features of the configuration of knowledge, and to integrate the previously mentioned forms of knowledge.[2] Traditionally handed down and learnt knowledge, as well as forms of knowledge that are contained in the human body or in material objects and lie beyond language, can be thought of in analogy to relationally connected spaces with transitions and intersections as well as in different kinds of scale. They surround the designers and researchers and bring forth a spatial occurence as a genesis of work and knowledge. As in other professions, the core of expertise can also be seen in the personal knowledge reservoir of designers and researchers in combination with skills.[3] This ultimately depicts the attempt to create long-term successful architectural-spatial ensembles and the promotion of this aim.

Reflexives Entwerfen findet eine seiner Artikulationen in der Befragung, Evaluation und kontinuierlichen Erweiterung persönlicher Wissensbestände. Der Wissenskorpus der Tradition ist als Konzept für die Charakterisierung der Formation von Wissensbeständen bereits seit Langem vertraut. In verschiedenen Diskursen der letzten Jahrzehnte werden zunehmend Momente von Wissenskörpern und Körperwissen bzw. verkörpertem Wissen (embodied knowledge) diskutiert.[1] Daneben lassen sich mit dem hier eingeführten Kompositum der Wissensräume insbesondere in den raumentwerfenden Disziplinen von Architektur, Städtebau und Landschaftsarchitektur gut verstehbare Eigenschaften der Konfiguration von Wissen umschreiben. Dabei ist es zudem möglich, die zuvor genannten Wissensformen zu integrieren.[2] Traditionell überliefertes und gelerntes Wissen ebenso wie Formen des Wissens, die im menschlichen Körper oder in materiellen Gegenständen enthalten sind und jenseits der Sprache liegen, können in Analogie zu relational verbundenen Räumen gedacht werden mit Übergängen und Schnittmengen sowie in Maßstäben unterschiedlicher Art. Sie umgeben die Entwerfenden und Forschenden und bringen ein Raumgeschehen als Werk- und Wissensgenese hervor. Wie auch in anderen Professionen kann darüber hinaus im persönlichen Wissensreservoir in Verbindung mit Fertigkeiten der Kern von Expertise gesehen werden.[3] Dieser bildet letztlich das Bestreben ab, langfristig gelungene baulich-räumliche Ensembles zu kreieren resp. dieses Ziel zu befördern.

In continuous development processes that incorporate new experiences, but which can also include routines and repetitions alongside structural change, there is an interplay of sensory perceptions, imagination and cognitive intellectual capacity.[4] It is a qualitative enrichment process. While the interconnection with the areas of knowledge of various crafting and technical, economic and logistical expert systems in architecture, urban and landscape design currently appears relevant and a matter of course, connections with the arts, philosophies and everyday cultures in spatial and creative everyday actions often come to the fore far less, despite prominent manifestations, for example, in the thinking and work of architects and artists of the Renaissance or in the context of the Bauhaus idea, in which art and technology were effectively postulated as essential poles within architecture.[5] This is also determined by the difficulty in describing this knowledge form that goes beyond solid abilities, is associated with aesthetic strategies and architectural-artistic forms of presentation and can shift the boundaries of the knowable. Overall, these knowledge spaces extend between explainable discursive practices or those presented in other ways or conveyed with different media.[6] Their specific compartments spring from many sources, whereby the practical realisation of architectures and spatial ensembles is only one of them. And they are associated with an interest orientated towards personal activities, which can include investigative research as well as design. Both manifest themselves, also in combination, as means of knowledge production with which realities and their complexity can be explored, understood and modified.[7]

In kontinuierlichen Entwicklungsprozessen, die neue Erfahrungen aufnehmen, aber auch Routinen und Wiederholungen ebenso einschließen können wie strukturellen Wandel, spielen dabei sinnliche Wahrnehmungen, Imaginationen und kognitives Denkvermögen zusammen.[4] Es handelt sich um einen qualitativen Anreicherungsprozess. Während die Verschränkung mit den Wissensbereichen verschiedener handwerklicher und technischer sowie ökonomischer und logistischer Expert:innensysteme in Architektur, Städtebau und Landschaftsarchitektur gegenwärtig naheliegend und selbstverständlich erscheint, treten Verbindungen zu den Künsten, zu Philosophien wie auch zu Alltagskulturen im baulich-räumlichen entwerferischen Alltagshandeln oftmals weit weniger hervor trotz prominenter Manifestationen beispielsweise im Denken und Schaffen von Architekten und Künstlern der Renaissance oder im Kontext der Bauhaus-Idee, mit der Kunst und Technik als essenzielle Pole der Architektur wirkungsstark postuliert wurden.[5] Dies ist auch bedingt durch die Schwierigkeit der Beschreibung dieser Art von Wissen, das ein festes Können überschreitet, mit ästhetischen Strategien und architektonisch-künstlerischen Darstellungsformen verbunden ist und Grenzen des Wissbaren verschieben kann. Insgesamt erstrecken sich die Wissensräume zwischen erklärbaren diskursiven und in anderer Weise dargebotenen bzw. mit anderen Medien vermittelten Praktiken.[6] Ihre spezifischen Kompartimente entspringen vielen Quellen, wobei die praktische Realisierung von Architekturen und räumlichen Ensembles nur eine davon ist. Und sie sind verbunden mit einem auf die persönlichen Aktivitäten gerichteten Interesse, welches das befragende Forschen ebenso einschließen kann wie das Entwerfen. Beide zeigen sich, auch in der Vermischung, als Wege der Wissensproduktion, mit der Wirklichkeiten in ihrer Komplexität erkundet, verstanden und verändert werden können.[7]

Going beyond the set of examples, concepts and activities that is described in professional associations as the knowledge that guides practice and determines works in space-designing disciplines, the contributions by Gennaro Postiglione, Andrea Canclini and Valerie Hoberg present different variants of knowledge forms and contribute to a better understanding of knowledge spaces as products of reflexive design and their production contexts in gradually differentiated ways. In his contribution, Gennaro Postiglione describes, based on the example of his own design and research activities, the relevance of personal participation as a vital component in the acts of understanding of knowledge genesis. Perceptions and actions such as visiting built architectures, urban spaces and territories, as well as reading books, are presented as fundamental features of the generation of design knowledge. In addition, it is the analysis, design and mediation levels of one's own drawings, photography and language that contribute to knowledge acquisition and stabilise it. The explanations also make clear that these experiences cannot be reduced to codified information but are rather formed individually. Beyond the learned conventions of the profession, these personal knowledge spaces were configured and interpreted through the experienced spatial environment and the perceiving and emotional connection to the valued architecture.[8] This sedimented, embodied and in part not linguistically explainable knowledge is updated in various situations or volitional actions and combined with explicit bodies of knowledge. In the activating practice, the examples, forms of thought and ways of acting are brought together as a personal repertoire and an attitude to architecture. In addition, attention is drawn to the performance of what is built, to consequences and effects associated with design actions. At the same time, it becomes clear how starting points can be created through the description and explanation of this genesis, which subsequently can extend the understanding of collective and individual knowledge spaces through comparison and analysis, even if these always remain bound up with selection processes.

Hinausgehend über das Set von Beispielen, Konzepten und Aktivitäten, das in professionellen Berufsverbänden als das die Praxis leitende und die Werke prägende Wissen der raumentwerfenden Disziplinen beschrieben wird, stellen die Beiträge von Gennaro Postiglione, Andrea Canclini und Valerie Hoberg verschiedene Varianten von Wissensformen vor und tragen dazu bei, Wissensräume als Produkte Reflexiven Entwerfens und ihre Produktionskontexte in graduell unterschiedlicher Weise besser zu verstehen. In seinem Beitrag beschreibt Gennaro Postiglione am Beispiel der eigenen entwerfenden und forschenden Tätigkeiten die Relevanz der persönlichen Partizipation als vitale Komponente in den Verstehensakten der Wissensgenese. Wahrnehmungen und Aktionen wie das Aufsuchen von gebauten Architekturen, Stadträumen und Territorien ebenso wie das Lesen von Büchern werden als grundlegende Eigenschaften der Erzeugung von Entwurfswissen vorgestellt. Darüber hinaus sind es die Analyse-, Entwurfs- und Vermittlungsebenen der eigenen dokumentierenden und interpretierenden Zeichnung, Fotografie und Sprache, die zum Wissenserwerb beitragen und diesen stabilisieren. Die Ausführungen verdeutlichen zudem, dass diese Erfahrungen nicht auf kodifizierte Informationen zu reduzieren sind, vielmehr individuell gebildet werden. Über die erlernten Konventionen der Profession hinaus wurden diese persönlichen Wissensräume durch die erfahrene baulich-räumliche Umwelt sowie die wahrnehmende und auch emotionale Verbindung zu der wertgeschätzten Architektur konfiguriert und interpretiert.[8] Dieses sedimentierte, verkörperte und in Teilen sprachlich nicht explizierbare Wissen wird in verschiedenen Situationen oder willentlichen Aktionen aktualisiert und verbunden mit expliziten Wissensbeständen. In der aktivierenden Praxis werden die Beispiele, Denkformen und Handlungsweisen verknüpft zu einem persönlichen Repertoire und einer Haltung zur Architektur. Zudem wird die Aufmerksamkeit auf die Performanz von Gebautem gelenkt, auf Konsequenzen und Wirkungen, die mit Entwurfshandeln verknüpft sind. Gleichzeitig wird deutlich, wie durch Beschreibung und Erklärung dieser Genese Ausgangspunkte geschaffen werden können, die im Weiteren durch Vergleich und Analyse das Verstehen kollektiver und individueller Wissensräume erweitern können, auch wenn diese stets mit Selektionsprozessen verbunden bleiben.

Based on the example of the Japanese architect Hiroshi Hara, Andrea Canclini shows the interlinking of (immaterial) ideas or notions with materially created entities. The exhibition 'Wallpapers', which philosophically and graphically interprets spatial concepts, goes back for example to experiences of field research on social and physical-material spatial formation processes within traditional villages and settlements in different parts of the world. These were associated with various philosophical ideas and introduced as a complex presentation of textual structures interwoven with graphic elements. In reflexive processes questioning conventional spatial forms, this revealed complex knowledge spaces that determine the design and subsequently also permeate the architect's built practice. The presented poietic overlaying acts as a mix of personality, creativity, perception, reflection and experience in the formation of products of an architectural-artistic nature. This also prompts the discussion of in what way theory and practice as well as knowledge spaces, are created and interrelate in continuous development processes and also include cultural contexts. It incorporates the situated, obvious cultural background of Japan, as well as the mixing with numerous references to other knowledge cultures of the world. In the exhibition, graphically drawn and linguistic traces show a connection between perception and thinking that intersect and overlap. As articulations, the wallpapers stimulate combinatorial interpretations. Furthermore, they allow their potential as generators of insights and knowing to become perceptible even in relation to the transfer potential that is difficult to grasp for realisation in architectures. The linking of thinking, action and experience, the inseparability of a certain type of being, and the way knowledge spaces appear show how widely divergent situations can also be temporarily synchronised in the dynamics of active life.[9]

Am Beispiel des japanischen Architekten Hiroshi Hara zeigt Andrea Canclini die Verschränkung von (immateriellen) Ideen oder Vorstellungen mit materiell kreierten Gebilden auf. Dies wird vorgestellt ausgehend von einer Raumkonzepte philosophisch und zeichnerisch interpretierenden Ausstellung ‚Wallpapers', die unter anderem auf Erfahrungen von Feldforschungen zu sozialen und physisch-materiellen Raumbildungsprozessen traditioneller Dörfer und Siedlungen in unterschiedlichen Teilen der Welt zurückgeht. Diese wurden mit diversen philosophischen Ideen verbunden und als komplexe Präsentation von mit zeichnerischen Anteilen durchwobenen textlichen Strukturen präsentiert. In einem herkömmliche Raumformen befragenden reflexiven Prozess wurden damit entwurfsprägende komplexe Wissensräume aufgezeigt, die in der Folge auch die gebaute Praxis des Architekten durchziehen. Die dargebotene poietische Überlagerung wirkt als eine Mischung von Persönlichkeit, Kreativität, Wahrnehmung, Reflexion und Erfahrung in der Ausprägung architektonisch-künstlerisch geprägter Produkte. Damit wird auch diskutiert, in welcher Weise Theorie und Praxis sowie Wissensräume in kontinuierlichen Entwicklungsprozessen entstehen und zusammenwirken und ebenfalls kulturelle Kontexte einschließen. Es findet sich dabei der situierte, naheliegende kulturelle Hintergrund Japans ebenso wie die Vermischung mit zahlreichen Bezügen zu anderen Wissenskulturen der Welt. In der Ausstellung wird durch grafisch gezeichnete und sprachliche Spuren eine Verbindung von Anschauung und Denken vor Augen geführt, die sich kreuzen und überlagern. Als Artikulationen stimulieren die Wallpapers kombinatorische Interpretationen. Im Weiteren werden auch Relationen zu dem nur schwer erfassbaren Transfer in die Realisierung von Architekturen wahrnehmbar. Die Verkettung von Denken, Handlung und Erfahrung, die Untrennbarkeit von einer bestimmten Art zu sein und die Art, wie die Wissensräume erscheinen, zeigen, wie in der Dynamik des aktiven Lebens auseinanderliegende Situationen vorübergehend auch synchronisiert werden können.[9]

Valerie Hoberg's contribution focusses in particular on the results of artistic processes in the context of architecture work, which seek novel possibilities and ways of understanding for architectural actions by taking distance to established routines and knowledge aspects. They are presented as different ways of trying out and of artistic experimentation, which include setting, planning and coincidental moments and contribute to extending knowledge spaces. This is presented in more detail using the Spanish architecture team Ensamble Studio as an example, who integrate artistic and performative forms of knowledge and styles of thought to a particularly high degree in their thinking, associations and experiments. Their experiments, also repeated methodically in series and modified, are created with a clear reference to real, material conditions of building practice but are also codetermined by intangible factors. They are referred to as the development of products (experimental models, videos) which can then be ranked and seen as bearers of knowledge.[10] The experimental models open up new possibilities of constructive, material and formal treatment, and the videos show the potential for the reflexive analysis of procedures. The structures and principles of production thereby become a product themselves.[11] At the same time, these artistic concepts and products encourage a plurality of possible interpretations and thereby enrich the self-understanding and understanding of the world, as well as the architecture-related knowledge spaces. The contribution can therefore also be an indication of the heterogeneity of knowledge forms as components of knowledge spaces, as well as of the associated questions, media and means of mediation and their interweaving. MB

Valerie Hobergs Beitrag fokussiert insbesondere die Resultate künstlerischer Prozesse im Kontext des Architekturschaffens, die über die Distanz zu etablierten Routinen und Wissensbestandteilen neuartige Möglichkeiten und Verständnisweisen für architektonisches Handeln suchen. Sie werden dargeboten als verschiedene Weisen des Ausprobierens und künstlerischen Experimentierens, die Setting, Planung und auch zufällige Momente einschließen sowie dazu beitragen, Wissensräume zu erweitern. Exemplarisch wird dies am Beispiel des spanischen Architekt:innenteams von Ensamble Studio vertieft, die im Denken, in Assoziationen und in Experimenten künstlerische und performative Wissensformen und Denkstile in besonders hohem Maße integrieren. Die auch in Reihungen methodisch wiederholten und modifizierten Experimente entstehen mit einem klaren Bezug zu realen, materiellen Bedingungen baulicher Praxis, werden aber von nicht fassbaren Faktoren mitbestimmt. Sie sind als Entwicklung von Produkten (experimentelle Modelle, Videos) gekennzeichnet, die dann als Trägerinnen von Wissen rangieren bzw. gesehen werden können.[10] Die experimentellen Modelle eröffnen neue Möglichkeiten der konstruktiven, materialen und formalen Behandlung, und die Videos das Potenzial der reflexiven Analyse von Vorgehensweisen. Die Strukturen und Prinzipien der Produktion werden dabei selbst zum Produkt.[11] Gleichzeitig ermuntern diese künstlerischen Konzepte und Produkte eine Pluralität möglicher Deutungen und bereichern so das Selbst- und Weltverständnis ebenso wie die architekturbezogenen Wissensräume. So kann der Beitrag auch gleichzeitig ein Hinweis sein auf die Heterogenität der Wissensformen als Komponenten von Wissensräumen wie auch der damit verbundenen Fragenkomplexe, Medien und Vermittlungsweisen und ihrer Verflechtungen. MB

1 Cf. e.g. | Vgl. beispielsweise Jan Ole Bangen/Henriette Hanky/Almut-Barbara Renger/Christoph Wulf, Körperwissen. Transfer und Innovation, in: Paragrana 25(2016), 13–19; Pierre Bourdieu, Meditationen. Zur Kritik der scholastischen Vernunft. Frankfurt a. M.: Suhrkamp 2001, 185; Georg Lakoff, Foreword, in: Benjamin K. Bergen, Louder than words: The new science of how the mind makes meaning, New York, NY: Basic Books 2012, s.p.; Michael Polanyi, Personal knowledge, Chicago: University of Chicago Press 2015, 57–64 and | und passim. **2** Cf. on this also | vgl. hierzu auch Günter Abel, Systematic knowledge research. Rethinking epistemology, in: Hans Jörg Sandkühler. Wissen. Wissenskulturen und die Kontextualität des Wissens, Frankfurt a. M. et al.: Peter Lang 2014, 17–27, 36 **3** Cf. | Vgl. Kees Dorst/Bryan Lawson, Design expertise, Oxford et al.: Elsevier 2009, 68–70, 128, 180–182 and | und passim; Geraldine Fitzpatrick, Emergent expertise sharing in a new community, in: Marc S. Ackerman/Volkmar Pipek/Volker Wulf (eds.), Sharing expertise. Beyond knowledge management, Cambridge, MA et al.: MIT Press 2002, 81–110, 101 **4** Cf. on this also | Vgl. dazu auch Olaf Breidbach, Anschauung denken, München: Fink 2011, 23 **5** For the interweaving of different forms of knowledge with expert systems, cf. | Zur Verschränkung verschiedener Wissensformen mit Expert:innensystemen vgl. Karin Knorr Cetina, Wissenskulturen. Ein Vergleich naturwissenschaftlicher Wissensformen, Frankfurt a. M.: Suhrkamp 2002, 17; on the position of the artist-architect in the Renaissance cf. zur Position des Künstler-Architekten in der Renaissance vgl. Rafael Moneo, Vom Entwurf zum Bauwerk, Brakel: Franz Schneider 2014, 11 **6** Cf. | Vgl. Frank Adloff/Katharina Gerund/David Kaldewey, Locations, translations, and presentations of tacit knowledge, in ids. (eds.), Revealing tacit knowledge. Embodiment and explication, Bielefeld: Transcript 2015, 7–17 **7** Cf. | Vgl. Margitta Buchert, Praktiken der kreativen Mischung, in: id. (ed.), Praktiken Reflexiven Entwerfens, Berlin: jovis 2016, 17–31, 25 **8** Cf. on this | Vgl. hierzu Michael Polanyi (2015), op. cit. (note | Anm. 1), XXVIII **9** For this interpretation of cognition cf. | Zu dieser Interpretation des Erkennens vgl. Humberto Maturana/Francisco Varela: Der Baum der Erkenntnis. Die biologischen Wurzeln menschlichen Erkennens, München: Goldmann 1984, 31 **10** Cf. | Vgl. Florian Dombois/Philip Ursprung, Kunst und Forschung. Ein Kriterienkatalog und eine Replik dazu, in: Kunst-Bulletin 4, 2006, 30–35, 33–34 **11** Cf. on this also | Vgl. hierzu auch Pierre Bourdieu, Outline of a theory of practice, Cambridge, UK: Cambridge University Press, 2010, 78–79

ARTEFACTS IN REFLEXIVE DESIGN
From formation to effect and meaning

Gennaro Postiglione

FRAMING THE CONTEXT   In my contribution, taking seriously and literally the suggestions of the Symposium, I interpret the formation, the effect and the meaning of products in Reflexive Design in architecture by reflecting on my specific understanding of those three fields of activity framed as follows. Formation is understood as something based on and related to the 'knowing' and to the body experience of architectural places; effect is understood as the perceived emotions and feelings connected to the experience of architectural places; and meaning is understood as the advancement of knowledge in architecture (discipline). In a first step, I evaluate some definitions related to the keyword of the symposium, product. My investigation is related to the framework of Italian language and culture, paving the way to introducing an alternative keyword, artefact, which is considered as more appropriate for my contribution when referring to architecture outcomes.

A NECESSARY SHIFT: FROM PRODUCTS TO ARTEFACTS   Quite significantly, both are "the result of an activity and/or a process (requiring labour)".[1] A product is "something that is made to be sold" while an artefact is "something showing human workmanship". As a result, product is therefore connected to consumption (that is, "about consuming something") and consequently to waste (that is, "a gradual loss or decrease of performance by consumption"). On the contrary, artefact is connected to use (that is, "about using something") and consequently to the creation of heritage (that is, "something transmitted by or acquired from a predecessor", or "created by the authorisation of its use"). Therefore, since an artefact shows human workmanship and is able to create heritage by the authorisation of its use, it better fits with architecture and its outcomes.

ARTEFAKTE IM REFLEXIVEN ENTWERFEN
Von der Entstehung zur Wirkung und Bedeutung

Gennaro Postiglione

RAHMUNG DES KONTEXTS   In meinem Beitrag, der die Anregungen des Symposiums ernst nimmt und wörtlich versteht, interpretiere ich die Formation, Wirkung und Bedeutung von Produkten im Reflexiven Entwerfen in der Architektur, indem ich über mein spezifisches Verständnis dieser drei Bereiche nachdenke. Die Formation wird als etwas verstanden, das auf der ‚Kenntnis' und der körperlichen Erfahrung architektonischer Orte basiert und damit verbunden ist; unter Wirkung werden die bei der Erfahrung architektonischer Orte wahrgenommenen Emotionen und Gefühle gefasst und die Bedeutung wird als die Weiterentwicklung des Wissens in der Architektur(-disziplin) verstanden. Zunächst erfolgt in einem ersten Schritt die Auswertung einiger Definitionen, die sich auf den Schlüsselbegriff des Symposiums, Produkte, beziehen. Meine Untersuchung bezieht sich auf den Rahmen der italienischen Sprache und Kultur und ebnet den Weg zur Einführung eines alternativen Schlüsselbegriffs, ‚Artefakte', der für meinen Beitrag in Bezug auf Ergebnisse der Architektur als geeigneter angesehen wird.

EIN NOTWENDIGER WANDEL: VON PRODUKTEN ZU ARTEFAKTEN
Bezeichnenderweise sind sowohl Produkte als auch Artefakte „das Ergebnis einer Tätigkeit und/oder eines Prozesses (der Arbeit erfordert)".[1] Das Produkt ist „etwas, das hergestellt wird, um verkauft zu werden", während das Artefakt etwas ist, „das menschliche Handwerk zeigt". Infolgedessen ist das Produkt mit Konsum (d. h. mit „etwas verbrauchen") und folglich mit Verschwendung (d. h. „einem allmählichen Verlust oder einer Abnahme der Leistung durch den Verbrauch") verbunden. Im Gegensatz dazu steht das Artefakt im

1 | Charles Eisen *Allegory of architecture* 1755

As Marco Biraghi writes in his book 'Questa è architettura', the labour (intellectual and physical) dedicated to the making of architecture manifests the philia (love) of its author for it.² This is well represented in the 1755 etching 'Allegory of Architecture' by Charles J. D. Eisen (fig. 1), later used by Marc-Antoine Laugier as the cover for the second edition of his 'Essai sur l'architecture'.³ In the etching, the mater (mother) admires with love (interpreted by the presence of Cupido) the primitive hut, presented as the archetype of any architecture. While probably stating, 'That is architecture!' A few years later, another architect made the same statement. It was Adolf Loos in the very last lines of his book 'Architektur'. "[...] If we find a mound in the forest that is six feet long and three feet wide... something tells us: someone is buried here. That is architecture."⁴

Laugier and Loos, like many others before and after, affirm that architecture always goes beyond its function, from which it always originates. Recently, Per Olaf Fjeld, in his book 'The Power of Circumstance', also touches upon the same subject and, referring to the work of his masters (namely, Louis Kahn, Sverre Fehn and Giancarlo De Carlo), brilliantly states, "The quality we appreciate today in their work dis not based on elements such as new materials, the technology used, their functionalism, etc. but on their ability to connect the knowledge available to their inner 'knowing'."⁵ In those works, we recognise the presence of a deep love (philia) for architecture that is manifested in its appearance, as something showing the human workmanship typical of artefacts. To conclude, I propose the following

Zusammenhang mit dem Gebrauch (d. h. mit „etwas zu gebrauchen") und folglich mit der Schaffung eines Erbes (d. h. mit „etwas, das von einem Vorgänger übertragen oder erworben wurde" oder „durch die Ermächtigung zum Gebrauch geschaffen wurde"). Da das Artefakt die menschliche Kunstfertigkeit zeigt und in der Lage ist, mittels seiner Befähigung zum Gebrauch ein Erbe zu erzeugen, passt es besser zur Architektur und ihren Ergebnissen.

Wie Marco Biraghi in seinem Buch ‚Questa è architettura' schreibt, ist die (intellektuelle und physische) Arbeit, die zur Herstellung von Architektur nötig ist, Ausdruck der Philia (Liebe) der Autorinnen und Autoren zu ihr.[2] Dies wird in der Radierung ‚Allegorie der Architektur' von Charles J. D. Eisen (Abb. 1) aus dem Jahr 1755 deutlich, die später von Marc-Antoine Laugier als Titelbild für die zweite Ausgabe seines ‚Essai sur l'architecture' verwendet wurde.[3] In der Radierung bewundert die Mater (Mutter) mit Liebe (interpretiert durch die Anwesenheit von Cupido) die primitive Hütte, die als Archetyp jeglicher Architektur dargestellt ist. Wahrscheinlich sagt sie dabei: „Das ist Architektur!" Ein paar Jahre später traf ein anderer Architekt die gleiche Aussage. Es war Adolf Loos in den allerletzten Zeilen seiner ‚Architektur'. „[...] Wenn wir im Walde einen Hügel finden würden, sechs Fuß lang und drei Fuß breit, [...] sagt etwas in uns: Hier liegt jemand begraben. Das ist Architektur."[4]

Laugier und Loos bekräftigen, wie auch viele andere vor und nach ihnen, dass Architektur immer über ihre Funktion hinausgeht, von der sie allerdings stets ausgeht. Kürzlich hat Per Olaf Fjeld in seinem Buch ‚The power of circumstance' dasselbe Thema aufgegriffen und unter Bezugnahme auf die Werke seiner Meister (Louis Kahn, Sverre Fehn und Giancarlo De Carlo) treffend festgestellt: „Die Qualität, die wir heute an ihren Werken schätzen, beruht nicht auf Elementen wie neuen Materialien, der verwendeten Technik, ihrem Funktionalismus usw., sondern auf ihrer Fähigkeit, verfügbares Wissen (knowledge) mit ihrer inneren ‚Kenntnis' (knowing) zu verbinden".[5] In diesen Werken erkennen wir die Präsenz einer tiefen Liebe (Philia) zur Architektur, die sich in ihrer Erscheinung manifestiert, als etwas, das die für Artefakte übliche menschliche Kunstfertigkeit zeigt. Abschließend schlage ich die folgenden Paare von miteinander verbundenen Dualitäten vor: Produkt vs. Artefakt führt zu Konsum vs. Gebrauch, d.h. Verschwendung vs. Erbe. Letztendlich ist das Produkt gleichbedeutend mit Abfall, während das Artefakt zum Erbe wird. Um die vorgeschlagene Verschiebung weiter zu verstärken, füge ich hinzu,

2 | San Domenico Maggiore Napoli (1283–1324)

pairs of connected dualities: Product vs artefact results in consumption vs use, that is to say, waste vs heritage. Ultimately, product is tantamount to waste, while artefact to heritage. To further strengthen the proposed shift, I add that product is the result of a finished work, while artefact is an open-end manifestation, almost as a process in itself (and this might be even more true if we refer to urban design or landscape architecture).

THE FORMATION OF ARTEFACTS IN REFLEXIVE DESIGN

As stated before, the Formation of Artefacts in Reflexive Design is understood as something based and related to the 'knowing' and the body experience of architectural places. My personal 'knowing' understands, probably due to my multiple being (at least a Practitioner, a Scholar, and a Teacher), formation as a process started during my education in architecture when/where, beside the typical transfer of visual and textual knowledge, body experiences of high-quality architectural places and their representation (by drawings, pictures and texts) were fundamental milestones for creating my 'individual knowing', to use Louis Kahn's definition.[6] Something not given one and for good, but an open-end process started during my university years and still lasting today, as part of the permanent process of updating and self-educating in architecture on which my tacit 'knowing' is built and cultivated. And in which my deep love (philia) for architecture and its manifestations is rooted (fig. 2). I need to clarify that this specific 'knowing' of architecture should not be confused nor identified with the attitude of some practitioners to look for architecture references since 'knowing' has no such direct and visual value. If knowledge consists of elements and solutions, 'knowing' consists of processes. Therefore, the history of architecture and its manifestations is not only understood as a repertoire of stories/people/buildings but also as world evidence that can be personally experienced, explored, and understood in its real physicality. This is exactly where my tacit 'knowing' was born, and it keeps nourishing itself: on the evidence of the artefacts and their multi-sensorial experiences and memories.

dass das Produkt das Ergebnis eines fertigen Werks ist, während das Artefakt eine Manifestation mit offenem Ende ist, fast wie ein Prozess an sich (und dies könnte sogar noch mehr zutreffen, wenn wir uns auf Stadtplanung oder Landschaftsarchitektur beziehen).

DIE BILDUNG VON ARTEFAKTEN IM REFLEXIVEN ENTWERFEN

Wie bereits erwähnt, wird die Bildung von Artefakten im Reflexiven Entwerfen als etwas verstanden, das auf der ‚Kenntnis' und der körperlichen Erfahrung von architektonischen Orten basiert und mit ihnen verbunden ist. Meine persönliche ‚Kenntnis' begann, wahrscheinlich aufgrund meiner Vielschichtigkeit (zumindest als Praktiker, Wissenschaftler und Lehrer), während meiner Architekturausbildung, als neben der gewöhnlichen Vermittlung von visuellem und textuellem Wissen Körpererfahrungen mit qualitätsvollen architektonischen Orten und deren Darstellung (durch Zeichnungen, Bilder und Texte) grundlegende Meilensteine für die Schaffung meiner „individuellen Kenntnis" waren, um die Definition von Louis Kahn zu verwenden.[6] Etwas, das nicht einmalig und für immer gegeben ist, sondern ein Prozess mit offenem Ende, der während meiner Studienzeit begann und bis heute andauert, als Teil des permanenten Prozesses der Aktualisierung und Selbstbildung in der Architektur, auf dem mein stilles ‚Wissen' aufbaut und kultiviert wird. Und etwas, in dem meine tiefe Liebe (Philia) zur Architektur und ihren Erscheinungsformen verwurzelt ist (Abb. 2). Ich muss klarstellen, dass diese spezifische ‚Kenntnis' über Architektur nicht mit der Haltung einiger Praktizierender verwechselt oder identifiziert werden sollte, die nach Architekturreferenzen suchen, da ‚Kenntnis' keinen solchen direkten und visuellen Wert hat. Wenn das Wissen aus Elementen und Lösungen besteht, so besteht die ‚Kenntnis' aus Prozessen. Daher wird die Geschichte der Architektur und ihrer Erscheinungsformen nicht nur als ein Repertoire von Geschichten/Menschen/Bauten verstanden, sondern auch als Weltzeugnisse, die in ihrer realen Körperlichkeit persönlich erfahren, erforscht und verstanden werden können. Genau hier wurde mein stilles ‚Wissen' geboren, und es nährt sich weiter: aus der Evidenz der Artefakte und ihrer multisensorischen Erfahrungen und Erinnerungen. Dieser erste Teil soll mit einem Hinweis auf die sogenannte Architekturethnografie und ihren wachsenden Einfluss auf die Architektur (Praxis, Kritik und Geschichte) schließen. Befördert durch die Pionierarbeit von Albena Yaneva bei OMA[7] und durch die wunderbare Produktion von Atelier Bow-Wow[8], betont die Architekturethnografie die Bedeutung der direkten und körperlichen Erfahrung architektonischer Orte für ein umfängliches Verständnis sowohl ihrer räumlichen Qualität als auch ihrer Nutzung.

Let me close this first chapter with reference to the so-called architectural ethnography and its growing influence and impact on architecture (practice, criticism and history). Promoted by the pioneering work of Albena Yaneva about OMA[7] and by the incredible production of Atelier Bow-How[8], architectural ethnography stresses the relevance of direct and body experience of architectural places for a thorough understanding of both their spatial quality and their uses. An understanding based upon the 'individual knowing' resulting from the physical experience of places intertwined with their visual and textual knowledge. Body, direct and participant observation are keywords for any ethnographer as they were and should still be for any architect. I would like, therefore, to underline that something that was fundamental for architectural education (the body experience and the 'individual knowing' of meaningful architectural places) has been completely lost to be, unexpectedly, re-discovered by other disciplines, namely architectural ethnography. What else, if not architectural ethnography, are all the reports (visual and textual) of architectural explorations (of all time and of all places), since all our experiences of places have always been transcribed in drawings, pictures, annotations (fig. 3)? What else do we need to understand the urgency to go back to our own foundations and traditions?

THE EFFECT OF ARTEFACTS IN REFLEXIVE DESIGN

The effect is understood, as stated at the beginning, as the perceived emotions and feelings connected to the experience of architectural places. In my understanding, the effect of artefacts in reflexive design is something strongly related to the impact architecture might have both in tangible and intangible terms. For tangible effects, I am not referring at all to its functions, but to a) the physical impacts both on the behaviours of its direct and indirect users (human and non-human) and on the artefacts and their surroundings; b) the built environment at large, including direct transformations of sites and their surroundings. For intangible effects, I refer to the perceived emotions and feelings connected to the experience of architectural places. And this is precisely what I consider architecture's primary effect and impact. Far too much has already been written on atmospheres, starting from the liminal work of the German philosopher Gernot Böhme[9] to the famous and well know pamphlet by Peter Zumthor[10], not to forget the phenomenology theory by Juhani Pallasmaa and the very dry interpretation given by the Italian philosopher Tonino Griffero who has

3 | Alison and Peter Smithson The Big Scrapbook, 261

Ein Verständnis, das auf der ‚individuellen Kenntnis' basiert, die sich aus der physischen Erfahrung von Orten ergibt, die mit ihrem visuellen und textuellen Wissen verwoben sind. Körperliche, direkte und teilnehmende Beobachtung sind Schlüsselbegriffe für die Ethnografie, wie sie es auch für alle Architekturschaffenden waren und sein sollten. Ich möchte daher betonen, dass etwas, das für die Architekturausbildung von grundlegender Bedeutung war (die Körpererfahrung und die ‚individuelle Kenntnis' von bedeutungsvollen architektonischen Orten), völlig verloren gegangen ist, um unerwartet von anderen Disziplinen wiederentdeckt zu werden, etwa der Architekturethnografie. Was sonst, wenn nicht Architekturethnografie, sind all die (visuellen und textlichen) Berichte von architektonischen Erkundungen (aller Zeiten und aller Orte), da alle unsere Erfahrungen von Orten immer in Zeichnungen, Bildern, Anmerkungen niedergeschrieben wurden (Abb. 3)? Was brauchen wir noch, um die dringliche Notwendigkeit dafür zu begreifen, dass wir zu unseren eigenen Grundlagen und Traditionen zurückkehren müssen?

DIE WIRKUNG VON ARTEFAKTEN IM REFLEXIVEN ENTWERFEN
Unter Wirkung werden hier, wie eingangs ausgeführt, die wahrgenommenen Emotionen und Gefühle verstanden, die mit der Erfahrung von architektonischen Orten verbunden sind. Nach meinem Verständnis ist die Wirkung von Artefakten im Reflexiven Entwerfen etwas, das stark mit den Auswirkungen zusammenhängt, die Architektur sowohl in materieller als auch in immaterieller Hinsicht haben kann. Bei den materiellen Effekten beziehe ich mich nicht auf die Funktionen, sondern auf a) die physischen Einwirkungen sowohl auf das Verhalten der direkten und indirekten (menschlichen und nicht menschlichen) Nutzenden als auch auf die Artefakte und ihre Umgebung; b) die gebaute Umwelt insgesamt, einschließlich der direkten Veränderungen der Orte und ihrer Umgebung. Als immaterielle Auswirkungen bezeichne ich die wahrgenommenen Emotionen und Gefühle, die mit der Erfahrung architektonischer Orte verbunden sind. Und das ist es auch, was ich als die primäre Wirkung und den Einfluss der Architektur betrachte. Über Atmosphären ist schon viel

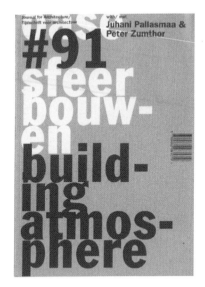

4 | Building Atmospheres OASE 91 (2014)

theorised atmospheres as spatial affordances due the co-creation process at stake between the artefact and the individual experiencing it: not fully embodied in the object neither in the subject but raising exactly at the moment of their meeting (fig. 4).[11] It is an opening towards an understanding of atmospheres as manifestations going beyond any planned 'effect' by the architect thanks to the co-creative and inventive agency of the subject. Taking his position as a starting point, I have further explored Griffero's theory, applying spatial affordances to architectural typology to further support what was stated at the beginning of my text: architecture goes always beyond its practical functions, from which, indeed, it originates.[12] In fact, by interpreting architecture as spatial articulation, it is easy to understand typology as spatial affordances, completely freeing architecture from any genealogy connecting it to its practical functionality. This is exactly what the whole history of architecture – of whatever place and whatever time – is continuously teaching us[13]: it is the active encounter between people and places that generates possible usages thanks to the powerful structure of architectural typology and the creative agency of its users (fig. 5). Architecture generates spatial quality, and there is no other goal in design, since the functional programme is only the reason and the starting point to deal with architecture per se.[14] This is crucial to produce artefacts and not products, to promote uses and not consumption, to achieve heritage and not waste.

THE MEANING OF ARTEFACTS IN REFLEXIVE DESIGN   As stated in the introduction, meaning is understood as the advancement of knowledge in architecture (discipline) and something strongly related to what I like to call its 'inner

5 | Diocletian's Palace Split (305 AD) 2004

zu viel geschrieben worden, angefangen mit der Arbeit des deutschen Philosophen Gernot Böhme[9] über das berühmte und bekannte Pamphlet von Peter Zumthor[10] bis hin zur phänomenologischen Theorie von Juhani Pallasmaa und der sehr trockenen Interpretation des italienischen Philosophen Tonino Griffero, der Atmosphären als räumliche Angebote skizziert hat, die im gemeinsamen Schaffensprozess zwischen dem Artefakt und den erlebenden Individuen entstehen: weder vollständig im Objekt noch im Subjekt verkörpert sind, sondern genau im Moment ihrer Begegnung (Abb. 4).[11] Es ist eine Öffnung hin zu einem Verständnis von Atmosphären als Manifestationen, die dank der mitschöpferischen und erfinderischen Kraft der Subjekte über jeden geplanten ‚Effekt' der Architekturschaffenden hinausgehen.

Ausgehend von seiner Position habe ich Grifferos Theorie weiter erforscht, indem ich räumliche Affordanzen auf die architektonische Typologie angewandt habe, um das zu untermauern, was zu Beginn meines Textes gesagt wurde: Architektur geht immer über ihre praktischen Funktionen hinaus, aus denen sie allerdings hervorgeht.[12] In der Tat ist es durch die Interpretation der Architektur als räumliche Artikulation einfach, die Typologie als räumliche Angebote zu verstehen. Das befreit die Architektur vollständig von jeder Genealogie, die sie in Verbindung zu ihrer praktischen Funktionalität setzt. Dies ist genau das, was uns die gesamte Geschichte der Architektur – unabhängig von Ort und Zeit – immer wieder lehrt: Es ist die aktive Begegnung zwischen Menschen und Orten, die dank der kraftvollen Struktur der architektonischen Typologie und der schöpferischen Kraft ihrer Nutzenden mögliche Funktionen hervorbringt (Abb. 5).[13] Architektur erzeugt räumliche Qualität. Es gibt kein anderes Ziel im Entwurf, da das Funktionsprogramm nur der Anlass und der Ausgangspunkt ist, um sich mit Architektur an sich zu beschäftigen.[14] Dies ist von entscheidender Bedeutung, um Artefakte und nicht Produkte zu produzieren, um die Nutzung und nicht den Verbrauch zu fördern, um ein Erbe und nicht die Verschwendung zu erreichen.

61

6-7 | Sigurd Lewerentz Petri Church Klippan (1962–1966) Markus Church Stockholm (1956–1960)

programme'. Also, Valerio Olgiati, together with Markus Breitschmid, refer to it in their book 'Non-referential architecture'[15] where they theorise the only scope of architecture is architecture itself, overcoming both function and uses. In my understanding, the 'Meaning of artefacts in reflexive design' relies on the capacity of their authors to activate design productivity able to tackle architecture foundations and/or elements and/or principles from within the discipline and via architecture. While, at the same time, answering to the specific programme from which they originate and have to – initially – respond to. It is a kind of double reflexivity: one by the authors and the other by architecture itself, transforming the author into a sort of 'minister of a profane cult'.[16] This is what I – as probably all architects – admire in the so-called masterpieces. It is not their functional programme, neither their performances nor their technological capacity, but it is the ability to connect the available knowledge to the 'individual knowing' of their authors.

This is exactly what Sigurd Lewerentz does, for instance, in his church building in Klippan (fig. 6), in the South of Sweden (1962-1966), where he engages in an investigation of the relationship between construction and decoration (traditionally, the latter is understood as a representation of the former)[17] already started a few years earlier in the design of Bjorkhagen parish church (fig. 7) in Stockholm (1956–1960). In Klippan, Lewerentz entrusts decoration with a completely new and different role: it carries, for the first time in the history of architecture, its own independent (from construction) values. And he does it recurringly to an extraordinary level of craftsmanship. Lewerentz disrupts the traditional role of decoration from inside the discipline of architecture, paradoxically using construction as a paradigm for manifesting its autonomy. He makes recourse to an orthodox and skilfully managed building knowledge in a completely non-orthodox way, transforming building knowledge into building 'individual knowing'. Nothing is what it seems to be at first glance.

8–9 | Sigurd Lewerentz Flower Kiosk Malmö East Cemetery Malmö (1968-1969)

DIE BEDEUTUNG VON ARTEFAKTEN IM REFLEXIVEN ENTWERFEN

Wie in der Einleitung formuliert, wird die ‚Bedeutung' als die Weiterentwicklung des Wissens in der Architektur(-disziplin) verstanden und steht in engem Zusammenhang mit dem, was ich als ihr ‚inneres Programm' bezeichnen möchte. Auch Valerio Olgiati bezieht sich in seinem gemeinsam mit Markus Breitschmid verfassten Buch ‚Nicht-Referenzielle Architektur' darauf.[15] Sie stellen die These auf, dass der einzige Anwendungsbereich der Architektur die Architektur an sich sei, die sowohl die Funktion als auch den Gebrauch überwinde. Meines Erachtens beruht die Bedeutung der Artefakte im Reflexiven Entwerfen auf der Fähigkeit ihrer Autor:innen, eine schöpferische Produktivität zu aktivieren, die sich mit den Grundlagen und/oder Elementen und/oder Prinzipien der Architektur innerhalb der Disziplin und mittels Architektur beschäftigt. Gleichzeitig antworten sie aber auch auf das spezifische Programm, aus dem sie hervorgehen und auf das sie – zunächst – reagieren müssen. Es handelt sich um eine Art doppelte Reflexivität: die der Autor:innen sowie die der Architektur selbst. Es findet eine Verwandlung der Autor:innen in eine Art ‚Bedienstete eines profanen Kults' statt.[16] Das ist es, was ich – wie wahrscheinlich alle Architekturschaffenden – an den sogenannten Meisterwerken bewundere. Es ist weder ihr funktionales Programm, noch sind es ihre Leistungen oder ihre technische Kapazität, sondern es ist die Fähigkeit, das vorhandene Wissen mit der ‚individuellen Kenntnis' ihrer Autor:innenschaft zu verbinden.

Genau das tut Sigurd Lewerentz zum Beispiel in seinem Kirchenbau in Klippan in Südschweden (1962–1966), wo er eine Untersuchung der Beziehung zwischen Konstruktion und Dekoration (traditionell wird Letztere als Repräsentation Ersterer verstanden)[17] vornimmt (Abb. 6), die bereits einige Jahre zuvor bei der Gestaltung der Bjorkhagen-Kirche in Stockholm (1956–1960) begonnen wurde (Abb. 7).[14] In Klippan vertraut Lewerentz der Dekoration eine

To measure nature in relation; to what picture you have on the wall –

looking upon architecture as in relation to nature, the intstetial, architecture became becomes a room of limitation, that can persue a precision within the resistance of natures room,

10 | Per Olaf Fjeld Architecture as an intermediate space and interplay with nature

And he goes even further, if possible, in his last work, the Flower Kiosk (fig. 8) at Malmö East Cemetery (1968–1969), where the dialectics between construction and decoration reaches the most sublime (built) representation. In Malmö, decoration is not used to express or deny any construction-related content; rather, it represents its completely autonomous values. It is pure aesthetics. In the Flower Kiosk, the material becomes materiality as is probably also the case for the La Congiunta by Peter Märkli (1992).

ARCHITECTURE AS AN EXTENSION OF OUR HUMANNESS   I want to conclude my reflections by quoting P.O. Fjeld (fig. 9), who has beautifully framed what I have tried to articulate so far in my contribution in a very clear and synthetic way. "If architecture is understood as an extension of our humanness, and not just as a commodity, architectural space must be able to make an emotional connection. Architectural spatial energy must be strong enough to influence our sense of being in a positive way. To place this type of responsibility and significance upon architecture is impossible without also having a strong, shared belief in architecture in itself."[18] The same belief we recognise in 'Allegory of Architecture' as in every single episode of its history since at least Stonehenge was erected, or even before.

völlig neue und andere Rolle an: Sie trägt zum ersten Mal in der Geschichte der Architektur ihre eigenen (von der Konstruktion) unabhängigen Werte. Und er tut dies wiederkehrend auf eine außergewöhnliche handwerkliche Weise. Lewerentz bricht mit der traditionellen Rolle der Dekoration innerhalb der Disziplin der Architektur, indem er paradoxerweise die Konstruktion als Leitbild für die Manifestation ihrer Autonomie benutzt. Er rekurriert auf eine völlig unorthodoxe Weise auf ein orthodoxes und fachkundiges Bauwissen, indem er das Bauwissen in eine ‚individuelle Baukenntnis' verwandelt. Nichts ist dabei so, wie es auf den ersten Blick scheint. Und er geht sogar noch weiter, sofern das überhaupt möglich ist: in seinem letzten Werk, dem Blumenkiosk (Abb. 8) auf dem Ostfriedhof von Malmö (1968–1969), bei dem die Dialektik zwischen Konstruktion und Dekoration den erhabensten (gebauten) Ausdruck erreicht. In Malmö wird die Dekoration nicht verwendet, um irgendeinen baulichen Inhalt auszudrücken oder zu dementieren; sie repräsentiert vielmehr ihre völlig autonomen Werte. Sie ist reine Ästhetik. Im Blumenkiosk wird das Material zur Materialität, wie es möglicherweise auch im Museum La Congiunta von Peter Märkli (1992) der Fall ist.

ARCHITEKTUR ALS ERWEITERUNG UNSERES MENSCHSEINS   Ich möchte meine Überlegungen mit einem Zitat von Per Olaf Fjeld abschließen, der das, was ich bisher in meinem Beitrag zu formulieren versucht habe, als klare Synthese auf den Punkt gebracht hat (Abb. 9): „Wenn Architektur als Erweiterung unseres Menschseins verstanden wird und nicht nur als Ware, dann muss der architektonische Raum in der Lage sein, eine emotionale Verbindung herzustellen. Die architektonische Raumenergie muss stark genug sein, um unser Lebensgefühl positiv zu beeinflussen. Es ist unmöglich, der Architektur diese Art von Verantwortung und Bedeutung zuzuschreiben, wenn man nicht auch einen starken, gemeinsamen Glauben an die Architektur selbst hat."[18] Es ist derselbe Glaube, den wir in ‚Allegorie der Architektur' wiedererkennen, ebenso wie in jeder einzelnen Episode ihrer Geschichte – mindestens seit der Errichtung von Stonehenge und vielleicht sogar noch früher.

1 All quoted dictionary definitions in this paper are taken from: | Alle zitierten Wörterbuchdefinitionen in diesem Artikel sind entnommen aus: Manlio Cortelazzo/Michele A Cortelazzo (eds.), DELI – Dizionario Etimologico della Lingua Italiana, Bologna: Zanichelli 2014   **2** Cf. | Vgl. Marco Biraghi, Questa è architettura, Turin: Einaudi 2021, 16   **3** Cf. | Vgl. Marc-Antoine Laugier, Essai sur l'architecture, Paris: Chez Duchesne 1753   **4** Adolf Loos, Architektur, in: id. Ornament and Crime: selected essays, Riverside, CA: Ariadne Press 1998, 20 (first published partly | teilweise Erstveröffentlichung in: Der Sturm, 42/1910)   **5** Per Olaf Fjeld, The Power of Circumstance, Copenhagen: Arkitekturforlaget B, 85   **6** Ibid., 45   **7** Cf. | Vgl. Albena Yaneva, Made by the OMA, Rotterdam: nai010 2009, passim.   **8** Cf. | Vgl. Momoyo Kaijima/ Laurent Stalder (eds.), Architectural Ethnography, Tokyo: TOTO 2018   **9** Cf. | Vgl. Gernot Böhme, Architektur und Atmosphäre, Paderborn: Wilhelm Fink 2006   **10** Cf. | Vgl. Peter Zumthor, Atmospheres, Basel: Birkhäuser 2006   **11** Cf. | Vgl. Tonino Griffero, Atmospheres, London: Routledge 2016   **12** 'Typological affordances – Architecture beyond function' is a research proposal edited in 2022 in collaboration with Andreas Lechner from TU Graz, and presented to the Call for international collaborations at DAStU Department – Politecnico di Milano. | ,Typologische Affordanzen – Architektur über Funktion hinaus' ist ein Forschungsantrag, der 2022 in Zusammenarbeit mit Andreas Lechner von der TU Graz bearbeitet und dem Call for international collaborations am DAStU Department, Politecnico di Milano vorgelegt wurde.   **13** Cf. |

Vgl. Aldo Rossi, L'architettura della città, Milan: CLUP 1978, passim.   **14** This has been actually the case of art practices until the 20th century vanguard movements. Any work of art, in fact, before last century, has always been commissioned by a client for a very practical reason. That is to say, to commemorate, to remember, to teach, etc. This specific functionalistic character of art production has never counter-acted on artists who have always been able to overcome the pragmatic determinism of any commission, transforming it into an opportunity to reflect and contribute to their own creative practice. This is what we see in any art work from any time in any cultural and geographical context. | Dies war in den Künsten bis zu den Avantgardebewegungen des 20. Jahrhunderts der Fall. Jedes Kunstwerk vor dem letzten Jahrhundert wurde immer aus einem sehr praktischen Grund durch Kundschaft in Auftrag gegeben. Also gedenken, sich erinnern, lehren usw. Dieser spezifisch funktionalistische Charakter der Kunstproduktion hat sich nie gegen die Kunstschaffenden gewandt, die stets in der Lage waren, den pragmatischen Determinismus eines Auftrags zu überwinden und ihn in die Gelegenheit zu verwandeln, zu reflektieren und damit zu ihrer eigenen kreativen Praxis beizutragen. Dies wird in jedem Kunstwerk aus jeder Zeit in allen kulturellen und geografischen Kontexten ersichtlich.   **15** Cf. | Vgl. Valerio Olgiati/Markus Breitschmid, Non-Referential Architecture, Zurich: Park Books 2019   **16** Marco Biraghi (2021) op. cit. (note | Anm. 2), 99   **17** Cf. | Vgl. Antonio Monestiroli, La metopa e il Triglifo, Bari: Laterza 2002   **18** Per Olaf Fjeld (2020) op. cit. (note | Anm. 5), 101

HIROSHI HARA: WALLPAPERS
Transcriptions about spatial concepts and modes

Andrea Canclini

BETWEEN 'THEOREIN' AND 'PRAXIS' IN ARCHITECTURE
Theory can be used as justification, as propaganda, as a guide for practice, as a set of
principles, as a vehicle of thought, as a platform for debate, and as an architectural
project in itself. Historically, theory has changed its role and relationship with practice,
thus being by no means unambiguous or stable in its understanding. The term 'theory' is
ambiguous: as a form of mediation between idea and reality, theory has been deployed
as an explanation or as a tool for critique; but it is even possible to consider an expanded
notion of theory in relation to architecture, given the role that theoretical production
has played in relation to both practice and broader social, political, and technological
currents. In the very beginning, in ancient Greek, the relation between 'theorein' and
'praxis' is not primarily functional or instrumental, since theory is not a function of
practice, nor is practice a heuristic instrument of theory, but they are in a generative
and foundational relationship.[1] The Greek word 'techne', derived from the verb 'tikto'
(to generate, to reveal, to bring into the world, the mode of being of 'poiesis'), is the
etymological root of both the words 'art' and 'technique', here more in the ideal meaning
of 'modes of knowledge' than in the sense of 'practical work'; in ancient Greece, this
meaning becomes apparent in the exactness of the design of the base of a classical
column, in which 'techne' imposes itself on nature with the only 'télos', the only goal,
of revealing itself, making its own perfection manifest.[2] 'Prássein', the verb from which
the noun 'praxis' is derived, does not simply mean to act or operate, but also to perform,
to travel, to walk, to cross; it has to do with the dynamic, daring and cunning action
of the Greek merchant and navigator.[3] 'Theoréin', in turn composed of 'theá' (spectacle)
and 'horân' (to observe), meant archaically to be a spectator at a religious festival.[4]

HIROSHI HARA: WALLPAPERS
Transkriptionen zu räumlichen Konzepten und Modi

Andrea Canclini

ZWISCHEN ‚THEOREIN‘ UND ‚PRAXIS‘ IN DER ARCHITEKTUR

Die Theorie kann als Begründung, als Werbung, als Leitfaden für die Praxis, als ein Zusammenschluss von Prinzipien, als Vehikel des Denkens, als Plattform für Debatten und als ein architektonisches Projekt in sich dienen. Historisch gesehen hat die Theorie ihre Rolle und ihre Beziehung zur Praxis verändert und ist damit in ihrem Verständnis keineswegs eindeutig oder stabil. Der Begriff Theorie ist mehrdeutig: Als eine Form der Vermittlung zwischen Idee und Realität wurde die Theorie als Erklärung oder als Werkzeug der Kritik entwickelt; aber angesichts der Rolle, die theoretische Produktionen sowohl gegenüber der Praxis als auch gegenüber breiteren sozialen, politischen und technischen Strömungen eingenommen haben, ist es auch möglich, einen erweiterten Theoriebegriff im Zusammenhang der Architektur zu betrachten. Schon im Altgriechischen ist die Beziehung zwischen ‚theorein‘ und ‚praxis‘ nicht in erster Linie funktional oder instrumentell, denn die Theorie ist weder eine Funktion der Praxis, noch ist die Praxis ein heuristisches Instrument der Theorie, sondern sie stehen in einer generativen und begründenden Beziehung.[1] Das griechische Wort ‚techne‘, abgeleitet vom Verb ‚tikto‘ (erzeugen, offenbaren, in die Welt bringen, die Seinsweise der ‚poiesis‘), liegt die etymologische Wurzel sowohl des Wortes ‚Kunst‘ als auch des Wortes ‚Technik‘, hier eher in der ideellen Bedeutung von ‚Erkenntnisweisen‘ als im Sinne von ‚praktischer Arbeit‘. In der griechischen Antike zeigt sich diese Bedeutung in der Genauigkeit der Gestaltung des Sockels einer klassischen Säule, in der sich die ‚techne‘ der Natur aufdrängt, mit dem einzigen ‚télos‘, dem einzigen Ziel, sich selbst zu offenbaren und die eigene Vollkommenheit zur Erscheinung zu bringen.[2] ‚Prássein‘, das Verb, von dem das Substantiv ‚praxis‘ abgeleitet ist, bedeutet nicht nur handeln oder agieren, sondern auch durchführen, reisen, gehen, kreuzen; es hat mit dem dynamischen, risikofreudigen und geschickten Handeln griechischer Kauf- und Seeleute zu tun.[3] ‚Theoréin‘, das sich wiederum aus ‚theá‘ (Schauspiel) und ‚horân‘ (beobachten) zusammensetzt, bedeutete ursprünglich, einem religiösen Fest als Publikum beizuwohnen.[4]

1 | Wallpapers exhibition catalogue Ichihara Lakeside Museum 2014

BETWEEN 'THEOREIN' AND 'PRAXIS' IN HIROSHI HARA'S WORK

Following these conceptual understandings, Japanese architect Hiroshi Hara prepared twenty-five 'Fragmentary Passages' for his exhibition 'Wallpapers', held in 2014 at the Ichihara Lakeside Museum of Art in Chiba, a small town at the end of a peninsula outside Tokyo. They were ways of expressing his personal 'Weltanschauung' he calls architecture, 25 modalities of interpreting spatial concepts used without boundaries or hierarchies (fig. 1). The curator, Fram Kitagawa, introducing the exhibition itself, states that: "The thing that I think is the best part [...] is that the display of the artworks illuminates an aspect of our society, that is to say, to eliminate distances".[5] The 25 'Fragmentary passages' Hara prepared, encourage him to continue, poetically asking: "Doesn't Hara continue to take such elements as space, words and 'the teachings of the villages', and from them construct as-yet unseen towers? Those are space-times in which light, air, earth, adverbs and adjectives resonate, and within them people in the form of silhouettes live in their own 'world scenery'".[6]

Hara writes on this translucent sketch paper his impeccably designed and erudite texts, which are layers of applied knowledge, meandering between anthropology and philosophy, mathematics and poetry, ranging from Greek mythology to Neoplatonic philosophy, from Upanishads to Spinoza's Ethica (fig 2–3). In a wallpaper dedicated to René Descartes, Hara rewrites passages from 'Principia Philosophiæ', using different colours to highlight words such as 'duratio', 'extensio', 'ordo', 'spatio', 'loco', in order to describe his spatial concept of 'extension': putting 'extensio' and 'cogito' together, we can assume that 'the world that surrounds us is ceaselessly expanding', and that it was the evocation of the observations as conducted through phenomenology.[7] In another wallpaper Hara quotes extensively from Spinoza's Ethica; if we read that the substance is nature, then all the changes that can be seen in nature are simply forms, and Hara highlights words such as 'mode' and 'modification'.[8]

2 | Wallpaper with reference to Aristoteles and metaphysical science

ZWISCHEN ‚THEORIE' UND ‚PRAXIS' BEI HIROSHI HARA

Diesen Begriffsverständnissen folgend, hat der japanische Architekt Hiroshi Hara 25 ‚Fragmentarische Passagen' für seine Ausstellung ‚Wallpapers' vorbereitet, die 2014 im Ichihara Lakeside Museum of Art in Chiba, einer kleinen Stadt am Ende einer Halbinsel vor Tokio, stattfand. Sie waren Ausdruck seiner persönlichen ‚Weltanschauung', die er als Architektur bezeichnet, 25 Modalitäten der Interpretation von Raumkonzepten, die ohne Grenzen oder Hierarchien eingesetzt werden (Abb. 1). Der Kurator Fram Kitagawa erklärt in seiner Einführung in die Ausstellung: „Was ich für das Beste halte [...], ist, dass die Ausstellung der Kunstwerke einen Aspekt unserer Gesellschaft beleuchtet, nämlich die Aufhebung von Distanzen".[5] Die 25 ‚Fragmentarischen Passagen', die Hara vorbereitet hat, regen ihn an, poetisch zu fragen: „Nimmt Hara nicht zudem Elemente wie den Raum, die Worte und die ‚Lehre der Dörfer' und konstruiert aus ihnen noch nicht gesehene Türme? Das sind Raumzeiten, in denen Licht, Luft, Erde, Adverbien und Adjektive mitschwingen und in denen die Menschen als Scherenschnitte in ihrer eigenen ‚Weltszenerie' leben".[6]

Auf durchscheinendes Skizzenpapier schreibt Hara seine formvollendeten und geistvollen Texte, die Schichten von angewandtem Wissen sind und zwischen Anthropologie und Philosophie, Mathematik und Poesie, von der griechischen Mythologie bis zur neuplatonischen Philosophie, von den Upanishaden bis zu Spinozas Ethica mäandern (Abb. 2–3). In einer René Descartes gewidmeten Tapete schreibt Hara Passagen aus ‚Principia Philosophiæ' um, wobei er Wörter wie ‚duratio', ‚extensio', ‚ordo', ‚spatio', ‚loco' farblich hervorhebt, um sein räumliches Konzept der ‚Ausdehnung' zu beschreiben: Wenn man ‚extensio' und ‚cogito' zusammennimmt, kann man davon ausgehen, dass „die Welt, die uns umgibt, sich unaufhörlich ausdehnt" und dass es sich dabei um die Heraufbeschwörung der Beobachtungen durch die Phänomenologie handelt.[7] In einem

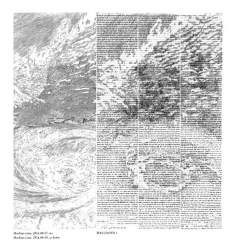

ホメロス『オデュッセイア』
Homer, *Odyssea* BC8C, English (tr. A. T. Murray)

ジェイムズ・ジョイス『ユリシーズ』
James Joyce, *Ulysses* 1922, English

第十二章
古代ギリシャのホメロスの手によるとされる世界最古の小説は、地中海世界を円環的にトラヴァーシングし、閉じた回路とする物語であった。テキストとしたのは「怪物スキュラと魔女カリュブディス」の一節。『オデュッセイア』に描かれたさまざまな情景図式は、ジョイスの『ユリシーズ』を筆頭に、2500年を経て超え数多くの創造的表現の源泉となっている。

第2部第9挿話（部分）
主人公がダブリンの街を円環的にトラヴァーシングする『オデュッセイア』と同じ構造をもつ「方法」、全18の神話は異なった記述法、文体のコラージュで記述される「方法2」、社会や芸術のさまざまな事象への言及が複雑に折り重ねられ、ときに物語は整理不能な混乱状態に陥る。これらは、カオスとコスモスが入り乱れる空間性への移行を描出するためにジョイスが採用した方法であろう。

Book XII
The world's oldest novel, written by Homer of Ancient Greece, is a story that traverses the span of the Mediterranean world in a closed circuit. The excerpt is relates to Scylla and Charybdis. The various schemata of scene in *Odyssey* have admirably withstood 2500 years, and have also become the source of many imaginative expressions, as exemplified by Joyce's *Ulyses*.

Episode 9
While the story has a similar structure to Odyssey with an account of the protagonist's encompassing traversal of the city of Dublin (Method 1), all 18 anecdotes used different notations – written with a collage of literary styles (Method 2). With its complicatedly overlapped references to society and various phenomena in the history of art, at times the story falls into an unintelligible state of confusion. These may have been selected by Joyce in order to portray the movement towards an extensity of the cosmos that has been sent into a shambles by chaos.

3 | Wallpapers 1 and 34 References to Homer's 'Odyssea' and James Joyce's 'Ulysse'

BETWEEN FIELD TRIPS WITH STUDENTS AND 'WALLPAPERS'

From the late 1960s to the mid-70s, Hara wrote a series of philosophical texts and books on architectural principles, from the 'porous body' theory to the 'floating architecture' and 'homogeneous space' that impacted Japanese architecture practice.[9] At the same time, instead of participating in the EXPO in 1970, he decided to conduct surveys around the world, an activity he continued with the Institute of Industrial Science at the University of Tokyo from 1972 to 1978, in traditional villages and settlements in Europe, Africa, the Middle East, Latin America, and South and South-East Asia.[10] On these trips, Hara analysed the relationships between individuals and their grouping in communities through direct observation, travelling with his students to over 200 villages in 40 countries. During the trips, he explored alternatives to what he saw as the rigid structure of modernist urbanism, namely the idea of universal space in vernacular communal dwellings. These reports would later be published as extra issues of 'Space Design' magazine from 1973 to 1975, and theorised into one hundred teachings for architecture in 'Kenchiku Bunka' magazine in 1987.[11] Hara draws theoretical tools from various sources to critically address this mass of information gathered on field trips with students. From Plotinus' 'Enneads', Hara highlights the concepts of 'prohodos' (one to many) and 'epistrophe' (many to one) to describe the urban development and history of another African village, the Algerian city of Ghardaïa, while using the topology of Dante's 'La Divina Commedia' to describe the Yemeni city of Bani Mourah (fig. 4), where the base of high-rise buildings is made of stone and the rest of mud bricks: Hara would use the same concept when designing the Umeda Sky Building (1993) in central Osaka, with its open-air observation deck at the top.

4 | Wallpaper 12 References to Dante's 'La Divina Commedia'

anderen ‚Wallpaper' zitiert Hara ausführlich aus Spinozas ‚Ethica'; wenn wir lesen, dass das Material die Natur ist, dann sind alle Veränderungen, die man in der Natur sehen kann, einfach Formen, und Hara hebt zudem Wörter wie ‚Modus' und ‚Modifikation' hervor.[8]

ZWISCHEN FELDFORSCHUNGEN MIT STUDIERENDEN UND ‚WALLPAPERS'
Von Ende der 1960er bis Mitte der 1970er Jahre schrieb Hara eine Reihe von philosophischen Texten und Büchern über architektonische Prinzipien, von der Theorie des ‚porösen Körpers' bis zur ‚schwebenden Architektur' und dem ‚homogenen Raum', welche die japanische Architekturpraxis beeinflussten.[9] Parallel beschloss er, statt an der EXPO 1970 teilzunehmen, Untersuchungen in der ganzen Welt durchzuführen. Dies setzt er gemeinsam mit dem Institute of Industrial Science der Universität Tokio von 1972 bis 1978 in traditionellen Dörfern und Siedlungen in Europa, Afrika, dem Nahen Osten, Lateinamerika sowie Süd- und Südostasien fort.[10] Bei diesen Reisen analysierte Hara die Beziehungen zwischen Individuen und ihren gemeinschaftlichen Gruppierungen durch direkte Beobachtung und reiste mit seinen Studierenden in über 200 Dörfer in 40 Ländern. Während dieser Reisen untersuchte er Alternativen zu der seiner Meinung nach starren Struktur des modernistischen Städtebaus, nämlich die Idee eines universellen Raums in den traditionellen Gemeinschaftshäusern. Diese Berichte wurden später als Sonderausgaben der Zeitschrift ‚Space Design' in den Jahren 1973 bis 1975 veröffentlicht und 1987 in der Zeitschrift ‚Kenchiku Bunka' in 100 Lehren für die Architektur theoretisiert.[11] Aus verschiedenen Quellen zieht Hara theoretische Hilfsmittel zur kritischen Auseinandersetzung mit dieser Masse an Informationen, die er auf seinen Exkursionen mit Studierenden gesammelt hatte. Aus Plotins ‚Enneaden' hebt Hara die Begriffe ‚prohodos' (einer zu vielen) und ‚epistrophe' (viele zu einem) hervor, um die städtebauliche Entwicklung und Geschichte der algerischen Stadt Ghardaïa zu beschreiben. Die Topologie von Dantes ‚Göttlicher Komödie'

5 | Sunset on the rooftop of Umeda Sky Building Osaka

It is precisely based on these experiences – his lifelong research, field investigations, and theoretical approach – that over the course of several years Hara designed these 25 'Transcripts' on spatial concepts and modalities, real fragments of discourse.[12] The first is titled 'Mode at Dusk' and 'Not-Not'. Hara here describes that "there is no more beautiful part of our 'Umwelt', the self-centred world, than the sky, which we have long shared. In particular, the sunset is a dramatic performance of 'mode at dusk' that sometimes tints the western sky with gold and sometimes burns in the dark clouds, color changing from moment to moment appearing in the shadows cast by nearby trees as it gradually becomes dark" (fig. 5–6).[13] This transcription is on the 'arazu-arazu', the 'not-not', the anti-western logic that is the apotheosis of Japanese culture.[14] Another one is titled 'Transcription', where Hara describes that "the type of text typically used for transcription is sacred scripture, which indicates something other than secular books. In that sense, the only sacred in 'Wallpapers' appears to be the 'Lotus Sutra'". Or, in the 'Mode at Dawn', where he quotes the Iranian philosopher Shahab al-Din Suhrawardi's 'The Philosophy of Illumination', he continues using these words: "a 'mode at dawn'. Light, shadow of light, Light of Lights. Plato, Aristotle. Light and clouds are integrated in the Book of Genesis, and William Morris, Franz Listz, Spinoza, Locke and Kant, Miyaza-wa's 'Night of Milky Way Railroad' and Eliot's 'Waste Land', the 'Radio Head' rock band, Giordano Bruno, Newton, Einstein, Leibniz, Riemann and Poincaré, the Upanishad as well as the Leibniz monad, Mark Twain and Henry David Thoreau, Edgard Allan Poe's 'The philosophy of composition' and 'The philosophy of furniture', the Joyce's 'Ulysses' with Homer's 'The Odyssey', closing with the Dante's 'The Divine Comedy".[15] Hara's effort is therefore clear: to look at and interpret the world from an architectural point of view.[16]

6 | Wallpaper Sunset above Tokyo

nutzt Hara wiederum, um die jemenitische Stadt Bani Mourah zu charakterisieren, wo die Basis der Hochhäuser aus Stein und der Rest aus Lehmziegeln besteht (Abb. 4). Das-selbe Konzept verwendet Hara bei der Gestaltung des Umeda Sky Building (1993) im Zentrum von Osaka mit seiner Aussichtsplattform unter freiem Himmel auf dem Dach.

Ausgehend von diesen Erfahrungen – seinen lebenslangen Forschungen, Feldforschungen, und theoretischen Ansätzen – hat Hara im Laufe mehrerer Jahre die 25 ,Transkripte' über räumliche Konzepte und Modalitäten, echte Diskursfragmente, entworfen.[12] Das erste trägt den Titel ,Modus in der Dämmerung' und ,Nicht-Nicht'. Hara beschreibt hier: „Es gibt keinen schöneren Teil unserer ,Umwelt', der selbstbezogenen Welt, als den Himmel, den wir seit langem teilen. Insbesondere der Sonnenuntergang ist eine dramatische Auf-führung des ,Modus in der Dämmerung', der manchmal den westlichen Himmel mit Gold färbt und manchmal in den dunklen Wolken brennt, wobei die Farbe von Augenblick zu Augenblick wechselt und in den Schatten erscheint, die von den nahen Bäumen geworfen werden, wenn es allmählich dunkel wird" (Abb. 5–6).[13] Diese Transkription befasst sich mit dem ,arazu-arazu', dem ,Nicht-Nicht', der anti-westlichen Logik, die die Apotheose der japanischen Kultur ist.[14] In diesem Sinne erscheint das Heilige in den ,Wallpapers' als das ,Lotus Sutra'. Oder im ,Modus in der Morgendämmerung', wo er ,Die Philosophie der Erleuchtung' des iranischen Philosophen Shahab al-Din Suhrawardi zitiert und mit diesen Worten fortfährt: „ein Modus in der Morgendämmerung". Licht, Schatten des Lichts, Licht der Lichter. Platon, Aristoteles. Integriert sind Licht und Wolken im Buch Genesis sowie Gedanken und Impulse von William Morris, Franz Listz, Spinoza, Locke und Kant, Miyazawas ,Eine Nacht in der Milchstraßenbahn' und Eliots ,Das wüste Land', die Rockband Radio-head, Giordano Bruno, Newton, Einstein, Leibniz, Riemann und Poincaré, die Upanishaden

7 | Wallpaper 9 Imabari at dawn with references to 'One thousand an one nights'

BETWEEN 'THEOREIN' AND 'PRAXIS' IN THREE PROJECTS   About this generative point of his poetic, as a relationship between 'theorein' and 'praxis', Hara wrote: "The designs for 'reflection houses', which includes my own house, were supported by the aesthetics of reduction as in 'Hojoki' and the image of 'embedding a city within a house' as inspired by 'The Fisherman and the Jinni', a story included in the 'One Thousand and One Nights'. Also at around the same time, I encountered many ruins and ancient structures in Iraq during my investigations of villages there, and I learned that in many places people have claimed throughout the ages to have seen visions of levitating gardens. Upon knowing these, I designed the Umeda Sky Building. The soccer court in the Sapporo Dome is a realization of the 'floating' concept, which I was led to by a magic spell in 'Arabian Nights'" (fig. 7).[17]

It is of some help to have a brief look at these three particularly representative buildings. First, the 'Hara House', built in Tokyo in 1974, the most representative work in the 'Reflection House' series (fig. 8–9). Firstly for the reason that the area is framed by the rectangular outer enclosure, that has been given a clearly recognisable valley-like topography. Secondly, the house is a clear expression of what he calls a 'nest structure', a smaller house nested within the house like Russian dolls, as well as an expression of his idea of embedding a city inside a house. Thirdly, the exterior of the house is simple in appearance, though this is difficult to see because of the trees, and the true façade is found inside. That is, the design is successful in expressing a reversal of inside and outside. About the design of his house, he wrote: "One simple detail was crucial to the design of this house: the 'second roof' made by acrylic panels installed in each of the rooms. [...] This second roof serves as a lightweight, cloud-like ceiling. As a result, each room in the building looks like a separate house. [...] Light enters each room via a window, but a skylight above the central

sowie die Leibniz'sche Monade, Mark Twain und Henry David Thoreau, Edgard Allan Poes ‚Die Philosophie der Komposition' und ‚Die Philosophie der Möbel', Joyce' ‚Ulysses' mit Homers ‚Odyssee' und abschließend Dantes ‚Die göttliche Komödie'.[15] Darin zeigt sich Haras Bestreben: die Welt mit architektonischen Augen zu betrachten und zu interpretieren.[16]

ZWISCHEN ‚THEOREIN' UND ‚PRAXIS' IN DREI PROJEKTEN Über diesen generativen Punkt seiner Poesie als Beziehung zwischen 'theorein' und 'praxis' schrieb Hara: „Die Entwürfe für ‚Reflektionshäuser', zu denen auch mein eigenes Haus gehört, wurden von der Ästhetik der Reduktion wie in ‚Hojoki' und dem Bild der ‚Einbettung einer Stadt in ein Haus' unterstützt, das inspiriert ist von ‚Der Fischer und der Dschinn', einer Geschichte aus ‚Tausendundeiner Nacht'. Etwa zur gleichen Zeit stieß ich im Irak bei meinen Nachforschungen in den dortigen Dörfern auf viele Ruinen und antike Strukturen und ich erfuhr, dass Menschen an vielen Orten im Laufe der Jahrhunderte artikulierten, Visionen von schwebenden Gärten gehabt zu haben. Mit diesem Wissen entwarf ich das Umeda Sky Building. Der Fußballplatz im Sapporo Dome ist eine Umsetzung des Konzepts des ‚Schwebens', zu dem mich ein Zauberspruch aus ‚Tausendundeiner Nacht' geführt hat" (Abb. 7).[17]

Es ist angezeigt, einen kurzen Blick auf diese drei besonders repräsentativen Gebäude zu werfen. Erstens das 1974 in Tokio errichtete ‚Hara House', das markanteste Werk der ‚Reflektionshaus'-Serie. (Abb. 8–9) Erstens, weil das Areal von der rechteckigen Außenhülle umrahmt wird, die mit einer deutlich ablesbaren, talähnlichen Topografie versehen wurde. Zweitens ist das Haus ein klarer Ausdruck dessen, was Hara eine ‚Neststruktur' nennt, ein kleineres Haus, das wie Matroschkas im Haus verschachtelt ist, sowie Ausdruck seiner Idee, eine Stadt in ein Haus einzubetten. Drittens ist das Äußere des Hauses einfach gehalten, auch wenn dies wegen der Bäume schwer zu erkennen ist, und die wahre Fassade befindet sich im Inneren. D.h., der Entwurf verkörpert eine Umkehrung von Innen und Außen. Über den Entwurf seines Hauses schrieb er: „Ein einfaches Detail war für den Entwurf dieses Hauses entscheidend: das ‚zweite Dach' aus Acrylplatten, die in jedem der Zimmer installiert sind. [...] Dieses zweite Dach dient als leichte, wolkenartige Decke. Dadurch wirkt jeder Raum des Gebäudes wie ein eigenes Haus. [...] In jeden Raum fällt Licht durch ein Fenster, aber ein Oberlicht über dem zentralen Durchgang erhellt den Raum auch durch das zweite Dach [...]. Diese Helligkeit unterstreicht sowohl die Idee der Umkehrung als auch das Konzept eines ‚kleinen Zentrums'. Wenn nachts das Licht in den Räumen brennt, leuchtet das zweite Dach aus Acrylplatten, und die Räume selbst werden zu Lichtquellen. [...] Später entdeckte ich eine ähnliche Beziehung in einer Anlage in Afrika, bei deren Formation jedes Familienmitglied als eigenständiges Individuum behandelt wurde".[18]

8–9 | Hara House Tokyo 1974

passage-way also illuminates the room through the second roof [...]. This brightness underscores the idea of reversal as well as the concept of a 'small centre'. When the lights are on in the rooms at night, the second roof of acrylic panels glows, and the rooms themselves become sources of light. [...] I later discovered a similar relationship in a compound in Africa, where in its formation each family member was treated as a distinct individual".[18]

A second representative architectural project by Hara is the Umeda Sky Building, built in Osaka in 1993 (fig. 10). This 'connected highrise' structure is comprised of a pair of office buildings whose design was chosen from a number of international proposals. The site is in the central district of Osaka, even if in an area that has not yet been fully developed, while one of the design conditions was that the buildings should be able to generate a high level of human activity. Hara commented: 'The history of tall buildings and surveys of villages show that people of many different regions and periods have envisioned hanging gardens. Here, I proposed three connected highrise buildings with an open-air observation deck on top'.[19]

The third building, the Sapporo Dome, was completed in 2001 in Sapporo (fig. 11). After hosting the 1972 Winter Olympics, Sapporo was selected as one of ten cities to host the Football World Cup in 2002. At the time of selection, the city had been preparing to construct an all-weather dome capable of handling World Cup football, with a convenient turf-changing system. The silvery egg-shaped dome will appear on Sapporo's scenic Hitsujigaoka in 2001, and has two distinctive characteristics. The first stems from the need to have a natural grass field within a dome for the World Cup. To satisfy this technical need, a 'dual arena' shape was designed, with open and closed arena areas facing each other. The football field is laid on what is also called a 'hovering stage', which can be raised by an air cushion and moved on wheels between the two arenas.

10 | Umeda Sky Building Osaka 1992   11 | Sapporo Dome Sapporo 2001

Ein zweites repräsentatives architektonisches Objekt Haras ist das Umeda Sky Building, das 1993 in Osaka errichtet wurde (Abb. 10). Dieses ‚zusammenhängende Hochhaus' besteht aus zwei Bürogebäuden, der Entwurf wurde aus einer Reihe von internationalen Vorschlägen ausgewählt. Der Standort liegt im Zentrum von Osaka, wenn auch in einem noch nicht vollständig erschlossenen Gebiet, und eine der Entwurfsbedingungen war, dass die Gebäude in der Lage sein sollten, ein hohes Maß an menschlicher Aktivität zu erzeugen. Hara kommentierte: „Die Geschichte der Hochhäuser und die Untersuchungen von Dörfern zeigen, dass die Menschen in vielen verschiedenen Regionen und Epochen hängende Gärten geplant haben. Hier habe ich drei miteinander verbundene Hochhäuser mit einer Aussichtsplattform unter freiem Himmel auf dem Dach vorgeschlagen".[19]

Das dritte Gebäude, der Sapporo Dome, wurde 2001 in Sapporo gebaut (Abb. 11). Nach der Austragung der Olympischen Winterspiele 1972 wurde Sapporo als eine von zehn Städten für die Ausrichtung der Fußballweltmeisterschaft 2002 ausgewählt. Zum Zeitpunkt der Auswahl bereitete die Stadt den Bau einer Allwetterkuppel vor, die für die Fußballweltmeisterschaft geeignet ist und über ein praktikables System zum Austausch der Spielfelder verfügt. Die silberne, eiförmige Kuppel wurde im Jahr 2001 auf dem malerischen Hitsujigaoka in Sapporo errichtet und weist zwei prägnante Merkmale auf. Das erste ergibt sich aus der Anforderung, für die Weltmeisterschaft ein Naturrasenfeld innerhalb einer Kuppel zu errichten. Um diesem technischen Erfordernis gerecht zu werden, wurde die Form einer ‚Doppelarena' entworfen, bei der sich offene und geschlossene Arenabereiche gegenüberstehen. Das Fußballfeld liegt zweitens auf einer sogenannten ‚schwebenden Bühne', die durch ein Luftkissen angehoben und auf Rädern zwischen den beiden Arenen bewegt werden kann. Zudem entlehnte Hara die Begriffe ‚Kontinuum' und ‚Individuum' aus der Mathematik von Bernhard Riemann, die er 1970 zum ersten Mal auf Japanisch las, wobei er von der Idee beeindruckt war, dass topologische

79

Hara also borrowed the terms 'continuum' and 'individuum' from Bernhard Riemann's mathematics, which he first read in 1970 in Japanese, being struck by the idea that topological concepts can help interpret the real world conveniently.[20] Consequently, Hara developed a mathematical model using points, groups, neighbourhoods, subsets and topological spaces in an attempt to unite the discrete and the continuous as social structural qualities in a single model. The key to the possibility of uniting these poles is his desire to avoid the Hegelian dialectic in order to resolve the apparent conflict between 'individuum' and 'continuum' using the Taoist concept of 'arazu-arazu', the 'not-not'. In his words: "Whereas in dialectics there is always a solution, in 'arazu-arazu' there is never a solution... dialectics incorporates a concept of order, [whereas in] 'not-not'... this is replaced by a concept of parallelism and simultaneous existence".[21]

RELATIONS   The Hegelian dialectic implies progress, whereas 'arazu-arazu' allows diversity without hierarchy; this understanding led Hara to search for topological models that translate the 'not-not' into architectural relationships. Bridging disciplines, Hara's reflexive design has the research as part of the design process itself: his practical research on West African savanna villages during the Eighties directly informs his design, after demonstrating that they constitute a semiotic paradigm made up of many elements.[22] As is clear in his 25 'Fragmentary passages' exhibited in the 'Wallpapers' exhibition and in his projects, Hara's architecture is rich in these connections, capable of distilling in their essentiality image and reality, historical stratification and phenomenological evidence, geography and human knowledge, whose particular measure is never mathematical or geometric, but reflexive to the point of coming together to merge into the fullness of existence.

Konzepte dabei helfen können, die reale Welt zu interpretieren.[20] Hara entwickelte daraufhin ein mathematisches Modell, das Punkte, Gruppen, Nachbarschaften, Teilmengen und topologische Räume verwendet, um das Diskrete und das Kontinuierliche als soziale Strukturqualitäten in einem einzigen Modell zu vereinen. Der Schlüssel zu der Möglichkeit, diese Pole zu vereinen, ist sein Wunsch, die Hegel'sche Dialektik zu vermeiden, um den scheinbaren Konflikt zwischen ‚Individuum' und ‚Kontinuum' mithilfe des taoistischen Konzepts ‚arazu-arazu', dem ‚Nicht-Nicht', zu lösen. Mit seinen Worten: „Während es in der Dialektik immer eine Lösung gibt, gibt es in ‚arazu-arazu' nie eine Lösung … die Dialektik beinhaltet ein Konzept der Ordnung, [während] im ‚Nicht-Nicht' [...] dieses durch ein Konzept der Parallelität und der gleichzeitigen Existenz ersetzt wird".[21]

R E L A T I O N E N   Die Hegel'sche Dialektik impliziert Fortschritt, während ‚arazu-arazu' Vielfalt ohne Hierarchie zulässt; dieses Verständnis veranlasste Hara, nach topologischen Modellen zu suchen, die das ‚Nicht-Nicht' in architektonische Beziehungen übersetzen. In Haras Reflexivem Entwerfen, das eine Brücke zwischen den Disziplinen schlägt, ist die Forschung Teil des Entwurfsprozesses: Seine praktische Forschung über westafrikanische Savannendörfer in den 1980er Jahren fließt direkt in sein Entwerfen ein, nachdem er herausgestellt hat, dass diese Dörfer ein aus vielen Elementen bestehendes semiotisches Paradigma darstellen.[22] Wie in seinen 25 ‚Fragmentarischen Passagen', die in der Ausstellung ‚Wallpapers' gezeigt werden, und in seinen Projekten deutlich wird, ist Haras Architektur reich an diesen Verbindungen, die in der Lage sind, in ihrer Essenz Bild und Realität, historische Schichtung und phänomenologische Evidenz, Geografie und menschliches Wissen zu destillieren, deren besonderes Maß niemals mathematisch oder geometrisch ist, sondern reflexiv bis zu dem Punkt, an dem sie zusammenkommen, um in der Fülle der Existenz aufzugehen.

1 Cf. e.g. | Vgl. z. B. Kate Nesbitt (ed.), Theorizing a new agenda for architecture: An anthology of architectural theory 1965–1995, New York, NY: Princeton Architectural Press 1996, 16   2 Cf. | Vgl. Neil Leach (ed.), Rethinking architecture. A reader in cultural theory, London: Routledge 1997, 103, 115–116   3 Cf. | Vgl. José Guilherme Abreu, Vivre la structure absolue: la pratique quotidienne entre action et non-action, in: Rencontres Abelio (2012), 1–23   4 Cf. | Vgl. Jean-Pierre Vernant, The origin of greek thought, Ithaca, NY: Cornell University Press 1984   5 Hiroshi Hara, Hiroshi Hara: Wallpapers. The 'Transcriptions' about spatial concepts and modes, Tokyo: Gendai Kikaku Shitsu 2014, 4   6 Ibid., 5   7 Ibid., 21   8 Cf. | Vgl. ibid., 22   9 Cf. in the next notes 10 and 11 and in | Vgl. dazu die folgenden Fußnoten 10 und 11 sowie in Botond Bognar, Hiroshi Hara: The floating world of his architecture, Hoboken, NJ: John Wiley 2001, passim   10 Cf. | Vgl. Hiroshi Hara, Learning from the villages: 100 lessons, in: id./Yukio Futagawa/ David B. Stewart (eds.), GA Architect 13 Hiroshi Hara, Tokyo: A.D.A. EDITA 1993, 88–91   11 The researches were done in the 'Hara Laboratory' in the Institute of Industrial Science at the University of Tokyo, published as 'Dwelling Group', series 1–5 'Space Design', 1973–1979. Later published in: 'Dwelling Group', Vol. I & II, Tokyo: Kajima Institute Publishing, 2006. The ideas Hara gathered from his village investigations were presented as a collection of dissertations at Tokyo University published in 'Kenchiku Bunka', April 1987, and then published as a book in 1998 by Shokokusha. | Die

Forschungen wurden im ‚Hara Laboratory' des Institute of Industrial Science an der University of Tokyo durchgeführt, veröffentlicht als ‚Dwelling Group', Serie 1–5 ‚Space Design', 1973–1979. Später veröffentlicht in: ‚Dwelling Group', Vol. I & II, Tokyo: Kajima Institute Publishing, 2006. Die Ideen, die Hara bei seinen Dorfuntersuchungen sammelte, wurden als eine Sammlung von Dissertationen an der Tokyo University präsentiert, die im April 1987 in ‚Kenchiku Bunka' veröffentlicht und dann 1998 bei Shokokusha als Buch veröffentlicht wurden. **12** Cf. | Vgl. Hiroshi Hara (2014), op. cit. (note | Anm. 5), 9–24 **13** Ibid., 12 **14** Cf. | Vgl. ibid., 20 **15** Cf. | Vgl. ibid., 82 **16** Cf. | Vgl. Yann Nussaume, Définition de l'architecte ou l'influence du rapport au monde dans le processus de création architecturale, in: Daruma, 14(2008), 25–33 **17** Hiroshi Hara, Reflection/Embedding, in: Botond Bognar (2001), op. cit. (note | Anm. 9), 34 **18** Hiroshi Hara (2014), op. cit. (note | Anm. 5), 42 **19** Ibid., 132 **20** See | Vgl. Ariel Genadt, Discrete continuity in the urban architectures of H. Hara & K. Kuma, in: Acadia (2020), 416–424 **21** Hiroshi Hara (2014), op. cit. (note | Anm. 5), 20 **22** Ibid., Hara wrote extensively in this text about this travels with students (including Kengo Kuma) between 1972 and 1979, research collated into a text titled 'Dwelling Group Domain Theory'. | Hara schrieb in diesem Text ausführlich über seine Reisen mit Studenten (darunter Kengo Kuma) zwischen 1972 und 1979. Die Recherchen wurden zu einem Text mit dem Titel ‚Dwelling Group Domain Theory' zusammengefasst.

PRODUCTIVE DISTANCES

Valerie Hoberg

Architecture can be understood as a producing discipline, as it conveys theoretical concepts through mostly physical and in any case aesthetically perceptible artefacts.[1] These are not only 'products' in a general, especially economic conceptual understanding of products, which views material things (or persons) as the end point of an action for fulfilling usage requirements.[2] The products of architecture can also be similar to creative products of artistic disciplines, which allow different types of sensory experiences: alongside the generation of a conscious perception of specific design qualities, individual ways of thinking and alternative perspectives, even critical stances can be conveyed.

PRODUCTION OF DIFFERENCE   In relation to artistic works, there is often a reference to the creation of the 'other', which signifies for example that things are treated, seen, shown or experienced differently.[3] The core operation is the production of difference, whereby the other can serve the conveying of alternative understandings of the world as a change of perspective.[4] In this respect, artistic work that various architects integrate into their practice can also be of significance for architecture. However, how this other is actually produced and specifically characterised is often difficult to describe and requires a consideration of examples.[5] The following is dedicated to the

PRODUKTIVE DISTANZEN

Valerie Hoberg

Die Architektur kann als produzierende Disziplin verstanden werden, da sie gedankliche Konzepte durch meist physische und in jedem Fall ästhetisch rezipierbare Artefakte vermittelt.[1] Diese sind nicht nur ‚Produkte' in einem allgemeinen, vor allem wirtschaftlichen Begriffsverständnis von Produkten, das materielle Dinge (oder Personen) als Endpunkt einer Handlung zur Erfüllung von Nutzungsbedürfnissen ansieht.[2] Die Produkte der Architektur können ebenso kreativen Produkten künstlerischer Disziplinen ähneln, anhand derer durch sinnliches Erleben Erfahrungen unterschiedlicher Art möglich werden: Neben der Erzeugung einer bewussten Wahrnehmung spezifischer gestalterischer Qualitäten können sich individuelle Denkweisen und alternative Perspektiven bis hin zu kritischen Haltungen vermitteln.

DIFFERENZPRODUKTION   Im Zusammenhang zum künstlerischen Arbeiten findet sich häufig ein Verweis auf eine Erzeugung des ‚Anderen', was zum Beispiel beinhaltet, dass Dinge anders behandelt, gesehen, gezeigt oder erfahren werden.[3] Kernoperation ist die Erzeugung von Differenz, wodurch das Andere zur Vermittlung alternativer Weltverständnisse als Wechsel der Perspektive dienen kann.[4] Darin kann künstlerisches Arbeiten, das verschiedene zeitgenössische Architekturschaffende in ihre Praxis integrieren, auch für die Architektur von Bedeutung sein. Wie dieses Andere allerdings produziert werden kann und spezifisch ausgeprägt ist, ist oft schwer zu beschreiben und bedarf beispielhafter Betrachtungen.[5] Im Folgenden wird sich dem Spektrum der Wirkungsweisen

1 | Ensamble Studio SGAE Santiago de Compostela Explorative mock-up inside the quarry 2007

spectrum of how artistic products take effect in architecture. Two products that can be described as artistic from the practice of the Spanish architecture office Ensamble Studio – experimental models as well as videos – serve the outlining of the 'other' in terms of its characterisation and effect on architectural design and research. Reflexive potentials are identified via creative-rational interplays, which can provide impulses for future-orientated action and produce insights.

ARTISTIC EXPERIMENT   Experiments play a significant role in art, especially with regard to products: along the production, a creative process is linked with interests in insights. Experiments allow artists to pursue questions in a target-oriented but nevertheless freely explorative manner. This provides experiences of the other, as those experimenting are confronted with an unpredictable creation and results that only gain meaning as a deviation from the rest. To reach an insight, exposure to this elusiveness is required, whereby for artistic experiments a relativisation of the self and one's own capacities are always conditional.[6]

THINKING WITH ONE'S HANDS   Experiments are often used in architecture as part of construction and material research, as in the case of Ensamble Studio.[7] They look for new constructive possibilities and combine this with a specific aesthetic, especially of the material. They produce material studies for this purpose as well as mockups of constructions that are structured but at the same time include modifiable parts (fig. 1–2). Ensamble Studio work with different, mostly easily modifiable, perhaps even obsolete materials and use the results as a starting point for building. They pursue two

2 | Ensamble Studio SGAE Santiago de Compostela Direct transfer of the mock-up to the built work 2007

künstlerischer Produkte in der Architektur gewidmet. Zwei als künstlerisch zu beschreibende Produkte der Praxis des spanischen Architekturbüros Ensamble Studio – experimentelle Modelle sowie Videos – dienen dazu, dem ‚Anderen' in seiner Charakterisierung und Wirkung für architektonisches Entwerfen und Forschen Kontur zu verleihen. Es lassen sich reflexive Potenziale anhand kreativ-rationaler Wechselwirkungen aufzeigen, die Impulse für zukunftsgerichtetes Handeln setzen und Erkenntnisse produzieren können.

KÜNSTLERISCHES EXPERIMENT   Experimente spielen für die Kunst eine große Rolle, insbesondere im Hinblick auf Produkte: Im Hervorbringen dieser verknüpft sich ein kreativer Prozess mit Erkenntnisinteressen. Experimente ermöglichen Kunstschaffenden, zielorientiert und dennoch frei explorativ Fragestellungen nachzugehen. Dabei entstehen Erfahrungen des Anderen, da die Experimentierenden konfrontiert werden mit einer Unvorhersehbarkeit des Hervorgebrachten und Ergebnissen, die erst als Abweichung vom Übrigen Bedeutung erlangen. Um zur Erkenntnis zu gelangen, muss sich diesen Unverfügbarkeiten ausgesetzt werden, wodurch für künstlerische Experimente immer eine Relativierung vom Selbst sowie den eigenen Kapazitäten Voraussetzung ist.[6]

DENKEN MIT DEN HÄNDEN   Experimente werden in der Architektur oft im Rahmen von Konstruktions- und Materialerforschungen eingesetzt, so auch bei Ensamble Studio.[7] Sie suchen nach neuen konstruktiven Möglichkeiten und verknüpfen dies mit einer spezifischen Ästhetik, insbesondere des Materials. Sie erzeugen dazu Materialstudien sowie Mock-ups von Konstruktionen, die zwar strukturiert werden, aber ebenso frei ausprobierende Anteile enthalten (Abb. 1–2). Ensamble Studio arbeiten mit

3 | Ensamble Studio Structures of landscape Model studies 2015

overarching paths that structure their entire work: on the one hand, they work with their hands – even think with them – and 'natural' materials such as earth, stone and especially concrete, and on the other hand, they work with prefabricated products, especially with constructional steel and concrete elements, for which e.g. staples are used in the model. The office founder Antón García-Abril and the co-owner Débora Mesa describe that they must absolutely be involved in the experimenting and that this is even the only activity that they cannot delegate.[8]

S E L F - D I S T A N C I N G   The artistic experimental model studies serve the finding of possible novel results regarding haptics, visuals and the plasticity of the material. They can be described as artistic insofar as they do not strive for a rationalisation of aesthetic properties but instead enable an openness to unpredictability by means of singular results and coincidence.[9] Forms, structures and spaces are explored in connection with material compositions and surfaces. For example for the project 'Structures of landscape' (Fishtail, MT, 2016), which consists of monumental concrete objects in the expanse of nature of the Tippet Rise Art Center, Ensamble Studio considers various natural formations through numerous models (fig. 3).[10] Through digging, filling with concrete and then digging out again (sometimes propping up), artefacts between sculpture and architecture are produced, not dissimilar to works of land art, whose final aesthetic properties are not predeter-mined but continue to incorporate coincidence artistically and experimentally (fig. 4–5).[11]

4–5 | Ensamble Studio Structures of landscape Domo, Fishtail MT 2016

unterschiedlichen, meist einfach modifizierbaren, vielleicht sogar obsoleten Materialien und nutzen die Ergebnisse als Ausgangspunkt für Gebautes. Sie verfolgen zwei übergeordnete Suchpfade, die ihr gesamtes Werk strukturieren: So arbeiten sie einerseits mit ihren Händen – denken gar mit diesen – sowie ‚natürlichen' Materialien wie Erde, Stein und insbesondere Beton und andererseits mit präfabrizierten Produkten, vor allem mit konstruktiven Stahl- und Betonelementen, wofür im Modell zum Beispiel Tackernadeln dienen. Der Bürogründer Antón Garcia-Abril und die Mitinhaberin Débora Mesa beschreiben, dass sie zwingend in das Experimentieren eingebunden sein müssen sowie dies sogar die einzige Tätigkeit sei, die sie nicht delegieren können.[8]

SELBSTDISTANZ   Die künstlerischen experimentellen Modellstudien dienen dem Finden möglicher neuartiger Resultate im Hinblick auf Haptik, Optik und Formbarkeit des Materials. Sie können insofern als künstlerisch beschrieben werden, als sie nicht nach einer Rationalisierung der ästhetischen Eigenschaften streben, sondern anhand singulärer Ergebnisse und durch den Zufall eine Offenheit für Unvorhersehbares ermöglichen.[9] Formen, Strukturen und Räume im Zusammenhang zu Materialzusammensetzungen und Oberflächen werden erkundet. So untersuchen Ensamble Studio zum Beispiel für das Projekt ‚Structures of landscape' (Fishtail, MT, 2016), das aus monumentalen Betonobjekten in der weiten Natur des Kunstzentrums Tippet Rise besteht, verschiedene natürliche Formationen mittels zahlreicher Modelle (Abb. 3).[10] Durch Graben, Verfüllen mit Beton und wieder Ausgraben (sowie manchmal Aufrichten) werden zwischen Skulptur und Architektur befindliche Artefakte produziert, Land-Art-Kunstwerken nicht unähnlich, deren finale ästhetische Eigenschaften nicht vorherbestimmt sind, sondern weiterhin künstlerisch-experimentell den Zufall integrieren (Abb. 4–5).[11] Die Architekturschaffenden treffen zwar Entscheidungen über Rahmenbedingungen, aber spezifische Eigenschaften des Materials bleiben durch sie indeterminiert. Das Material wird in den Arbeiten sogar als Agens betont, mit dem Eindruck eigener Aktivität und Vitalität (Abb. 6).[12] Im gebauten Werk wird diese vermittelte Transformabilität durch Natureinwirkungen wie Verwitterung und sich ansiedelnde Pflanzen zur Realität.

6 | Ensamble Studio Structures of landscape Non-designable material surface

Although the architects make decisions about framework conditions, specific properties of the material remain undetermined by them. The material is even emphasised as a vital agent in the works, with the impression of proper activity and vitality (fig. 6).[12] In the built work, this conveyed transformability becomes reality through effects of nature such as weathering and the proliferation of plants. Ensamble Studio describe this giving up of complete authorship and maybe even a distance to one's own capacities as necessary, in order to be able to find new constructions and material properties through the models. Mesa states that it is only when letting go of control and trusting in improvisation and adaptation, which usually are more a feature of art, works are created with design properties that cannot be designed.[13] Established systems are consciously given up in order to achieve new possibilities and ways of understanding.[14] In the model studies, this distancing is materialised, in the context of design they form distanced and distancing intermediary steps. In these, what is familiar is shown differently in an artistic way and based on these a plurality of architectural interpretations becomes possible.

DOCUMENTATION AND INTERPRETATION   The various videos they make for the majority of their works can be regarded as a further artistic product in the work of Ensamble Studio.[15] They rarely thematise spatial qualities of the built work: the videos show the idea by means of the construction process and the site as well as, depending whether it is a realised project or not, the model construction or the construction phase, and sometimes even both together. The recordings seldom have original sound, instead they are often set to pieces of music by the father of García-Abril, who was a well-known Spanish composer, or other pieces of classical music. By means of the editing technique and the camera perspective, the filmic documentations are reinforced and interpreted (fig. 7–9). For example, stop-motion technology, time lapses or slow motion are used. Together with the musical backdrop, the focus is placed on the movements of the people, the materials and the constructional elements.

7–9 | Ensamble Studio The truffle Screenshots from construction video Costa da morte 2010

Dieses Aufgeben von der vollständigen Autorenschaft und vielleicht sogar einer Distanz von den eigenen Kapazitäten beschreiben Ensamble Studio als notwendig, um mittels der Modelle neue Konstruktionen und Materialeigenschaften finden zu können. Mesa konstatiert, dass erst im Loslassen der Kontrolle hin zu einem Vertrauen in Improvisation und Anpassung, die üblicherweise eher in der Kunst vorkämen, Werke mit gestalterischen Eigenschaften entstehen, die nicht entwerfbar seien.[13] Etablierte Systeme werden bewusst aufgegeben, um zu neuen Möglichkeiten und Verständnisweisen zu gelangen.[14] In den Modellstudien materialisiert sich dieses Distanznehmen, im Kontext von Entwurfstätigkeiten bilden sie distanzierte sowie distanzierende Zwischenschritte. In ihnen wird auf künstlerische Weise Bekanntes anders gezeigt und von ihnen ausgehend eine Pluralität architektonischer Interpretationen ermöglicht.

DOKUMENTATION UND INTERPRETATION   Als ein weiteres künstlerisches Produkt im Werk Ensamble Studios können die verschiedenen Videos betrachtet werden, die sie zum überwiegenden Teil ihrer Arbeiten anfertigen.[15] Nur wenig thematisieren sie räumliche Qualitäten des fertig Gebauten: Die Videos zeigen die Idee mittels des Konstruktionsprozesses und dafür das Grundstück sowie, je nachdem ob realisiertes Projekt oder nicht, den Modellbau oder die Konstruktionsphase und manchmal auch beides zusammen. Selten haben die Aufnahmen Originalton, sondern sind häufig unterlegt mit Musikstücken des Vaters Antón García-Abrils, der ein bekannter spanischer Komponist war, oder anderen klassischen Musikstücken. Mittels der Schnitttechnik und der Kameraperspektive werden die filmischen Dokumentationen verstärkt und interpretiert (Abb. 7–9). Es kommen zum Beispiel Stop-Motion-Technik, Zeitraffer oder schnelle Zeitlupen zum Einsatz. Gemeinsam mit der musikalischen Untermalung wird so der Fokus auf die Bewegungen der Menschen, der Materialien und des Konstruktionsgeräts gelegt.

Darin können Ensamble Studios Videos an Werke der Performancekunst erinnern.[16] Diese intendiert eine Entfernung vom Objektcharakter der Kunst und betont die singuläre, direkte Erfahrung: Es sind aufgeführte Inszenierungen, wobei die Körper der Agierenden

10 | Ensamble Studio Casa del lector Inserted bridges visible in window Madrid 2010

In this respect, Ensamble Studio's videos can be evocative of works of performance art.[16] Their purpose is a distancing from the object character of art, emphasising a singular, direct experience: they represent performed staging, whereby the bodies of the actors and recipients are set in a spatial relationship as a medium in the unfolding action.[17] After the one-time performance, they only continue to exist in the memories of the public, as well as videos and photographs, and rarely in fragments of the works that enter exhibition contexts as documentations of the transient and enable a discourse. This results in independent forms of work that feed off the difference, the otherness between what is pictured and real experience on site.[18]

EXPERIENCE AND EVENT   These videos can influence the reception of what is built. They flow like a memory into its spatial configuration: for example, the U-shaped concrete supports that are shoved through the windows at the 'Casa del lector' in Madrid (2007) are given an inscribed story through the video (fig. 10). Their position in the spatial building configuration is endowed with significance through the videos; the movement of sliding explains their relation to the overall system (fig. 11-13). Through Ensamble Studio, these bridges are thought of as a dissonant sound that interrupts the previously existing (constructive) harmony of the building – an impression that is in turn reinforced by the video and the musical accompaniment.[19] The construction is shown as a sequence of movement with a choreographed effect. The presentation of the performance – the building activity – is the actual work according to this understanding, which is recounted by what is built as a 'remainder'. The building procedure, its documentation in the video and the experience on site come together as an overall event, in which the relations between the spatial components and the temporal levels are overlayed.[20] The videos as an artistic product convey an alternative reality.

11–13 | Ensamble Studio Casa del lector Screenshots from construction video Madrid 2010

und Rezipierenden als Medien im gegenwärtigen Geschehen räumlich in Beziehung gesetzt werden.[17] Sie bestehen nach dem einmaligen Aufführen lediglich in Erinnerungen des Publikums sowie Videos oder Fotografien und selten in Fragmenten der Werke fort, die als Dokumentationen des Vergänglichen in Ausstellungskontexte eingehen und einen Diskurs ermöglichen. Dabei entstehen eigene Werkformen, die sich aus der Differenz, der Andersartigkeit zwischen Abgebildetem und realer Erfahrung vor Ort, speisen.[18]

ERFAHRUNG UND EREIGNIS   Diese Videos können Einfluss auf die Rezeption des Gebauten nehmen. Sie gehen wie ein Gedächtnis in dessen Raumkonfiguration ein: So erhalten zum Beispiel die Beton-U-Träger, die in die Casa del lector in Madrid (2007) durch die Fenster eingeschoben werden, durch das Video eine ihnen eingeschriebene Geschichte (Abb. 10). Ihre Position in der räumlichen Gebäudekonfiguration wird durch die Videos mit Bedeutung belegt; die Bewegung des Schiebens erklärt ihren Bezug zum Gesamtsystem (Abb. 11–13). Durch Ensamble Studio werden die Brücken als dissonanter Ton gedacht, der die vorher bestehende (konstruktive) Harmonie des Gebäudes unterbricht – ein Eindruck, der wiederum durch das Video und die musikalische Untermalung unterstützt wird.[19] Die Konstruktion wird als choreografiert wirkende Bewegungsabfolge gezeigt. Die Aufführung der Performance – das Bauen – ist in diesem Verständnis das eigentliche Werk, wovon das Gebaute als ‚Überbleibsel' erzählt. Der Bauvorgang, dessen Dokumentation im Video und

93

INTERIM SPACES   If one takes a comparative look at these two artistic products, a parallel emerges. While the material experiments serve the finding or invention of possible material qualities and construction methods, even not yet existent methods, the videos generate post-project interpretations that recount associations and a story about the work, thereby diversifying its perception. In both cases, what is familiar and known – knowledge about handling of material, technical skills, constructional habits, built reality – becomes something still unknown. It is not about a radical reinvention but about a breaking down of the familiar in order to put it back together anew and furthermore extend or amend it.[21] What is decisive is that it is not a polar opposite but something that oscillates in between. The artistic products materialise this interim space and therefore set framework conditions for making it possible to show what is not yet known.[22]

(Self-)distances therefore manifest in the artistic products: by removing their own control through the experiments, Ensamble Studio can make out coincidental finds in the results. A 'Failing' is necessarily part of it and a condition for those finds that reveal productivity in the serendipity of missing a target.[23] The videos also have a retroactive effect of unfolding the imagination, which as an additional layer distances reception from the actual built reality. They could also reflect back into the design by acting as a different perspective on the construction: the leading question could be not so much how a specific end result can be achieved but, vice versa, which material traces are created through a script of construction measures.[24] The artistic product ensures that the architects distance themselves – from abilities, control, reality or constructional habits and also from themselves. External recipients can also have these experiences of distance based on the works that thematise the subject of being made, and subsequently gain insights themselves.[25]

die gegenwärtige Erfahrung vor Ort verdichten sich zu einem gemeinsamen Ereignis, indem sich die Beziehungen zwischen den räumlichen Bestandteilen und die zeitlichen Ebenen überlagern.[20] Die Videos als künstlerisches Produkt vermitteln eine alternative Realität.

Z W I S C H E N R Ä U M E   Wird nun auf diese beiden künstlerischen Produkte im Vergleich geblickt, zeigt sich eine Parallele. Während die Materialexperimente dazu dienen, mögliche Materialqualitäten und Konstruktionsweisen bis zu noch nicht existenten Techniken zu (er-)finden, werden mit den Videos Postprojekt-Interpretationen erzeugt, die Assoziationen und eine Geschichte zum Werk erzählen und so dessen Wahrnehmung vervielfältigen. In beiden Fällen wird von etwas Bekanntem – Wissen über Materialbehandlungen, handwerklichen Fähigkeiten, konstruktiven Gewohnheiten, gebauter Realität, etwas Gewusstem – zu etwas noch Unbekanntem gelangt. Es geht nicht um eine radikale Neuerfindung, sondern um eine Zerlegung des Bekannten, um es neu zusammenzusetzen und darüber zu erweitern oder zu verändern.[21] Entscheidend ist, dass es nicht um einen polaren Gegensatz, sondern etwas dazwischen Oszillierendes geht. Die künstlerischen Produkte materialisieren diesen Zwischenraum und setzen damit Rahmenbedingungen dafür, dass noch nicht Bekanntes sich überhaupt zeigen kann.[22]

In den künstlerischen Produkten manifestieren sich also (Selbst-)Distanzen: Indem sich Ensamble Studio durch die Experimente der eigenen Kontrolle entzieht, kann das Büro in den Resultaten zufällige Funde ausmachen. Dabei ist ein ‚Scheitern' zwangsläufig inbegriffen und Voraussetzung für jene Funde, die als Serendipität in der Zielverfehlung Produktivität entdecken.[23] Die Videos haben zudem eine nachträgliche Wirkung der Imaginationsvervielfältigung, die als zusätzlicher Layer die Rezeption von der eigentlichen gebauten Realität distanziert. Sie könnten außerdem in das Entwerfen zurückwirken, indem sie als andere Perspektive auf das Bauen wirken: Es könnte weniger die Frage leitend sein, wie ein spezifisches Endergebnis erreicht werden kann, und umgekehrt die Frage danach, welche materiellen Spuren durch ein Skript von Konstruktionshandlungen erzeugt werden.[24] Jeweils sorgt das künstlerische Produkt dafür, dass sich die Architekturschaffenden distanzieren – von sich selbst, von Fähigkeiten, Kontrolle, der Realität oder konstruktiven Gewohnheiten. Auch externe Rezipierende können diese Distanzerfahrungen anhand der Werke machen, die das Gemachtsein thematisieren, und, dies nachvollziehend, selbst Erkenntnisse gewinnen.[25]

This allows a significance to be discerned for artistic products in architecture that goes beyond a purely inspirational effect that stimulates the imagination: in the distancing that they describe lies the possibility of gaining a reflexive perspective on one's own work; a possibility afforded by art especially since modern times.[26] In the context of practice, reflexivity refers to a stance that reflects on what is produced in order to obtain something new and insights. The distancing to the self, one's own conditions and own products is of great significance.[27] If the distancing is consolidated through the repetition of the singular event as a method, it can also have externalisable knowledge-producing potential. The recurring approaching and distancing, which repeatedly give up control and then regain it through selection, sorting and framing, are intended to unravel existing ways of understanding and to redefine them. This takes effect especially when the artistic products are reworked and reconveyed for example as part of exhibitions or publications. The understanding of an 'other' therefore includes an awareness of the starting framework as well as creative-projective changes.

PRODUCTS AS PROCESS WITNESSES   Artistic work is therefore not (only) a contemplative departure from other work in architecture. On the one hand, it serves the working out of design properties and the unfolding of the imagination and, on the other hand, the reflection on established routines, conditions or possibilities. They are questioned and transformed. The resulting products are essential for this: they manifest and materialise the interim space – of what is mastered and not mastered, of one thing and another – which can be filled imaginatively and extended to new projects. The products incorporate both one and the other by going against previously known ordering systems and indicating new ones, which, however, must be transferred in turn to architecture, whereby they remain open. They create distances that are experienced aesthetically in the products.

Damit lässt sich für künstlerische Produkte in der Architektur eine Bedeutung ausmachen, die über eine rein inspirative, imaginativ anregende Wirkung hinausgeht: In den durch sie beschriebenen Distanzbewegungen liegt die Möglichkeit, eine reflexive Perspektive auf das eigene Arbeiten zu gewinnen; eine Möglichkeit, die der Kunst vor allem seit der Moderne eingeschrieben ist.[26] Mit Reflexivität ist in Praxiskontexten eine Haltung gemeint, die das Produzierte reflektiert, um davon ausgehend zu Neuem und Erkenntnissen zu gelangen. Das Distanzieren zum Selbst, den eigenen Bedingungen und den eigenen Produkten ist von wesentlicher Bedeutung.[27] Werden die Distanzbewegungen in der Wiederholung vom singulären Ereignis zur Methode verstetigt, können sie auch externalisierbare wissens-produzierende Potenziale haben. Die retournierenden Annäherungs- und Distanzierungs-bewegungen, die wiederholt Kontrolle abgeben und sie durch Auswahl, Sortierung und Rahmung wiedererlangen, intendieren bestehende Verständnisweisen aufzutrennen, um diese neu zu prägen. Dies wird insbesondere wirksam, wenn die künstlerischen Produkte zum Beispiel im Rahmen von Ausstellungen oder Publikationen erneut aufbereitet und vermittelt werden. Im Verständnis eines ‚Anderen' sind dann sowohl ein Bewusstsein über die Ausgangsrahmung inbegriffen als auch kreativ-projektive Veränderungen.

PRODUKTE ALS PROZESSZEUGEN   Das künstlerische Arbeiten ist damit nicht (nur) ein kontemplativer Ausflug vom sonstigen Arbeiten in der Archi-tektur. Es dient einerseits zur Erarbeitung gestalterischer Eigenschaften und Verviel-fältigung von Imaginationen sowie andererseits zur Reflexion etablierter Routinen, Voraussetzungen oder Möglichkeiten. Sie werden befragt und transformiert. Die resul-tierenden Produkte sind dafür essenziell: In ihnen manifestiert und materialisiert sich der Zwischenraum – von Gekonntem und Ungekonntem, vom Einen und Anderen –, der imaginativ gefüllt werden und zu neuen Projekten ausgebaut werden kann. Die Produkte inkorporieren sowohl das Eine als auch das Andere, indem sie bislang bekannte Ordnungssysteme durchkreuzen und neue andeuten, die allerdings wiederum in die Architektur übertragen werden müssen, wodurch sie offen verbleiben. Sie sind selbst und sie schaffen Distanzen, die in den Produkten ästhetisch erfahren werden.

1 On the importance of media products in architectural design cf. | Zur Bedeutung medialer Produkte im Architekturentwurf vgl. Margitta Buchert (ed.), Entwerfen gestalten. Skizzierungen. Shaping design. Delineations, in: Entwerfen gestalten: Medien der Architekturkonzeption. Shaping Design: Media of architectural conception, Berlin: jovis 2020, 14–33, passim and the contributions of the publication | sowie die Beiträge des Bandes   **2** Cf. | Vgl. https://wirtschaftslexikon.gabler.de/definition/produkt-42902/version-266242, 06.07.2022   **3** Cf. in relation to Peter Sloterdijk | Vgl. in Bezug auf Peter Sloterdijk Margitta Buchert, Anderswohnen, in: id./Carl Zillich (eds.), Performativ? Architektur und Kunst, Berlin: jovis 2007, 40–49, 40   **4** Cf. | Vgl. Niklas Luhmann, Die Kunst der Gesellschaft, Frankfurt a. M.: Suhrkamp 2017, 229–241, or | oder Dieter Mersch, Kunst und Episteme, in: what's next?, September 2013 on: | auf: http://whtsnxt.net/102 23.09.2021; Or to the similarly understood 'new' | Oder zum ähnlich zu verstehenden ‚Neuen' Thomas Lehnerer, Methode der Kunst, Würzburg: Königshausen & Neumann 1994, 24   **5** Cf. e.g. on the 'other' in the work of architect Rem Koolhaas | Vgl. z. B. zum ‚Anderen' in der Arbeit des Architekten Rem Koolhaas Margitta Buchert (2007), op. cit. (note | Anm. 3), passim   **6** Cf. | Vgl. Nicolas Constantin Romanacci, Experimentieren, Fremderfahrung, Selbstrelativierung. Eine philosophische Untersuchung in Bezugnahme auf eine sprachanalytisch-anthropologische Studie von Ernst Tugendhat und Nelson Goodmans Symbol- und Erkenntnistheorie, in: Werner Fitzner (ed.), Kunst und Fremderfahrung: Verfremdungen, Affekte, Entdeckungen, Image, Bielefeld: Transcript 2016, 119–140, 119–120   **7** Cf. | Vgl. Albert Kirchengast/Ákos Moravánszky, Experimentalismen. Zur Einführung, in: ids. (eds.), Experiments: Architektur zwischen Wissenschaft und Kunst, Berlin: jovis 2011, 6–23, 10–16; or | oder Michael Schumacher, Forschen heißt machen, in: Margitta Buchert (ed.), Praktiken Reflexiven Entwerfens, Berlin: jovis 2016, 93–103   **8** Cf. / Vgl. Iker Gil/Antón García-Abril/Débora Mesa, Iker Gil in conversation with Ensamble Studio, in: Iker Gil (ed.), Radical logic. On the work of Ensamble Studio, MAS Context 2021, 49–164, 148   **9** Cf. | Vgl. Dieter Mersch, Was heißt, im Ästhetischen forschen?, in: Kathrin Busch (ed.), Anderes Wissen, Paderborn: Wilhelm Fink 2016, 102–120, 117–118   **10** Cf. | Vgl. Iker Gil et al. (2021), op. cit. (note | Anm. 8), 130–137   **11** On the comparison between the Structures of landscape and Land art artworks cf. | Zum Vergleich zwischen den Structures of landscape und Land art-Kunstwerken vgl. Philip Ursprung, Earthwards, in: Moisés Puente (ed.), Ensamble Studio, 2G, Revista International de Arquitectura 82 Köln: König 2021, 4–11, 9   **12** Cf. on

the idea of 'vibrant matter' | Vgl. zur Idee ‚lebhafter Materie' Jane Bennett, Vibrant matter, A political ecology of things, London: Duke University Press 2010, esp. | bes. 110–122 and | und passim **13** Cf. | Vgl. Iker Gil et al. (2021), op. cit. (note | Anm. 8), 79 **14** On the production of knowledge through experiments cf. | Vgl. zu Erkenntnisproduktionen durch Experimente Romanacci (2016), op. cit. (note | Anm. 6), 131 **15** With just a few exceptions, the videos introduce the project presentations on the office's website. Cf. | Mit wenigen Ausnahmen leiten die Videos die Projektvorstellungen auf der Bürowebsite ein. Vgl. https://www.ensamble.info/projects, 03.07.2022 **16** Cf. | Vgl. Iker Gil et al. (2021), op. cit. (note | Anm. 8), 76 **17** Cf. | Vgl. Yve-Alain Bois, Oldenburg and happenings, in: Hal Foster et al. (eds.), Art since 1900: modernism, antimodernism, postmodernism, London: Thames & Hudson 2016, 520–525, 522–523; as well as | sowie Margitta Buchert, Performativ? Körper Raum Architektur Kunst, in: id./Carl Zillich (eds.) (2007), op. cit. (note | Anm. 3) 9–12, 11 **18** Cf. | Vgl. Geraldine Spiekermann, Performance-déjà-vu, in: Verena Krieger/Sophia Stang (eds.), Wiederholungstäter: die Selbstwiederholung als künstlerische Praxis in der Moderne, Köln: Böhlau 2017, 209–224, 213–214 **19** Cf. | Vgl. Antón García-Abril (2012), Stones and beams (Lecture | Vortrag 18.10.2012), Stockholm: KTH Arkitekturskolan, on: | auf: https://www.youtube.com/watch?v=_feog95gi_Q&t=20s, 18.12.2017 **20** Cf. | Vgl. Christoph Brunner, Krisis und Invention: Die Notwendigkeit, der Gegenwart zu widerstehen. Oder: Die Reihe Inventionen als Ereignis, in: Johannes M. Hedinger/Torsten Meyer (eds.), what's next? Kunst nach der Krise. Ein Reader, Berlin: Kulturverlag Kadmos 2013, 99–105, 99 **21** On experimenting as a confrontation with the existing cf. | Zum Experimentieren als Auseinandersetzung mit Vorhandenem vgl. Kirchengast/Moravánszky (eds.) (2011), op. cit. (note | Anm. 7), 18 **22** Cf. | Vgl. Hans-Jörg Rheinberger, Über Serendipität. Forschen und Finden, in: Emmanuel Alloa et al. (eds.), Imagination: Suchen und Finden, Paderborn: Fink 2014, 233–243, 233 **23** Cf. | Vgl. ibid., 236 **24** Cf. on script | Vgl. zu Skript Iker Gil et al. (2021), op. cit. (note | Anm. 8), 79 **25** Cf. | Vgl. Georg W. Bertram, Kunst als menschliche Praxis: eine Ästhetik, Berlin: Suhrkamp 2018, 139–146 **26** Cf. | Vgl. Arno Schubbach, Selbstbezügliches Schwarz? Zur Reflexivität von Bildern, in: Reflexivität in den Künsten, Zeitschrift für Ästhetik und Allgemeine Kunstwissenschaft, 55, 2 (2010), 287–300, 287 **27** Cf. | Vgl. Margitta Buchert, Reflexives Entwerfen? Topologien eines Forschungsfeldes, in: id. (ed.), Reflexives Entwerfen. Entwerfen und Forschen in der Architektur, Berlin: Jovis 2014, 24–49, 35–37 and | und passim

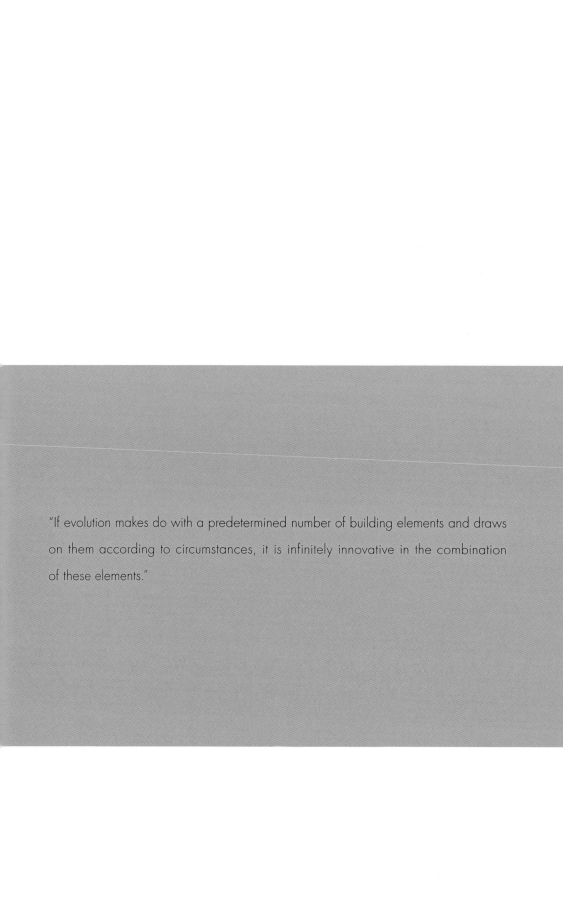

"If evolution makes do with a predetermined number of building elements and draws on them according to circumstances, it is infinitely innovative in the combination of these elements."

„Wenn die Evolution mit einer vorbestimmten Zahl von Bausteinen auskommt und je nach Gegebenheit auf diese zugreift, so ist sie in der Kombination dieser Elemente unendlich innovativ."

Enrico Coen

TYPEN VON TYPEN
TYPES OF TYPES

In the following discourses about products of reflexive design, it is not primarily about a science of types to be understood as taxonomy, nor about a set of rules with limitations or a canon of works perceived as exemplary. Even so, the contributions revolve around objectifiable and codifiable aspects, around the essentially invariant, as a potential means of knowledge genesis and of knowledge transfer, with the aim of promoting the design and planning of high-quality habitats. Architectural ways of thinking and acting are presented and discussed, which research, structure, construct and interpret empirical materials through doing and its relations to knowledge. It is the respective project that can be presented as a product of reflexive design, whether as something conceived, built, designed, researched, drawn, staged or written.[1] An exploration of types is inherent in the projects. As socially shared, collective background knowledge – alongside semantic levels of type relating to architypes such as tent, nest, hut and cave, field, park and square, or to typing in the sense of prefabricated elements in the industrial building of the modern era and in the algorhythmic-parametric designing of the present – numerous interpretations have evolved that see the formation of a building or spatial ensemble in relation to its social use as generated historically and view it as a qualitative design objective.

In den folgenden Diskursen zu Produkten Reflexiven Entwerfens geht es vorrangig nicht um eine als Taxonomie zu verstehende Wissenschaft von den Typen und auch nicht um ein Regelwerk mit Begrenzungen oder einen Kanon vorbildhaft empfundener Werke. Und doch kreisen die Beiträge um objektivierbare und auch kodifizierbare Aspekte, um essenziell Invariantes, als potenzielles Mittel der Wissensgenese und des Wissenstransfers mit dem Ziel, Entwurf und Planung qualitätsvoller Habitate zu befördern. Präsentiert und diskutiert werden architektonische Denk- und Handlungsweisen, die im Machen und seinen Relationen zum Wissen empirische Materialien erforschen, strukturieren, konstruieren und interpretieren. Es ist das jeweilige Projekt, das als Produkt des Reflexiven Entwerfens dargeboten werden kann, ob als Konzipiertes, Gebautes, Entworfenes, Erforschtes, Gezeichnetes, Inszeniertes oder Geschriebenes.[1] Den Projekten inhärent ist eine Erkundung von Typen. Als sozial geteiltes kollektives Hintergrundwissen haben sich neben Bedeutungsebenen von Typus, bezogen auf Archetypen wie Zelt, Nest, Hütte und Höhle, Feld und Platz, oder Typisierungen im Sinne vorgefertigter Elemente im industriellen Bauen der Moderne und im algorithmisch-parametrischen Entwerfen der Gegenwart auch zahlreiche Interpretationen eingenistet, die die Formation eines Gebäudes oder räumlichen Ensembles in Relation zu seinem sozialen Gebrauch als historisch generiert und als qualitatives Entwurfsziel betrachten.

With its rationalised, grid-based classification system for building types presented in analytical plans and profiles according to practical functions, the taxonomic interpretation by the French architect Jean-Nicolas-Louis Durand has strongly influenced the understanding of type since the beginning of the 19th century.[2] The typology concepts of the neorationalists of the 1960s and 1970s proved equally influential, developed based on the formation of principles for spatial and organisational design, with the addition of relations to the town and territory as factors. Typological interpretations refer to building and construction forms, to spatial organisations, as well as to building elements, building components and decorations. They can function equally as an analysis and design tool.[3] They support self-understandings of the discipline, forge collective identities and reach towards notions of typologies as the core of architecture, even if the concepts of type and typology are repeatedly discussed very controversially.[4] Such conventions of a discipline act as patterns of perception, understanding and action and are also described as habitus in anthropological, sociological, cultural and scientific theory discourses.[5] They have the ability to be adaptable and to form collective resources. For example, prototypes can be reactivated accordingly in the sense of first samples and become a starting point for variable interpretations. They enable the handling of changing situations and various tasks, while at the same time ensuring recognisability. They can also be questioned, modified, extended and potentially replaced by being stimulated to think beyond the familiar and through the suggestion of new architectural manifestations.

Mit seinem rationalisierten, in abstrakten analytischen Plänen und Schnitten dargebotenen rasterbasierten Klassifikationssystem für Gebäudetypen nach den praktischen Funktionen hat die taxonomische Interpretation des französischen Architekten Jean-Nicolas-Louis Durand seit Beginn des 19. Jahrhunderts das Typusverständnis stark geprägt.[2] Ebenso wirkungsstark zeigten sich die auf Prinzipienbildung für räumliche und organisatorische Gestaltung entwickelten Typologiekonzepte der Neorationalisten der 1960er und 1970er Jahre, bei denen Relationen zu Stadt und Territorium als Faktoren hinzutraten. Typologische Interpretationen beziehen sich dabei auf Gebäude- und Konstruktionsformen, auf Raumorganisationen, aber ebenso auch auf Bauelemente, Bauteile und Dekorationen. Sie können als Analyse- und Entwurfsinstrument gleichermaßen wirken.[3] Sie stützen Selbstverständnisse der Disziplin, prägen kollektive Identitäten bis hin zu Vorstellungen von Typologien als Kern der Architektur, wenngleich die Konzepte von Typus und Typologie immer wieder auch sehr kontrovers und vielfältig diskutiert werden.[4] Solche Konventionen einer Disziplin wirken als Schemata der Wahrnehmung, des Verstehens und der Aktion und werden in anthropologischen, soziologischen und kultur- und wissenschaftstheoretischen Diskursen auch als Habitus bezeichnet.[5] Sie haben die Kompetenz, anpassungsfähig zu sein und kollektive Ressourcen zu bilden. So beispielsweise können Prototypen im Sinne erster Exemplare entsprechend reaktiviert und zu einem Ausgangspunkt werden für variable Interpretationen. Sie ermöglichen, mit wechselnden Situationen und diversen Aufgabenstellungen umzugehen und gleichzeitig eine Wiedererkennbarkeit zu gewähren. Sie können aber auch befragt, modifiziert, erweitert und potenziell ersetzt werden durch die Anregung, das Bekannte erweitert zu denken, sowie den Vorschlag neuer architektonischer Manifestationen.

With the title 'Counterintuitive Products', Andreas Lechner already evokes the critical-questioning character of his contribution, as 'intuition' is often associated with notions of unconditional creativity. Based on the example of a book that emerged from his habilitation research on architectural building theory, he shows how the strengthening of canonisation endeavours of good architecture can be understood through typological arrangements in the sense of orientation aids and tools for designing. At the same time, however, he presents them, following cultural-critical questioning, as dynamic relations of synchronous and diachronic differentiations and combines them with new perspectives. In the concept of the presented proposal of a building theory, the primate of form remains. In the curated layout and the selection and sequence of the presented projects, the development of variants within building typology groupings is emphasised and thereby the emergence of differences between the general and specific. The chosen medium was layouts, profiles and elevations in black and white, as well as brief text characterisations of the buildings by various international authors. In addition, there are brief lists of various functional buildings by the groups assigned to the respective categories, as well as comprehensive disourse contextualisation surrounding the topic of the typology concept and formation in architecture, whereby typological themes are also discussed as tools of political and economic powers and control. When wandering through and looking in more depth at the linguistic and pictorial levels and their influence, the unusual constellations induce comparisons, extensions and modifications. In this way, a contemporary typological position is presented as an unconventional and undogmatic, more creative orientation and knowledge basis.

Bereits mit dem Titel ‚Kontraintuitive Produkte' evoziert Andreas Lechner den kritisch befragenden Charakter seines Beitrags, da ‚Intuition' vielfach mit Vorstellungen bedingungsfreier Gestaltung verbunden wird. Am Beispiel eines Buches, das aus seiner Habilitationsforschung zur architektonischen Gebäudelehre hervorgegangen ist, zeigt er, wie die Stärkung von Kanonisierungsbestrebungen guter Architektur durch typologische Anordnungen im Sinne von Orientierungshilfen und Instrumenten zum Entwerfen verstanden werden kann. Gleichzeitig aber stellt er sie, kulturell-kritisch befragt, als dynamische Relationen von synchronen und diachronen Differenzierungen vor und verbindet sie mit neuen Perspektiven. Im Konzept des präsentierten Entwurfs einer Gebäudelehre bleibt das Primat der Form bestehen. Im kuratierten Layout und der Selektion und Abfolge der dargestellten Projekte wird die Variantenbildung innerhalb von gebäudetypologischen Gruppierungen hervorgehoben und damit die Differenzbildung zwischen Generellem und Spezifischem. Als Medien sind in Schwarz-Weiß gehaltene Grundrisse, Schnitte und Ansichten sowie textliche Kurzcharakterisierungen der Bauten von diversen internationalen Autor:innen gewählt worden. Dazu treten kurze Listen diverser Funktionsbauten der den jeweiligen Kategorien zugeordneten Gruppen sowie umfangreiche Diskurskontextualisierungen zum Themenkreis des Typologiekonzepts und der Formbildung in der Architektur, wobei typologische Themen auch als Instrumente der politischen und ökonomischen Macht sowie der Steuerung diskutiert werden. Im Durchschweifen wie im Vertiefen der sprachlichen und bildlichen Ebenen und ihrer Durchdringung werden über die ungewöhnlichen Konstellationen Vergleiche, Erweiterungen, Modifikationen angeregt. In dieser Weise wird eine zeitgenössische typologische Position als unkonventionelle und undogmatische, vielmehr kreative Orientierung und Wissensbasis vorgestellt.

The practice-based architectural research shown by Diana Gouveia directs attention to a still 'anonymous architecture', to local and regional perspectives of the lived public space in connection with architectural configurations of transition and of spaces in between indoors and outdoors. The typological studies aim to understand small-scale and privately and collectively effective spatial elements such as balconies, verandas, entrance stairs or arcades. Active appropriation levels of such typological elements in small town and village communities are emphasised, explored graphically and presented. This research is also about the morpho-typological, the connection between activities, spaces and spatial relations, forms and formlessness. It is about a guided finding process whose products are on the one hand manifestations of the analysis and on the other building blocks of the design, which also contain correlations of history, the present and the future. The attempt to find out atmosphere and significance factors in the context of 'experienced space' through the slowly observing graphic representation and to become aware of what elements and constellation this allows is targeted towards an extension of the scopes of knowing through the integration of what can scarcely be grasped by logic alone. The attentive perception and empathy that have been interpreted and studied increasingly since the 19th century and again in recent decades as a form of understanding also flows into the context of empirical design research as a modality.[6] It is at the same time emotional and rational components that are rethought and reimagined here for contemporary relevant questions about the future of regional, rural areas as differentiated sensitisation from a type-related perspective.[7]

Die von Diana Gouveia gezeigte praxisbasierte Architekturforschung richtet die Aufmerksamkeit auf eine noch ‚anonyme Architektur', auf lokale und regionale Perspektiven des gelebten öffentlichen Raums im Zusammenhang mit architektonischen Konfigurationen des Übergangs bzw. der Zwischenräume von Innen und Aussen. Die typologischen Studien zielen darauf, kleinmaßstäbliche und im privaten wie im kollektiven Raum wirksame räumliche Elemente wie Balkone, Veranden, Eingangstreppen oder Arkadengänge zu erfassen. Hervorgehoben, zeichnerisch erkundet und dargeboten werden dabei aktive Aneignungsebenen solcher typologischen Elemente in kleinstädtischen und dörflichen Gemeinschaften. Auch bei diesen Forschungen geht es um Morphotypologisches, um die Verbindung von Tätigkeiten, Räumen und Raumrelationen, um Formen und Formlosigkeit. Es handelt sich um einen geleiteten Findeprozess, dessen Produkte zum einen Manifestationen der Analyse, zum anderen Bausteine des Entwerfens sind, die so auch Korrelationen von Geschichte, Gegenwart und Zukunft beeinhalten. Die Versuche, Stimmungs- und Bedeutungsfaktoren im Kontext des ‚gelebten Raumes' über die langsam beobachtende zeichnerische Erfassung herauszufinden und wahrzunehmen, welche Elemente und Konstellationen diese ermöglichen, richten sich als Anliegen auf eine Erweiterung von Wissensräumen durch Integration des allein logisch kaum Fassbaren. Die aufmerksame Wahrnehmung und die Empathie, wie sie verstärkt seit dem 19. Jahrhundert und erneut in den letzten Jahrzehnten als Form des Verstehens interpretiert und erforscht wurden, spielen als Modalitäten mit in den Kontext der empirischen Entwurfsforschung hinein.[6] Es sind gleichzeitig emotionale und rationale Komponenten, die hier für zeitgenössisch relevante Fragen nach der Zukunft regionaler, ländlicher Räume als differenzierte Sensibilisierung aus einer typusbezogenen Perspektive neu gedacht bzw. konzipiert werden.[7]

Based on the example of her doctoral project, Susan Jebrini presents how already the research design can be interpreted as a product of reflexive design. The enabling of a spatial prototype for contemporary 'new' music guides her studies. Through a combination of test designs and performances, which oscillate between artistic and scientific experimentation, and investigation phases on the research contexts and typologies of the music theatre and the opera, she discusses the genesis of insights on new type concepts for the musical performances. The architectural formations and the architecturally and musically staged performative events in existing built spaces, which could also be referred to as spatial sound events, are examples of practice-based aesthetic principal research in architecture. They are targeted towards raising the perceptions and experiences of the musicians and those experiencing them as listeners in terms of quality and showing how new types of sound spaces and spatial sounds can be generated. They integrate architecture and music science cognition processes sequentially with the aesthetic-artistic exploratory generation of building blocks.[8] Media of research expression are mock-up and installation, staging and performance, as well as language, diagram and photography. The curated research procedure therefore contains the creation of further products or interim products through practices of differentiation. The results then form levels of the poietic that can, as a potential transitional station, subsequently also lead to singularly articulated types.[9] MB

Am Beispiel ihres Promotionsprojekts stellt Susan Jebrini vor, wie bereits das Forschungsdesign als Produkt Reflexiven Entwerfens interpretiert werden kann. Die Ermöglichung eines räumlichen Prototyps für zeitgenössische ‚neue' Musik leitet ihre Untersuchungen. Im Ineinandergreifen von Testentwürfen und Performances, die zwischen künstlerischem und wissenschaftlichem Experimentieren changieren, und Recherchephasen zu den Forschungskontexten und Typologien des Musiktheaters und der Oper diskutiert sie die Genese von Erkenntnissen zu neuen Typenkonzepten für die musikalischen Darbietungen. Die architektonischen Formationen und performativ im baulichen Bestand architektonisch und musikalisch inszenierten Ereignisse im Raum, die auch als Raumklanggeschehen bezeichnet werden könnten, sind Beispiele für praxisbasierte ästhetische Grundlagenforschung in der Architektur. Sie sind darauf gerichtet, die Wahrnehmungen und Erfahrungen der Musiker:innen und der zuhörend Erlebenden qualitativ zu steigern und aufzuzeigen, wie neue Typen von Klangräumen und Raumklängen erzeugt werden können. Dabei integrieren sie architektur- und musikwissenschaftliche Erkenntnisprozesse in einer Abfolge mit ästhetisch-künstlerisch herantastender Entwicklung von Bausteinen.[8] Medien des forschenden Ausdrucks bilden Mock-up und Installation, Inszenierung und Performance sowie Sprache, Diagramm und Fotografie. So beinhaltet der kuratierte Forschungsverlauf die Entstehung weiterer Produkte oder Zwischenprodukte über Praktiken der Differenzierung. Die Resultate bilden dann Ebenen der Poiesis aus, die im Weiteren aber ebenfalls als potenzielle Übergangsstation zu jeweils singulär artikulierten Typen führen können.[9] MB

1 Cf. on this also | Vgl. hierzu auch Mats Alvessen/Kaj Sköjdberg, Reflexive methodology. New vistas for qualitative research, London et al.: SAGE 2013, 9   **2** Cf. also | Vgl. auch Chris Abel, The extended self. Architecture, memes and minds, Manchester: Manchester University Press 2015, 129–148   **3** Cf. | Vgl. Sylvain Malfroy, Die morphologische Betrachtungsweise von Stadt und Territorium, Zürich et al.: Triest 2018, 134–135   **4** For the controversial discourses cf. | Zu den kontroversen Diskursen vgl. Rafael Moneo, On typology, in: Tiago B. Borges/Anja Fröhlich/Martin Fröhlich/Sebastian F. Lippok et al. (eds.), Plans and images. An archive of projects on typology in architecture, Zürich: Park Books 2019, 336–345; Alexander Pellnitz, Ratio und Evokation in der Architekturtheorie von Giorgio Grassi, Berlin: TU 2011, 64–91; Angelika Schnell, Aldo Rossis Konstruktion des Wirklichen. Eine Architekturtheorie mit Widersprüchen, Basel et al.: Birkhäuser 2019, 277–284   **5** Cf. | Vgl. Loïc Wacquant, Toward a social praxeology. The structure and logic of Bourdieu's sociology, in: Id/Pierre Bourdieu, An invitation to reflexive sociology, Chicago, IL: University of Chicago Press 1992, 1–59, 15–18   **6** Cf. on this | Vgl. hierzu Daniel Kurz/Martin Steinmann, Erlebter Raum (Interview), on: | auf: https://www.artlog.net/it/node/149361, 8.8.2022   **7** Cf. | Vgl. Margitta Buchert, Design knowledges on the move, in: Lara Schrijver, The tacit dimension. Architecture knowledge and scientific research, Leuven: Leuven University Press 2021, 83–96, 86–88   **8** For this mixture cf. also | Zu dieser Mischung vgl. auch Henk Borgdorff, Wo stehen wir mit der künstlerischen Forschung, in: Gerald Bast/Jürgen Mittelstraß/Janet Ritterman (eds.), Kunst und Forschung. Können Künstler Forscher sein? Art and research. Can artists be researchers? Wien: Springer 2011, 29–79, 30–33   **9** For the difference practices cf. | Zu den Differenzpraktiken vgl. Silvia Henke/Dieter Mersch/Nicolai van der Meulen/Thomas Strässle/Jörg Wiesel, Manifest der künstlerischen Forschung. Eine Verteidigung gegen die Verfechter. Manifesto of artistic research. A defense against its advocates, Zürich: Diaphanes 2020, 40; John Zeisel, Inquiry by design, New York et al.: W. W. Norton 2006, 81

A COUNTERINTUITIVE PRODUCT

Andreas Lechner

Architectural designs are hybrid products that move between the 'production of signs' and the 'production of events'. They are mediations – of a technical as well as of a social and cultural nature. This tension lies at the heart of their fundamentally relational character and keeps them in motion as 'products', under present-day globalisation and digitisation dynamics, in a culture of cross references. No matter whether it is in more or less reflexive design projects – the hybridity of designs results from the 'in-between' of the ongoing referencing and transforming of architecture-related knowledge, but which continuously blurs disciplinary boundaries and responsibilities, competences and intel-lectual property. A prominent cultural theory characterisation of artistic-creative means of production at the end of the 1990s stated accordingly: "Hybrid is everything that owes its existence to a mixing of traditions or chains of signifiers, that combines different discourses and technologies, that emerges from the techniques of collage, sampling, and bricolage."[1] In the following description of my book 'Thinking Design: Blueprint for an Architecture of Typology' I clarify this hybridity as a fundamental characteristic of design actions. As a product of and for design research, the book provides a conscious sounding board that offers architecture production, which is currently globally fluctuating as media content, a dialogue of forms and functions reduced to drawings and texts, which can be continuously further developed or appropriated for new localised usages.

EIN KONTRAINTUITIVES PRODUKT

Andreas Lechner

Architekturentwürfe sind hybride Produkte, die sich zwischen der ‚Produktion von Zeichen' und der ‚Produktion von Ereignissen' bewegen. Sie sind Mediationen – sowohl technischer als auch sozialer und kultureller Natur. Dieses Spannungsverhältnis begründet ihren grundsätzlich relationalen Charakter und hält sie als ‚Produkte' unter heutigen Globalisierungs- und digitalisierungsbedingten Dynamiken in einer Kultur der Querverweise in Bewegung. Ob in mehr oder weniger reflexiven Entwurfshandlungen – die Hybridität von Entwürfen resultiert aus diesem ‚Dazwischen' fortlaufender Referenzierung und Transformierung von architekturbezogenem Wissen, das aber disziplinäre Grenzen und Zuständigkeiten, Kompetenzen und intellektuelles Eigentum fortlaufend verschwimmen lässt. Eine prominente kulturtheoretische Charakterisierung künstlerisch-gestalterischer Produktionsweisen lautete Ende der 1990er Jahre entsprechend: „Hybrid ist alles, was sich einer Vermischung von Traditionslinien oder Signifikantenketten verdankt, was unterschiedliche Diskurse und Technologien verknüpft, was durch Techniken der ‚collage', des ‚samplings', des Bastelns zustande gekommen ist."[1] In der folgenden Beschreibung meines Buches ‚Entwurf einer architektonischen Gebäudelehre' verdeutliche ich diese Hybridität als grundsätzliche Charakteristik von Entwurfshandlungen. Als Produkt aus und für die Entwurfslehre liefert das Buch eine bewusste Reibefläche, die der heute als Medieninhalte global fluktuierenden Architekturproduktion einen auf Zeichnung und Text reduzierten Dialog aus Formen und Funktionen anbietet, der fortlaufend für erneut ortsgebundene Einsätze weiterverarbeitet oder wiederangeeignet werden kann.

1–2 | Thinking Design. Blueprint for an Architecture German table of content

THE GENERAL AND THE SPECIFIC   The book undertakes a closer definition of the hybrid, by proposing an updating of architecture typology questions and of the classical 'type' as an analytical and generative tool for the structuring and articulation of architectural knowledge. The hybrid, as well as design actions, draw on the collective knowledge of architecture in different ways. These resources are knowledge and transformation processes, which are, however, linked 'counterintuitively' in the book both graphically and in terms of content. As a 'product' of design actions, the book does not present direct design results as regards content, nor does it consider the industry-compatible bases of modern building as current building theory. Graphically, the publication presents a division into two parts that can be read or considered independently (fig. 1–2). One part comprises three essays that form chapters – 'Tectonics', 'Type' and 'Topos'. The other consists of drawings of 144 architecture projects with their ground plan, section and axonometric view or elevation, with brief explanatory texts. The chapter texts and their associated projects are only loosely related, however. Neither the three unnumbered chapters nor the also unnumbered twelve usage contexts 'Theatre', 'Museum', 'Library', 'State', 'Office', 'Leisure', 'Religion', 'Retailing', 'Factory', 'Education', 'Control' and 'Hospital' follow a specific order beyond the chronological. The drawings of 144 buildings, from antiquity to the 21st century, are in a dialogue determined by their position that interrupts the three chapter texts four times respectively, thereby producing a hybrid, city-like juxtaposition – both as a diachronic grouping of 144 project and as a vis-à-vis of projects and texts (fig. 3). This vis-à-vis aspect in the design of the book therefore offers a clear indication of cultural and social aspects that are always related to a position and place, which designs draw on by means of mimesis or a metaphorization of architecture as an ultimately ineluctable level of thinking.[2] What the text and drawing parts therefore have in common is that they as a hybrid product emphasise the form as the core of the design discipline of architecture and in their function as a stage and background for human cohabitation – both in terms of content and through the constellation of this content (fig. 4) –, while still remaining 'open' to access.

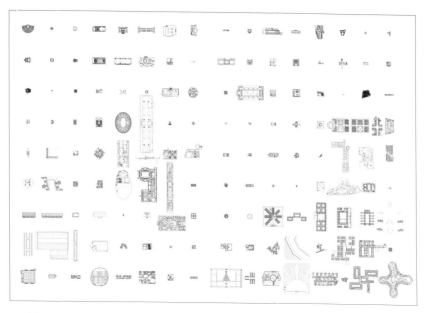

3 | Outlines of the 144 projects in twelve usage contexts on the same scale

ALLGEMEINES UND BESONDERES   Das Buch unternimmt eine nähere
Bestimmung des Hybriden, indem es eine Aktualisierung architekturtypologischer Fragestellungen bzw. des klassischen Typus als analytisches und generatives Werkzeug zur Strukturierung und Artikulation architektonischen Wissens vorschlägt. Dafür greift es, ebenso
wie Entwurfshandlungen, auf unterschiedliche Art und Weise auf das kollektive Wissen
der Architektur zu. Diese Zugriffe sind Wissens- und Transformationsprozesse, die im Buch
allerdings sowohl inhaltlich als auch grafisch kontraintuitiv verknüpft werden. Als Produkt
aus Entwurfshandlungen stellt das Buch inhaltlich weder direkte Entwurfsergebnisse vor,
noch befasst es sich näher mit den industriekompatiblen Grundlagen modernen Bauens als
aktualisierte Gebäudelehre. Grafisch liefert die Publikation eine Gliederung in zwei Teile, die
unabhängig voneinander gelesen oder betrachtet werden können (Abb. 1–2). Der eine Teil
umfasst drei kapitelbildende Aufsätze – ‚Tektonik', ‚Typus' und ‚Topos'. Der andere besteht
aus Zeichnungen von 144 Architekturprojekten in Grundriss, Schnitt und Ansicht mit kurzen
Erläuterungstexten. Die Kapiteltexte und die ihnen zugeordneten Projekte sind aber nur
lose aufeinander bezogen. Weder die drei unnummerierten Kapitel noch die ebenso unnummerierten zwölf Nutzungszusammenhänge ‚Theater', ‚Museum', ‚Bibliothek', ‚Staat', ‚Büro',
‚Freizeit', ‚Religion', ‚Einzelhandel', ‚Fabrik', ‚Bildung', ‚Kontrolle' und ‚Krankenhaus' folgen
über ihre chronologische Sortierung hinaus einer spezifischen Reihenfolge. Die Zeichnungen
von 144 Gebäuden, von der Antike bis zum 21. Jahrhundert, stehen so in einem positions-
bedingten Dialog, der je viermal die drei Kapiteltexte unterbricht und so ein hybrides, stadt-
ähnliches Nebeneinander – sowohl als diachrone Gruppierung von 144 Projekten als auch
als Gegenüber von Projekten und Texten – produziert (Abb. 3). Dieses Nebeneinander in der
Gestaltung des Buches liefert somit einen deutlichen Hinweis auf immer positions- und
ortsgebundene, kulturelle und gesellschaftliche Aspekte, auf die Entwürfe mittels Mimesis
oder einer Metaphorisierung der Architektur als letztlich unhintergehbare Ebene des Denkens zurückgreifen.[2] Text- und Zeichnungsteilen ist daher gemeinsam, dass sie als hybrides
Produkt die Form als Kern der Gestaltungsdisziplin Architektur und ihrer Funktion als Bühne

121

4 | Andreas Lechner Thinking Design. Blueprint for an Architecture of typology Selected pages

Because alongside the analogy of a topological design aspect in the book form itself, the tension between 'general' and 'specific' is to remain in the foreground with the form fundus of twelve projects in twelve functional contexts and in the three chapters, as is fundamental in building design – as a conventional level of architectural and professional responsibility – and in the building theory lectures on public usage contexts held annually since 2013 by the author. The representational focus chosen for the projects in the book consciously disregards technical details, as well as historical or local particularities, even though these levels of materialisation and typical local features as well as their urban context of course represent important aspects of architectural qualities or dialogues. However, this enables a kind of reversed attention. What the selection and presentation focus on allows the 'general' of the physical body of architecture – the fact that they are singular, i.e. built and localised – to come to the fore, with the particular circumstance that they achieve it through repetition. Both the elements and building components – walls, ceilings, roofs, supports, stairs, windows and doors etc. – as well as the spatial relations that it uses for the organisation of various usage contexts – corridors, atria, loggias, enfilades, halls, towers, courtyard houses etc. – are constantly reused by being repeated. It is from this field of tension, between originality and repetition, that design draws its creative power – the book reinforces this through its panorama of architectural, i.e. creatively multi-layered and still intentionally linked forms and usage relations (fig. 5). For the selection of projects, the focus was the intention to make exemplary works of architecture and building history accessible for design work in an informative and inspirational way, for which I drew on Nikolaus Pevsner's historical building theory in 'A History of Building Types', Kenneth Frampton's longstanding 'Modern architecture:

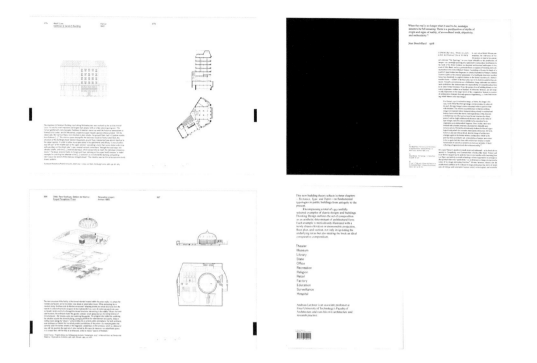

und Hintergrund menschlichen Zusammenlebens betonen – sowohl inhaltlich als auch durch die Konstellation dieser Inhalte (Abb. 4) –, dabei aber trotzdem für Zugriffe ‚offen' bleiben. Denn neben der Analogie eines topologischen Entwurfsaspekts in der Buchform selbst soll mit dem Formenfundus aus zwölf Projekten in zwölf Funktionszusammenhängen und in den drei Kapiteln das Spannungsfeld aus ‚Allgemeinem' und ‚Besonderem' im Vordergrund bleiben, wie es im Gebäudeentwurf – als konventioneller Ebene architektonischer und professioneller Zuständigkeit – und in den seit 2013 jährlich gehaltenen Gebäudelehrevorlesungen zu öffentlichen Nutzungszusammenhängen des Autors tragend wird. Der für die Projekte im Buch gewählte Darstellungsfokus blendet technische Details ebenso wie historische oder lokale Besonderheiten bewusst aus, obwohl diese Ebenen der Materialisierung und des Ortstypischen natürlich wesentliche Aspekte architektonischer Qualitäten bzw. Dialoge darstellen. Dadurch wird aber eine Art umgekehrte Aufmerksamkeit ermöglicht. Worauf sich Auswahl und Darstellung konzentrieren, lässt das ‚Allgemeine' der physischen Körper der Architektur – dass sie singulär, d.h. gebaut und ortsgebunden sind – mit jenem besonderen Umstand in den Vordergrund treten, dass sie das durch Wiederholung erreichen. Sowohl die Elemente und Bauteile – Wände, Decken, Dächer, Stützen, Stiegen, Fenster und Türen etc. – als auch die räumlichen Relationen, die sie zur Organisation verschiedener Nutzungszusammenhänge einsetzt – Korridore, Atrien, Loggien, Enfiladen, Hallen, Türme, Hofhäuser usw. – werden immer wieder neu verwendet, indem sie zugleich wiederholt werden. Aus diesem Spannungsfeld zwischen Originalität und Wiederholung bezieht das Entwerfen seine gestalterische Kraft – das Buch untermauert das durch sein Panorama architektonischer, d.h. gestalterisch vielschichtiger und dennoch intentional verknüpfter, Formen und Nutzungszusammenhänge (Abb. 5). Für die Projektauswahl stand

A critical history' and the comprehensive study by the French architect and historian Jacque Lucan, published in 2012, 'Composition, non-composition: architecture et théories, XIXe–XXe siècles' (engl. 'Composition, non-composition: Architecture and theory in the nineteenth and twentieth centuries') as central bases.[3] Of course, the collective knowledge about architecture cannot be restricted to the predominantly western architecture history here, just as vernacular or anonymous architecture cannot simply be omitted. With the ultimately made selection, for me it is not about perpetuating the white-male-western architecture canon, which is urgently to be broken up, into the 21st century, but about creative access and the productive further development of this comprehensively and critically available knowledge for design theory and architecture production. Such a selection is therefore necessarily fragmentary and exemplary and, in the contemporary, also more subjective and biographically motivated and correspondingly open to debate.

COMPARATIVE CONSIDERATION   Photos of the drawn projects are insignificant for the central argument of the book – not only because a millisecond of research is sufficient for providing thousands of more or less beautified images for each of the projects which, however, can never replace a personal visit on site, but also because this part of the book consciously relies on the abstract systematisation of codified architecture representation, as only this provides the key to typological knowledge in architecture. Because drawings are typical not only as a notation form of ideas for the discipline of architecture. Beyond this general function of the drawing, architectural drawings also harbour the potential of storing architectural knowledge and making it transferable. My theory is therefore that this knowledge in architecture is by no means only depicted in the drawings but only forms reflexively, i.e. from the interplay between codified architecture representation and design-relevant research – outlined here with the chapters 'Tectonics', 'Type' and 'Topos'. The publication would like to offer sounding boards and research indicators for such a reflexive understanding of designing and thinking and for this purpose, similar to Giulio Camillo's Theatre of Memory, turns the stage function around and delivers tableaux for comparative considerations (fig. 5). However, these drawn compositions of constructional elements and spatial relations are relatively open and ambiguous. They elude an unequivocal, i.e. modern 'building theory', precisely because their functional grouping and categorisation is not imperative. Each of the twelve functional categorisations corresponds to social and therefore linguistic conventions which are changeable in principle. Some of the 144 projects are also indeed conversions and could therefore be shifted in the order logic of the tableaux on the same scale at the beginning of the twelve building groupings – from Hospital to Education, from Factory to Museum etc. However, the relationship of form and function inherent in them is by no means arbitrary, instead, it is rather inconclusive, even though many typical spatial configurations recur very reliably in certain contexts of use – just think of housing construction which is not thematised here.

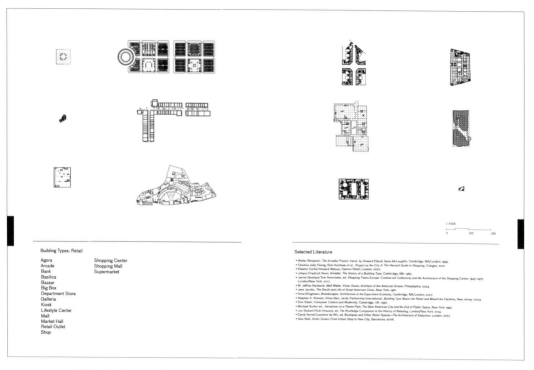

Building Types: Retail

Agora	Shopping Center
Arcade	Shopping Mall
Bank	Supermarket
Basilica	
Bazaar	
Big Box	
Department Store	
Galleria	
Kiosk	
Lifestyle Center	
Mall	
Market Hall	
Retail Outlet	
Shop	

Selected Literature

• Walter Benjamin, The Arcades Project, transl. by Howard Eiland, Kevin McLaughlin, Cambridge, MA/London: 1999.
• Chuihua Judy Chung, Rem Koolhaas et al., Project on the City II: The Harvard Guide to Shopping, Cologne: 2001.
• Eleanor Curtis/Howard Watson, Fashion Retail, London: 2007.
• Johann Friedrich Geist, Arcades, The History of a Building Type, Cambridge, MA: 1985.
• Janina Gosseye/Tom Avermaete, ed. Shopping Towns Europe: Commercial Collectivity and the Architecture of the Shopping Centre, 1945–1975, London/New York: 2004.
• M. Jeffrey Hardwick, Mall Maker: Victor Gruen, Architect of the American Dream, Philadelphia: 2004.
• Jane Jacobs, The Death and Life of Great American Cities, New York: 1961.
• Anna Klingmann, Brandscapes: Architecture in the Experience Economy, Cambridge, MA/London: 2007.
• Stephen A. Kliment, Vilma Barr, Jerde Partnership International, Building Type Basics for Retail and Mixed-Use Facilities, New Jersey: 2004.
• Don Slater, Consumer Culture and Modernity, Cambridge, UK: 1997.
• Michael Sorkin ed., Variations on a Theme Park: The New American City and the End of Public Space, New York: 1992.
• Jon Stobart/Vicki Howard, ed. The Routledge Companion to the History of Retailing, London/New York: 2019.
• David Vernet/Leontine de Wit, ed. Boutiques and Other Retail Spaces—The Architecture of Seduction, London: 2007.
• Alex Wall, Victor Gruen: From Urban Shop to New City, Barcelona: 2006.

5 | 'Retail' with layouts of the twelve projects on the same scale and literature references

die Absicht, exemplarische Werke der Architektur- und Baugeschichte für die Entwurfs-arbeit informativ und inspirativ zugänglich zu machen, im Vordergrund, wofür ich auf Nikolaus Pevsners historische Gebäudelehre in ‚A History of Building Types' (dt. ‚Funktion und Form'), Kenneth Framptons bewährte ‚Architekturgeschichte der Moderne' und die umfangreiche, 2012 erschienene Studie des französischen Architekten und Historikers Jacques Lucan, ‚Composition, non-composition: architecture et théories, XIXe–XXe siècles' (engl. ‚Composition, Non-Composition: Architecture and Theory in the Nineteenth and Twentieth Century'), als zentrale Grundlagen zurückgriff.[3] Natürlich kann das kollektive Wissen über Architektur ebensowenig auf die hier vornehmlich westliche Architektur-geschichte beschränkt werden, wie dabei ‚vernacular' oder anonyme Architektur ein-fach ausgespart werden darf. Mit der letztlich getroffenen Auswahl geht es mir nicht darum, den dringlich aufzusprengenden weiß-männlich-westlichen Architekturkanon auch noch ins 21. Jahrhundert hinein fortzuschreiben, sondern um entwerferischen Zugriff und produktive Weiterentwicklung dieses ebenso umfangreich wie kritisch vor-handenen Wissens für die Entwurfslehre und Architekturproduktion. Eine solche Auswahl ist daher notwendigerweise fragmentarisch und exemplarisch und im Zeitgenössischen auch stärker subjektiv und biografisch motiviert und entsprechend beeinspruchbar.

VERGLEICHENDE BETRACHTUNG   Fotos der gezeichneten Projekte sind für das zentrale Argument des Buches unbedeutend – nicht nur weil eine Millise-kundenrecherche ausreicht, um Tausende mehr oder weniger geschönte Bilder zu jedem der Projekte zu liefern, die einen eigenen Besuch vor Ort dennoch nie ersetzen können, sondern weil dieser Teil des Buchs bewusst auf die abstrakte Systematisierungsleistung

6 | Plan and section of the projects in 'Theatre', 'Museum', 'Library' and 'State'

der kodifizierten Architekturdarstellung vertraut, da nur diese den Schlüssel zu typologischem Wissen in der Architektur bereitstellt. Denn für die Disziplin Architektur sind Zeichnungen nicht nur als Notationsform von Ideen typisch. Architekturzeichnungen besitzen über diese generelle Funktion der Zeichnung hinaus zudem noch das Potenzial, architektonisches Wissen zu speichern und übertragbar zu machen. Meine These lautet daher, dass dieses Wissen der Architektur keineswegs nur in den Zeichnungen abgebildet wird, sondern sich erst reflexiv, d.h. aus dem Wechselspiel zwischen kodifizierter Architekturdarstellung und entwurfsrelevanter Recherche – hier mit den Kapiteln ‚Tektonik‘, ‚Typus‘ und ‚Topos‘ umrissen –, bildet. Für ein solcherart reflexiv verstandenes Entwerfen und Nachdenken möchte die Publikation Reibeflächen und Recherchehinweise anbieten und dreht dafür, ähnlich wie Giulio Camillos Gedächtnistheater, die Bühnenfunktion um und liefert so Tableaus zur vergleichenden Betrachtung. Allerdings sind diese gezeichneten Kompositionen aus baulichen Elementen und räumlichen Relationen relativ offen und vieldeutig. Sie entziehen sich einer eindeutigen, d.h. einer modernen, ‚Gebäudelehre‘, gerade weil ihre funktionale Gruppierung und Zuordnung nicht zwingend sind. Jede der zwölf funktionalen Zuordnungen entspricht sozialen und damit sprachlichen Konventionen, die grundsätzlich veränderlich sind. Einige der 144 Projekte sind auch tatsächlich Umnutzungen und könnten daher in der Ordnungslogik der maßstabsgleichen Tableaus zu Beginn der zwölf Gebäudegruppierungen verschoben werden – von Krankenhaus zu Bildung, von Fabrik zu Museum etc. Arbiträr ist das ihnen inhärente Verhältnis von Form und Funktion deswegen aber keineswegs, es ist vielmehr uneindeutig, obwohl sich viele typische räumliche Konfigurationen in bestimmten Nutzungszusammenhängen sehr verlässlich wiederholen – denkt man etwa an den hier nicht thematisierten Fachbereich Wohnungsbau. Die scheinbar konventionelle Versammlung von zwölf Bautypen wird durch die Gruppierungen ‚Staat‘, ‚Freizeit‘ und ‚Kontrolle‘ unscharf. Nicht nur versammeln diese Gruppierungen selbst eine Vielzahl völlig unterschiedlicher Bautypen, sondern sie verdeutlichen zugleich abstraktere, politische Prinzipien, die allgemeiner als etablierte Konventionen baulicher Vergesellschaftungsformen sind. Obwohl ‚Staat‘ hier nicht als Oberklasse für die Repräsentationsbauten in den Rubriken ‚Theater‘, ‚Museum‘ und ‚Bibliothek‘ verwendet wird, liegt der bauliche Zusammenhang der Monumentalbauten mit der Nationenbildung im 19. Jahrhundert natürlich nahe (Abb. 6). Obwohl im zweiten Kapitel ‚Freizeit‘ nicht als Reproduktionsverpflichtung oder als Antithese zu den mehr und weniger freiwilligen Verpflichtungszusammenhängen – ‚Büro‘, ‚Religion‘ und ‚Einzelhandel‘ – dialektisch festgelegt wird, legt die Spätmoderne ein derart gegenüberliegendes Nebeneinander mit allen seinen Widersprüchen nahe.

7 | The cover indicates the design and type discussions

The seemingly conventional collection of twelve building types becomes unclear through the groupings of 'State', 'Recreation' and 'Surveillance'. Not only do these groupings gather an array of completely different building types, they also show more abstract, political principles that are more general than established conventions of constructional socialisation forms. Although 'State' is not used here as a super class for the representation buildings in the categories of 'Theatre', 'Museum' and 'Library', the constructional connection of monumental buildings with the formation of nations in the 19th century is of course close (fig. 6). Although in the second chapter 'Recreation' is not dialectically set out as a reproduction obligation or as an antithesis to the more or less voluntary obligation contexts – 'Office', 'Religion' and 'Retail' – late modernity presents such a juxtaposition with all its contradictions.

At the latest with 'Surveillance', among the last four typologies, it becomes clear that the discipline of architecture, as well as its central element – the wall –, represents a highly ambivalent mechanism. Spatial repression on one side and more or less forced or voluntary subjugation on the other – these balancing acts between critical distance and offensive collaboration has scarcely been set in built, imagined and written scenes more prominently than by Rem Koolhaas, for example in 1972 with his work 'Exodus, or the voluntary prisoners of architecture', based on a study of the Berlin Wall, a conversion design of a panopticon prison that never functioned as such, about which he comments in 1980 that: "[c]hanges in regime and ideology are more powerful than the most radical architecture – a conclusion both alarming and reassuring for the architect", and of course with the plainly 'post-critical' architecture type of the skyscraper as a surrealistic stack of functions, that neither have a necessary connection internally nor provide suitable architectural-moral information through the façade.[4] Koolhaas's works are also by far the most frequent in the drawing section of this book, as his firm often further investigated the radical questioning of building typology in modern architecture. What the three categories of 'State', 'Recreation' and 'Surveillance', which are completely vague in terms of building typology, are supposed to do here is just to clearly indicate this fundamentally social level, i.e. the consistently socio-political dimensions of spatial-constructional contexts, than the perhaps more familiar, conventional and sometimes dusty building types do (fig. 7).

Spätestens mit ‚Kontrolle', bei den letzten vier Typologien, wird deutlich, dass die Disziplin der Architektur ebenso wie ihr zentrales Element – die Mauer – einen hochgradig ambivalenten Mechanismus darstellt – räumliche Repression auf der einen und mehr oder weniger erzwungene oder freiwillige Unterwerfung auf der anderen Seite. Diese Gratwanderungen zwischen kritischer Distanz und offensiver Kollaboration hat kaum jemand prominenter in gebaute, gedachte und geschriebene Szenen gesetzt als Rem Koolhaas, etwa 1972 mit seiner auf einer Studie zur Berliner Mauer beruhenden Arbeit ‚Exodus, or the voluntary prisoners of architecture', im Umbauentwurf eines als solches nie funktionierenden Panoptikum-Gefängnisses, zu dem er 1980 anmerkt, dass „[c]hanges in regime and ideology are more powerful than the most radical architecture – a conclusion both alarming and reassuring for the architect"; und natürlich mit dem schlechthin ‚post-kritischen' Architekturtypus des Wolkenkratzers als surrealistischem Stapel von Funktionen, die weder intern einen notwendigen Zusammenhang aufweisen, noch über die Fassade architektonisch-moralisch angemessen Auskunft geben.[4] Koolhaas' Arbeiten kommen auch im Zeichnungsteil dieses Buches mit Abstand am häufigsten vor, da sein Büro vielfach an den gebäudetypologisch radikalen Infragestellungen der modernen Architektur weiterarbeitete. Was die drei gebäudetypologisch völlig unscharfen Kategorien ‚Staat', ‚Freizeit' und ‚Kontrolle' hier leisten sollen, ist, nur deutlicher auf diese grundsätzlich soziale Ebene, d.h. auf die immer gesellschaftspolitischen Dimensionen räumlich-baulicher Zusammenhänge, hinzuweisen, als es die vielleicht vertrauteren, konventionellen und mitunter verstaubten Bautypen tun (Abb. 7).

TYPEN UND TYPOLOGIEN   Das Austesten innerer und äußerer Möglichkeitsformen und räumlicher Relationen wird im ersten Kapitel als Quintessenz architektonischer Entwurfsarbeit beschrieben und in der ‚Tektonik' des Buchs zu einer Sammlung an typischen Mustern zur Raumbildung gefügt, die sich zur vergleichenden Betrachtung, zur Inspiration von Eigenerecherche oder als Grundlage für transformative Bearbeitungen in neue und erneute Vorschläge für konkrete, gemeinschaftliche Orte anbieten. Angelehnt an Anthony Vidlers bekannte Unterscheidung architektonischer Typusverständnisse verfolgt das zweite Kapitel – ‚Typus' – das idealistische Typusverständnis der Aufklärung im Übergang zu den technisch-pragmatischen Zugängen einer sich formierenden modernen Industrie- und Massengesellschaft. Entsprechend nimmt auch das Ausnahmewerk von Jean-Nicholas-Louis Durand hier eine prominente Rolle ein, weil es als umfassendes Architekturlehrgebäude illustriert, wie Technik und Moral, wirtschaftlicher Hausverstand und gesellschaftliche Rangbemessung in allen architekturrelevanten Maßstabs- und Betriebsebenen als modern-nachhaltiges Staats- und Gesellschaftsverständnis formuliert werden konnte – von einem globalen Atlas der Baugeschichte über die Elemente, Bauteile und Gebäudetypen bis hin zu Musterentwürfen für alle notwendigen öffentlich-baulichen

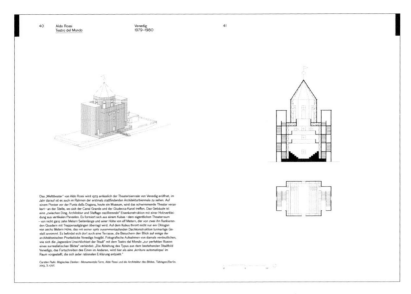

8 | Double page with Aldo Rossi's 'Teatro del Mondo'

TYPES AND TYPOLOGIES   The trying out of internal and external forms of possibility and spatial relations is described in the first chapter as the quintessence of architectural design work and brought together in the 'Tectonics' of the book as a collection of typical models of spatial formation that are useful for a comparative consideration, as inspiration for one's own research or as a basis for transformative revisions into new and renewed proposals for concrete communal places. In reference to Anthony Vidler's well-known distinction between architectural type understandings, the second chapter – 'Type' – traces the Enlightenment's idealistic understanding of type in its transition to the technical-pragmatic approaches for an emerging modern industrial and mass society. Accordingly, the exceptional work by Jean-Nicholas-Louis Durand takes on a prominent role here, because it illustrates as a comprehensive architecture education project how technology and morals, economic common sense and social ranking could be formulated on all architecture-relevant scales and operative levels as a modern and sustainable understanding of state and society – from a global atlas of building history to elements, building components and building types, to design templates for all necessary public and constructional contexts. However, the critique of the normative understanding of building typologies and of 'naïve' functionalism, as described by Georges Teyssot as a gradual transformation of the classical 'type' into a modern 'typological' thinking, can start here.[5] The traditional term 'type' indicates an original genesis in architecture that repeats the principles of the ancient form continuously. This embodiment of ideals in the architectural form – through nature and time – was indicated by classical principles and rules that recognizably gave a building authority. This physical and embodied remembrance capability of form is in contrast to the modern 'typology', whose morphogenesis led to a disembodied abstraction – simple calculation and laws of evolution. The modern 'typologies' went hand in hand with the abolition of the mimesis, the institutionalisation of the norm, the repetition of the same and the obligation for 'something new'.[6]

Zusammenhänge. Hier lässt sich aber bereits die Kritik am normativen Verständnis von Gebäudetypologien bzw. am ‚naiven' Funktionalismus ansetzen, wie sie etwa Georges Teyssot als allmähliche Umwandlung der klassischen ‚Typentheorie' in ein modernes ‚typologisches' Denken beschreibt.[5] Der klassische Begriff des Typus verweist auf eine Ur-Genese in der Architektur, die Prinzipien der antiken Form fortlaufend wiederholte. Auf diese Verkörperung von Idealen in der architektonischen Form verwiesen – durch Natur und Zeit hindurch – klassische Prinzipien und Regeln, die einem Gebäude wiedererkennbar Autorität verliehen. Diese körperliche und verkörperlichte Erinnerungsfähigkeit der Form steht im Gegensatz zur modernen ‚Typologie', deren Morphogenese zu einer entkörperlichten Abstraktion – simple Berechnung und Gesetze der Evolution – führte. Mit den modernen Typologien ging die Abschaffung der Mimesis, die Institutionalisierung der Norm, die Wiederholung des Gleichen und die Verpflichtung auf ‚Neues' einher.[6]

Im dritten Kapitel, ‚Topos', gehe ich der postfunktionalistischen bzw. urbanistisch-atmosphärischen Kritik an den mit der Moderne semantisch entleerten Typologien mit u.a. Aldo Rossis und Robert Venturis 1966 erschienenen Klassikern postmoderner Architekturtheorie nach (Abb. 8). Was diese mit ihrer Forderung nach einem komplexeren Verständnis von Architektur und Städtebau etablierten, war die Einsicht, dass es keine Alternative zu den provisorischen, nie abschließend klärbaren Herstellungsverfahren der Architektur gibt. Diese zentrale Einsicht verdeutlichte nicht nur für das Entwerfen, dass es hybride Produkte herstellt, sondern bildet auch das zentrale Argument für eine disziplinär anspruchsvolle Lehre im ‚Entwurf einer architektonischen Gebäudelehre': Architektonisches Entwerfen ist sowohl konservativ, weil es immer wieder auf Lösungen zurückgreift, die sich in langen Prozessen stillschweigenden Austestens bewährt haben, als auch kreativ, weil es diese Lösungen an den ständigen Wandel von Bedingungen anpassen muss. Diese Spannung aus Wiederholung und Originalität verdeutlicht, wie Geschichte als selektiver und subjektiver Zugriff seit jeher in den Architekturentwurf einfließen muss, nämlich als Auseinandersetzung des ‚Entwurfspersonals' mit Werken der Architektur, die sich weder auf ‚kanonische' oder persönlich auserkorene Meisterwerke noch auf empirische Messungen oder Alltagsbeobachtungen beschränken lassen muss. Auch wenn Dogmen, Heldenverehrung und Normativitäten den Zeitaufwand für die Entwurfs- und Lehrarbeit deutlich zu verringern helfen, so bleibt es für die Qualität eines Entwurfs letztlich aber einerlei, wie gestalterische Zweifel beseitigt wurden, da jedenfalls gilt: „Bricolage ist keine Alternative zur Architektur. Sie ist in allen Entwürfen, in jeder Gestaltung vorhanden."[7]

In the third chapter, 'Topos', I pursue the post-functionalist and urbanistic-atmospheric criticism of the semantically depleted 'typologies' in modern times with e.g. Aldo Rossi's and Robert Venturi's classics of postmodern architecture theory published in 1966 (fig. 8). What they established with their call for a more complex understanding of architecture and urban development was the insight that there is no alternative to the provisional design processes of architecture that are never conclusively clarified. This central insight showed not only for design that it produces hybrid products but also forms the central argument for a challenging disciplinary theory in the book. Architectural design is both conservative, because it keeps drawing on solutions that have proven themselves in long processes of tacit testing, and creative, because it must adapt these solutions to constantly changing conditions. This tension between repetition and originality shows how history has always had to flow into architectural design as a selective and subjective aspect, namely as an engagement of the 'design personnel' with works of architecture that must neither be limited to 'canonical' or personally chosen masterpieces nor to empirical measurements or everyday observations. Even if dogmas, hero worshipping and normativities significantly help to reduce the time needed for design and teaching work, it ultimately remains immaterial for the quality of a design how design doubts were resolved, as the following applies: "Bricolage is not an alternative to architecture. It is present in all designs, in every creation."[7]

DESIGNING FURTHER   As a practical, theoretical, artistic and technologically multi-layered field of tension, architecture does not provide binding conditions. The book does not seek to resolve this tension between the objective and subjective. As a collection of vignettes of design scopes of public buildings, it rather emphasises this tension when it recommends the 'collection' of projects and texts. In the English first edition published in 2021 and the revised German second edition, a booklet with extracts of twelve Master's theses supervised by me is enclosed. Like the 144 projects in the book, the works show as line drawings – compressed onto a double page with a brief text – how organised public spaces can be critically considered further (fig. 9). They further build on existing buildings and infrastructures, on products of the real estate industry and on urbanisation landscapes to become more sustainable, socially and ecologically responsible and aesthetically pleasing. By linking, combining, densifying and multiplying forms and functions of a technical as well as social and cultural nature, they emphasise the central design aspect of the composition as an important form of architectural correlation. No matter whether collage, sampling, stacking or layering techniques are used –, the composition as an aesthetic determination of the architectural form creates a design aspect that – before (or after) questions of function and atmosphere – can outlast times and usage cycles and therefore product cycles and lifecycles. What the book and the selection of twelve times twelves architectural projects provides as fundamental visual material and discusses in the chapters as fundamental design dialogues is therefore nothing other than possible development lines in design that can continuously be productively and newly combined.

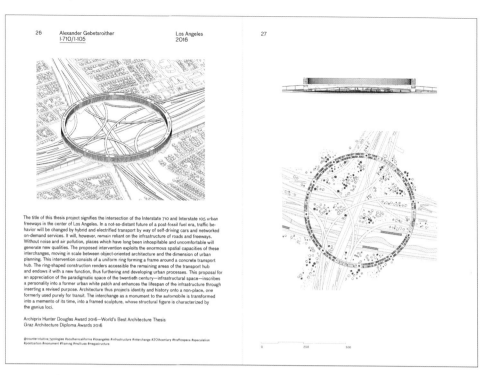

The title of this thesis project signifies the intersection of the Interstate 710 and Interstate 105 urban freeways in the center of Los Angeles. In a not-so-distant future of a post-fossil fuel era, traffic behavior will be changed by hybrid and electrified transport by way of self-driving cars and networked on-demand services. It will, however, remain reliant on the infrastructure of roads and freeways. Without noise and air pollution, places which have long been inhospitable and uncomfortable will generate new qualities. The proposed intervention exploits the enormous spatial capacities of these interchanges, moving in scale between object-oriented architecture and the dimension of urban planning. This intervention consists of a uniform ring forming a frame around a concrete transport hub. The ring-shaped construction renders accessible the remaining areas of the transport hub and endows it with a new function, thus furthering and developing urban processes. This proposal for an appreciation of the paradigmatic space of the twentieth century—infrastructural space—inscribes a personality into a former urban white patch and enhances the lifespan of the infrastructure through inserting a revised purpose. Architecture thus projects identity and history onto a non-place, one formerly used purely for transit. The interchange as a monument to the automobile is transformed into a memento of its time, into a framed sculpture, whose structural figure is characterized by the genius loci.

Archiprix Hunter Douglas Award 2016—World's Best Architecture Thesis
Graz Architecture Diploma Awards 2016

@counterintuitive_typologies #southerncalifornia #losangeles #infrastructure #interchange #20thcentury #trafficspace #speculation #postcarbon #monument #framing #nullius #megastructure

0   250   500

9 | Extract from Alexander Gebetsroither's thesis 'I-710/I-105'

WEITERENTWERFEN   Als ein praktisch, theoretisch, künstlerisch und technologisch vielschichtig verwobenes Spannungsfeld stellt die Architekturproduktion keine verbindlichen Voraussetzungen bereit. Diese Spannung aus Objektivem und Subjektivem versucht auch das Buch nicht aufzulösen. Als Sammlung von Vignetten zu gestalterischen Bandbreiten öffentlicher Bauten betont es diese vielmehr, wenn es das ‚Zusammenlesen' von Projekten und Texten empfiehlt. In der 2021 erschienenen englischen Erstausgabe und der überarbeiteten deutschen Zweitauflage ist dem Buch ein Heft mit Auszügen von zwölf von mir betreuten Masterarbeiten beigelegt. Wie die 144 Projekte im Buch zeigen die Arbeiten als Linienzeichnungen – auf eine Doppelseite mit Kurztext komprimiert –, wie Räume einer organisierten Öffentlichkeit kritisch weitergedacht werden können (Abb. 9). Sie bauen an vorhandenen Bauten und Infrastrukturen, an Produkten der Immobilienwirtschaft und an Verstädterungslandschaften zukunftsfähiger, gesellschaftlich und ökologisch verantwortungsvoller und ästhetisch anspruchsvoller weiter: Indem sie Formen und Funktionen sowohl technischer als auch sozialer und kultureller Natur verknüpfen, verbinden, verdichten und vervielfältigen, betonen sie den zentralen Entwurfsaspekt der Komposition als wesentliche Form architektonischer Verknüpfung. Ob dabei Techniken der Collage oder des Samplings, des Stapelns oder des Überlagerns zum Einsatz kommen – die Komposition bildet als ästhetische Festlegung der architektonischen Form einen Entwurfsaspekt, der – vor (oder nach) Fragen nach Funktion und Atmosphäre – Zeiten und Nutzungszyklen und damit Produkt- und Lebenszyklen überdauern kann. Was das Buch und die Auswahl von zwölf mal zwölf architektonischen Projekten als grundlegendes Anschauungsmaterial zur Verfügung stellt und in den Kapiteln als grundsätzliche Entwurfsdialoge bespricht, sind also nichts anderes als mögliche Entwicklungslinien im Entwerfen, die sich immer wieder produktiv und neu verbinden lassen.

1 Elisabeth Bronfen/Benjamin Marius, Hybride Kulturen. Einleitung zur anglo-amerikanischen Multikulturalismusdebatte, in: ids./Therese Steffen (eds.), Hybride Kulturen. Beiträge zur anglo-amerikanischen Multikulturalismusdebatte, Tübingen: Stauffenburg 1997, 1–30, 14   **2** Cf. | Vgl. Hans Blumenberg, Paradigmen zu einer Metaphorologie, Frankfurt a. M.: Suhrkamp 1998   **3** Nikolaus Pevsner, A history of building types, Princeton, NJ: Princeton University Press 1979, German | dt.: Funktion und Form. Die Geschichte der Bauwerke des Westens, Hamburg: Rogner & Bernhard/ Zweitausendeins 1998; Kenneth Frampton, Die Architektur der Moderne – Eine kritische Baugeschichte (ext. And revised version of the 8th ed. | erw. u. überarb. Fassung d. 8. Aufl.), München: DWA 2010; Jacques Lucan, Composition, non-composition: Architecture and theory in the nineteenth and twentieth centuries, London: Routledge 2012 **4** Rem Koolhaas, Revision – Study for the renovation of a panopticon prison, in: OMA/Rem Koolhaas/Bruce Mau, S, M, L, XL, New York, NY: Monacelli Press 1995, 235–253, 239   **5** Cf. | Vgl. Georges Teyssots, A topology of everyday constellations, Cambridge, MA/London: MIT Press 2013, 31–82, 69   **6** The architecture typology discussion is pointed at on the book cover with the Caribbean hut of Gottfried Semper, which illustrated his theory on the anthropological origin of architecture: four elements of architecture, which he defined as archetypal types – roof, wall, floor and hearth – and transfers in his metabolism theory into a scientific model of the hybridization of handicrafts. The doctrine of the building types as a building task, which is based on the social status and the political role of the client, can be found – from church building and palace to prison and animal stables – in the synopsis of Nikolaus Goldmann and Leonhard Christoph Sturms 'Complete instruction to the civil Baukunst' (1699) as the third figure on the cover. Le Corbusier's perspective view of the prototype of the Maison Dom-Ino (1914) presents the archetype of most 20th-century buildings. The allegorical representation of the primal hut

in Marc Antoine Laugier's 'Essai sur l'architecture' from 1755 contrasts the whims of the rococo with an archetype and fifth figure that is botch classicistic and committed to nature. | Auf die architekturtypologischen Diskussion wird auf dem Buchcover mit der karibischen Hütte Gottfried Sempers hingewiesen, die seine Theorie zum anthropologischen Ursprung der Architektur illustrierte: vier Elemente der Baukunst, die er als Ur-Typen – Dach, Wand, Boden und Feuerstelle – in seiner Stoffwechseltheorie in ein naturwissenschaftliches Modell der Hybridisierung der Kunsthandwerke überträgt. Die Lehre von den Gebäudetypen als Bauaufgabe, die sich aus dem sozialen Status und der politischen Rolle des Bauherren begründet, findet sich – vom Kirchenbau und Palast bis hin zu Gefängnis und Tierstall – in der Inhaltsangabe von Nikolaus Goldmann und Leonhard Christoph Sturms ,Vollständige Anweisung zu der Civil-Baukunst' (1699) als dritte Abbildung auf dem Cover. Le Corbusiers perspektivische Darstellung des Prototyps der Maison Dom-Ino (1914) präsentiert den Archetyp der meisten Bauten im 20. Jahrhundert. Die allegorische Darstellung der Urhütte in Marc-Antoine Laugiers ,Essai sur l'architecture' von 1755 stellt den Launen des Rokokos einen sowohl klassizistischen als auch der Natur verpflichteten Archetypen und fünfte Abbildung entgegen.   **7** Cf. | Vgl. Irénée Scalbert, Der Architekt als Bricoleur, in: Candide. Journal for Architectural Knowledge 4(7/2011), 69–88, 86. The film still from Georges Méliès' 'Journey to the moon' from 1902 as the first illustration on the book cover refers to the basically tinkering character of all design actions. The still shows the landing of the space capsule in the right eye of the man in the moon and at the same time an anthropomorphic viewer of the earth in the age of the Anthropocene. | Auf den grundsätzlich bastelnden Charakter aller Entwurfshandlungen verweist am Buchcover das Film-Still aus Georges Méliès' ,Die Reise zum Mond' von 1902 als erste Abbildung. Das Still zeigt die Landung der Raumkapsel im rechten Auge des Mannes im Mond und damit zugleich einen anthropomorphen Betrachter der Erde im Zeitalter des Anthropozäns.

ANALYTICAL COMPONENTS OF THE INHABITED FAÇADE

Diana Gouveia Amaral

In design and research, we are constantly rethinking the existent and responding in new ways to different questions. We talk about continuous processes of multiple scales until the result is reached. 'Products' is aligned with a vision in which the arts, as a whole, are responsible for combining aesthetics and quality, remembering that every action has an impact. We, architects and designers, are called to look beyond the object produced, focusing on the process and its impact on the place where it is inserted, aiming above all to strengthen knowledge within the disciplines with a view to reflective user-oriented design. Transposing to the scale of a residential building, the architect develops a process until the moment of construction, but can the construction of the building be considered the product of this process? Is this process the product itself? Is the result the same as the product or is it the appropriation by the user that ultimately creates it?

When we open a window, we open the inside of the house to the world and let the outside get into our space (fig. 1). The capacity of an act as simple as opening a window to enable such significant transformations exemplifies how the appropriations of constructive elements represent a change of the architectural space. Understanding the architectural project as something that can be appropriated and modified by the user allows us to create new dynamics from the scale of the house to the scale of the street. Sustainability and well-being as a basic argument of urban intervention is the pretext for the return of dialogue between architecture and urbanism. In a three-dimensional approach to the city, the aim is to explore the façade element as a transitional space (between interior-exterior) that welcomes collective uses. Consequently, it potentiates different qualities in the interior space and in the street, thereby multiplying the possible uses. Starting from the formality of the elements of architecture to the ambiguity of the appropriations, the project will use a model of urban reading to be applied in medium-sized European cities that starts from the decomposition and graphic exploration of the elements through drawing, a tool of both disciplines, architecture and urbanism.

ANALYTISCHE KOMPONENTEN
DER BEWOHNTEN FASSADE

Diana Gouveia Amaral

In Entwurf und Forschung denken wir Bestehendes immer wieder neu und antworten auf unterschiedliche Fragestellungen neu. Es sind kontinuierliche Prozesse in unterschiedlichen Maßstäben bis zum Erreichen des Ergebnisses. Die Perspektive auf Produkte orientiert sich an einer Vorstellung, derzufolge die Künste als Ganzes dafür verantwortlich sind, Ästhetik und Qualität zu verbinden, eingedenk dessen, dass jede Handlung eine Wirkung hat. Wir, Architekturschaffende und Entwerfende, sind dazu aufgerufen, den Blick über das produzierte Objekt hinaus auf den Prozess und seine Wirkung vor Ort zu richten und vor allem das Wissen innerhalb der Disziplinen im Hinblick auf eine reflektierte, nutzungsorientierte Gestaltung zu stärken. Auf den Maßstab eines Wohnhauses übertragen, entwickeln Architekturschaffende einen Prozess bis zum Moment der Bauausführung, aber kann der Bau des Gebäudes als Produkt dieses Prozesses betrachtet werden? Ist dieser Prozess das Produkt selbst? Ist das Ergebnis dasselbe wie das Produkt oder ist es die Aneignung durch die Nutzenden, die es letztendlich schafft?

Wenn wir ein Fenster öffnen, öffnen wir das Innere des Hauses zur Welt und lassen das Äußere in unsere Räume eindringen (Abb. 1). Die Fähigkeit einer so einfachen Handlung wie das Öffnen eines Fensters, signifikante Transformationen zu ermöglichen, veranschaulicht, wie die Aneignung konstruktiver Elemente eine Veränderung des architektonischen Raums darstellt. Das Verständnis des architektonischen Projekts als etwas, das durch die es nutzenden Menschen angeeignet und verändert werden kann, ermöglicht es, neue Dynamiken vom Maßstab des Hauses bis zum Maßstab der Straße zu schaffen. Nachhaltigkeit und Wohlbefinden als Hauptargumente für urbane Eingriffe sind ein Anlass dafür, den Dialog zwischen Architektur und Urbanismus wieder aufleben zu lassen. In einer dreidimensionalen Annäherung an die Stadt soll das Fassadenelement

1 | Johannes Vermeer Soldier and laughing girl ca 1657   2 | Diana Araújo Living City Napoli 2021

THE SUSTAINABLE CITY IS A LIVELY CITY   Projects of architecture or urbanism are processes that cross different principles, references and inspirations and that, by reading the existing, seek to rethink and design an ideal, a solution. In Europe, public and private entities, architects, designers and artists are called upon to rethink cities with a view to greater sustainability and higher quality. Movements such as the 'New Bauhaus' seek a critical and transdisciplinary thinking that combines science and research, technology and construction, redefining how to design and intervene in different contexts. It strives for an approach of an innovative Europe with common principles, with a distinctive identity where the quality of life is prioritised and aesthetic values present in all artistic forms are respected.[1] On an urban scale, European principles are aligned with the construction of a sustainable city, with other concepts emerging, which point to new concerns and approaches, both in research and in design. Concepts such as urban regeneration, smart cities, 15-minute city, rehabilitation, reuse, urban experience, etc. demonstrate a change towards the lived city where, besides looking at the infrastructures, the users are valued. Of these concepts, the one that appears with a new prominence is the urban experience, which demonstrates the importance of understanding the place beyond what was designed by the architect, and thus valuing the perceptions of the individual. If the 'experience is often associated with the different atmospheres created on the route through the layout and formal configuration', the description of the city is based on each person's individual perception of the surroundings.[2] The experience that one has in the city is reinforced to qualify the urban environment (fig. 2). Knowing that the experience is related to both public and private spaces, sustainable

erforscht werden als kollektive Nutzungen fördernder Übergangsraum (zwischen innen und außen). Dabei potenziert es unterschiedliche Qualitäten im Innenraum und auf der Straße und vervielfältigt die Nutzungsmöglichkeiten. Von der Formalität der Architekturelemente bis zur Mehrdeutigkeit der Aneignungen verwendet das Forschungsprojekt ein Modell des urbanen Lesens, das in mittelgroßen europäischen Städten anwendbar ist und mit der Zerlegung sowie grafischen Erforschung der Elemente durch Zeichnen arbeitet, einem Werkzeug der beiden Disziplinen Architektur und Städtebau.

DIE NACHHALTIGE STADT IST EINE LEBENDIGE STADT
Projekte der Architektur oder des Städtebaus bestehen aus Prozessen, die verschiedene Prinzipien, Referenzen und Inspirationen kreuzen und die durch das Lesen des Bestehenden versuchen, dieses zu überdenken, und ein Ideal, eine Lösung zu entwerfen. In Europa sind öffentliche und private Einrichtungen, Architektur-, Design- und Kunstschaffende aufgerufen, Städte im Hinblick auf mehr Nachhaltigkeit und höhere Qualität neu zu denken. Bewegungen wie das New Bauhaus streben ein kritisches und transdisziplinäres Denken an, das Wissenschaft und Forschung, Technik und Konstruktion verbindet und neu definiert, wie man in verschiedenen Kontexten entwirft und interveniert. Es strebt nach einem Ansatz für ein innovatives Europa mit gemeinsamen Prinzipien, mit einer unverwechselbaren Identität, in der die Lebensqualität einen hohen Stellenwert einnimmt und ästhetische Werte, die in allen künstlerischen Formen vorhanden sind, hoch geachtet werden.[1] Auf städtischer Ebene sind diese europäischen Prinzipien ausgerichtet auf die Errichtung einer nachhaltigen Stadt, wobei andere Konzepte entstehen, die auf neue Anliegen und Ansätze sowohl in der Forschung als auch im Entwurf hinweisen. Konzepte wie Stadterneuerung, Smart Cities, 15-Minuten-Stadt, Sanierung, Wiederverwendung, Stadterlebnis usw. demonstrieren einen Wandel hin zur gelebten Stadt, in der neben der Betrachtung der Infrastrukturen auch die Nutzenden wertgeschätzt werden. Unter diesen Konzepten erfährt das urbane Erleben eine neue Bedeutung. Es zeigt, wie wichtig es ist, den Ort über das hinaus zu verstehen, was von Architekturschaffenden entworfen wurde, und somit die Wahrnehmung der einzelnen Person zu schätzen. Wenn das „Erlebnis oft mit den unterschiedlichen Atmosphären verbunden ist, die auf dem Weg durch den Grundriss und die formale Konfiguration entstehen", dann baut die Beschreibung der Stadt auf der individuellen Wahrnehmung der Umgebung jeder einzelnen Person auf.[2] Das Erlebnis, das man in der Stadt hat, wird gestärkt, um so das städtische Umfeld zu qualifizieren (Abb. 2).

In dem Wissen, dass sich die Erfahrung sowohl auf öffentliche als auch auf private Räume bezieht, sind nachhaltige Anliegen nicht nur auf territorialer und städtischer Ebene, sondern auch auf der Ebene des architektonischen Bauens zu denken. Das mit dem Pritzker-Preis 2021 ausgezeichnete Architekturbüro Lacaton & Vassal verfolgt Prinzipien wie

3 | Lacaton & Vassal Housing in Bordeaux 2018

concerns are, besides being present at the territorial and urban scale, visible at the scale of architectural construction. The Pritzker Prize 2021-awarded architects Lacaton & Vassal transpose principles such as 'reuse' into the building, not forgetting the individual perception and everyday use, thus being aligned with the vision of a lived city also representing a sustainable city. In the press release of the Pritzker Awards regarding the 2021 winners, the jury states that "Lacaton and Vassal reexamine sustainability in their reverence for pre-existing structures, conceiving projects by first taking inventory of what already exists. By prioritizing the enrichment of human life through a lens of generosity and freedom of use, they are able to benefit the individual socially, ecologically, and economically, aiding the evolution of a city" (fig. 3).[3] With Lacaton & Vassal's architecture reiterating freedom of use as a qualitative informal element in architectural design, it is important to realise the role of this approach, coupled with urban experience, in the construction of the city. Where is the freedom of appropriation in urban space?

FAÇADE AS INHABITED SPACE   Acknowledging that the spaces most conducive to free use are those that are in between, between the public and the private domain, between indoor and outdoor, between sun and shadow, or between heat and cold, it allows us to focus on the façades as an element of transition. So, through this framework, the transition spaces stand out as elements to explore in a project, combining technology and construction with configuration, atmospheres and human interactions. These transitional spaces created by the façade are spaces of permanence, with particular characteristics that relate to the adjacent spaces. In D. W. Winnicott's concept of transitional spaces, "transitional space (intermediate area, third area) is that space of experiencing, between the inner and outer worlds, and contributed to by both, in which primary creativity (illusion) exists and can develop".[4] With Winnicott we assume that the transition space is not only physical but also psychological, related to the reality

,Wiederverwendung' in Gebäuden, ohne dabei die individuelle Wahrnehmung und alltägliche Nutzung zu vernachlässigen, und orientiert sich so an der Vision einer gelebten Stadt, die gleichzeitig eine nachhaltige Stadt ist. In der Pressemitteilung des Pritzker-Preises zu den Ausgezeichneten stellt die Jury fest, dass „Lacaton & Vassal die Nachhaltigkeit mit ihrem Respekt vor bestehenden Strukturen neu befragen. Sie konzipieren Projekte, indem sie zunächst eine Bestandsaufnahme dessen machen, was bereits vorhanden ist. Indem sie der Bereicherung des menschlichen Lebens durch Großzügigkeit und Nutzungsfreiheit Vorrang einräumen, können sie den Einzelnen sozial, ökologisch und wirtschaftlich zugute kommen und die Entwicklung einer Stadt unterstützen" (Abb. 3).[3] Vor dem Hintergrund des wiederholten Einsatzes der Nutzungsfreiheit als qualitatives, informelles Element in der architektonischen Gestaltung von Lacaton & Vassal ist zu befragen, welche Rolle dieser Ansatz in Verbindung mit urbanem Erleben für das Bauen der Stadt spielt. Wo existiert Aneignungsfreiheit im urbanen Raum?

FASSADE ALS BEWOHNTER RAUM   Wenn wir anerkennen, dass die Räume, die einer freien Nutzung am förderlichsten sind, diejenigen sind, die zwischen dem öffentlichen und dem privaten Bereich, zwischen Innen und Außen, zwischen Sonne und Schatten oder zwischen Hitze und Kälte liegen, können wir uns auf die Fassaden als ein Übergangselement konzentrieren. Durch diese Rahmung lassen sich die Übergangsräume als Elemente herausstellen, die in einem Projekt erforscht werden können, indem sie Technik und Konstruktion mit Konfiguration, Atmosphären und menschlichen Interaktionen kombinieren. Diese durch die Fassade geschaffenen Übergangsräume sind Räume der Beständigkeit mit besonderen Merkmalen, die in Relation zu den angrenzenden Räumen stehen. In D. W. Winnicotts Konzept der Übergangsräume ist der „Übergangsraum (intermediate area, third area) jener Erfahrungsraum zwischen Innen- und Außenwelt, der von beiden mitgestaltet wird und in dem eine primäre Kreativität (illusion) existiert und sich entfalten kann".[4] Mit Winnicott gehen wir davon aus, dass der Übergangsraum nicht nur physisch, sondern auch psychologisch ist und sich auf die Realität jedes einzelnen Menschen bezieht. Folglich kann angenommen werden, dass diese physischen Räume auch ein dynamischer Prozess des Übergangs von einem Punkt zum anderen sind und somit eine Atmosphäre ausbilden. Der durch die Fassade geschaffene Raum erweist sich als bewohnbar, aber sind es die Architekturschaffenden, die daran denken? Oder haben städtebauliche Planungen diese städtische Konfiguration im Sinn?

Die Fassade ist ein architektonisches Element mit Dicke und Tiefe, die sie flexibel und zuträglich für die Anpassungsfähigkeit an unterschiedliche Nutzungen machen, die notwendig ist, um die Beziehung zwischen den beiden angrenzenden Räumen zu stärken. In der Architekturgeschichte ist die Tiefe der Fassade als ein bewohnbarer Raum

of each individual. Hence, we can assume that these physical spaces are also a dynamic process of transition from one point to another, thus creating an atmosphere. So, the space created by the façade reveals itself capable of being inhabited, but is it the architects who think about it? Or do urban plans have this configuration of the city in mind?

The façade is an element of architecture with thickness and depth, making it flexible and conducive to the adaptability of uses necessary to enhance the relationship between the two spaces adjacent to it. In the history of architecture, the depth of the façade as an inhabitable space is present in traditional constructions as a filter between the private and the public, in the accesses to dwellings, or between the sacred and the mundane, in the case of churches and other religious structures. Looking at the Japanese culture, there is a transition space between the interior private space and the exterior garden space, this space is called 'Engawa' and appears associated to the façade and its thickness. 'Engawa' is a covered and paved space that extends from the façade built of sliding doors. It is a space in-between that allows a gradual transition between the interior and the exterior and that, simultaneously, accommodates different occupations by the dwellers. Although it has no defined programme, it allows the user multiple appropriations and assumes an important social role by being the place where guests are hosted and where one is in relation with the outside and nature, important to the Japanese.

This concept is fundamental in traditional Japanese construction, allowing us to look at the capacity of a transitional space to qualify the dwelling and the fact that elements such as the door, floor and roof of these spaces are determinant for the multiplicity of uses.[5] We can then understand how this element often considered the limit of the street is, after all, an element that incorporates it and gives it a cadence of spaces and qualifies it.[6] Thus, with a view to the sustainable city, it becomes imperative to associate this new approach of living spaces not only to public spaces, but also to collective spaces, public or private, adjacent to them and to the articulation between both, as shown by 'Engawa' (fig. 4). Looking at the city through its intermediate spaces associated with the façade and the way they are defined and created allows us, consequently, to situate ourselves between two project scales, the built scale and the urban scale, promoting architecture projects committed to the city and the public space, remembering architecture and urbanism as intrinsically related disciplines.

OBSERVING - SYNTHESISING - (RE)THINKING   It is necessary to think of the project as a process, which is built up of different parts, from the observation of the existing on the site, to the synthesis, (re)thinking and testing to reaching the built object, which is not the final result. The final result then depends on a new phase: the appropriations by the users, that is, the product of design is not only the architect's project but the conjunction of the project with the appropriation. The perception of the

bekannt aus traditionellen Konstruktionen, als Filter zwischen dem Privaten und dem Öffentlichen, in den Zugängen zu Wohnungen oder zwischen dem Sakralen und dem Weltlichen im Fall von Kirchen und anderen religiösen Strukturen. In der japanischen Kultur gibt es einen Übergangsraum zwischen dem privaten Innenbereich und dem äußeren Gartenbereich; dieser Raum wird ‚Engawa' genannt und ist mit der Fassade und ihrer Tiefe verbunden. Der Engawa ist ein überdachter und gepflasterter Raum, der hinter der aus Schiebetüren gebildeten Fassade liegt. Es ist ein Zwischenraum, der einen fließenden Übergang zwischen Innen und Außen ermöglicht und unterschiedliche Aktivitäten der dort Wohnenden beherbergen kann. Obwohl der Engawa kein definiertes Programm hat, ermöglicht er vielfältige Aneignungen und übernimmt eine wichtige soziale Rolle, indem er der Ort ist, an dem Besuch bewirtet wird und wo man in Beziehung zur Außenwelt und zur Natur steht, was in Japan von großer Bedeutung ist.

Dieses Konzept ist grundlegend in der traditionellen Bauweise Japans und ermöglicht es, die Fähigkeit eines Übergangsraums zur Qualifizierung der Wohnung sowie die entscheidenden Wirkungen zu betrachten, die Elemente wie Tür, Boden und Dach dieser Räume für eine Nutzungsvielfalt innehaben.[5] Es kann so ein Verständnis dafür entstehen, dass dieses Element, das oft als Begrenzung der Straße betrachtet wird, eigentlich ein Element ist, das sie räumlich zusammenschließt, ihr einen räumlichen Rhythmus verleiht und sie qualifiziert.[6] Daher ist es mit Blick auf die nachhaltige Stadt unerlässlich, diesen neuartigen Ansatz der gelebten Räume nicht nur auf öffentliche Räume, sondern auch auf die daran angrenzenden, öffentlichen wie auch privaten, kollektiven Räume anzuwenden sowie auf die Artikulation zwischen beiden, so wie es sich beim Engawa zeigt (Abb. 4). Eine Betrachtung der Stadt über ihre Zwischenräume, die in Verbindung zur Fassade stehen, und die Art und Weise, wie sie definiert und geschaffen werden, ermöglicht folglich eine Situierung zwischen zwei Projektmaßstäben – dem gebauten Maßstab und dem städtischen Maßstab – und eine Förderung von Architekturprojekten, die der Stadt und dem öffentlichen Raum verpflichtet sind. Architektur und Städtebau erscheinen wieder als eng miteinander verbundene Disziplinen.

BEOBACHTEN – SYNTHETISIEREN – (UM-)DENKEN Das Forschungsprojekt wird als Prozess verstanden, der aus verschiedenen Teilen aufgebaut ist, von der Beobachtung des Vorhandenen vor Ort über die Synthese und das (Um-)Denken sowie das Testen bis zum Erreichen des gebauten Objekts, das nicht das Endergebnis ist. Das Endergebnis hängt dann von einer neuen Phase ab: Die Aneignung durch die Nutzenden, d.h. das Entwurfsprodukt, ist nicht nur das Projekt der Architekturschaffenden, sondern es besteht aus der Verbindung des Projekts mit der Aneignung. Die Wahrnehmung der Nutzenden, die aktiv in die Stadt eingreifen können, ist ein Konzept, das allen ein Begriff ist, die sich mit Erdgeschossnutzungen und dem Zusammentreffen der Tür mit der Straße

4 | Coffee Place London 2021   5 | Mixed uses Pontevedra 2022

user capable of actively intervening in the city is a concept known to all those associated with ground floor uses and the meeting of the door with the street, such as cafés, other shops and houses that extend the interior to the exterior. Thus, it is important that reflexive design considers that the project does not end when the work is completed but is something that transforms and recreates itself through the uses.[7]

Let us now look at medium-sized European cities, which represent more than 80% of the urban environment in Europe, that have in their morphology ambiguous spaces created by the façade that allow multiple transitions between building and street and try to find examples that allow us to quantify their influence on the city. In Pontevedra, Spain, for example, by reducing the presence of the car in the urban environment through a new mobility plan, the municipality has enhanced new dimensions of collective space.[8] In the ongoing research, we have analysed how this change in accessibility has affected informal appropriation by the individual, the community or the establishments, and we observed that formal elements such as stairs or arcades have served as a canvas for the free appropriations that are now unique elements that make the city a model and a successful case study. These appropriations combined with mobility enhance the quality of life in the city and make it resilient for the future (fig. 5).[9]

In exceptional situations like the pandemic, which we were going through in 2020/2021, spaces like balconies and windows are also considered as places of conviviality and social life, even though they are private spaces and located at a different level from the street level. This principle leads us to a three-dimensional approach to the city, in which the encounter between the street (plan) and the building (section and elevation) demonstrates that the urban is not only experienced on the ground floor but also on different floors.[10] Through the research that considers reflexive design, we can rethink ways to promote or inhibit the modes of appropriation that arise from the architectural project. In order to have interventions that are more engaged with the surrounding environment, design is considered

beschäftigen, wie es bei Cafés, anderen Geschäften und Häusern, die den Innenraum nach außen erweitern, der Fall ist. Daher sollte Reflexives Entwerfen berücksichtigen, dass das Projekt nicht endet, wenn die Konstruktion abgeschlossen ist, sondern etwas ist, das sich durch die Nutzungen verändert und darüber wiederholt erschaffen werden kann.[7] Betrachten wir nun mittelgroße europäische Städte, die mehr als 80 Prozent des städtischen Umfelds in Europa ausmachen und in ihrer Morphologie mehrdeutige, durch die Fassaden erzeugte Räume aufweisen, die verschiedene Übergänge zwischen Gebäude und Straße ermöglichen, und versuchen, Beispiele dafür zu finden, die uns erlauben, ihren Einfluss auf die Stadt zu ermitteln. In Pontevedra, Spanien, zum Beispiel hat die Gemeinde durch die Reduzierung der Präsenz des Autos in der städtischen Umgebung durch einen neuen Mobilitätsplan neue Formate kollektiver Räume geschaffen.[8] In der laufenden Forschung haben wir analysiert, wie sich diese Veränderung der Zugänglichkeit auf die informelle Aneignung durch die einzelnen Menschen, die Gemeinschaft oder die jeweiligen Einrichtungen ausgewirkt hat. Es wurde beobachtet, dass formale Elemente wie Treppen oder Arkaden als leere Leinwand für die freie Aneignung dienten und als besondere Elemente die Stadt in eine Vorbildposition bringen und damit zu einer erkenntnisreichen Fallstudie machen. Diese Mittel in Kombination mit Mobilität steigern die Lebensqualität in der Stadt und machen sie zukunftsfähiger (Abb. 5).[9]

Durch Ausnahmesituationen wie die Pandemie, die wir 2020/21 durchgemacht haben, werden auch Räume wie Balkone und Fenster als Orte des Zusammenseins und des sozialen Lebens angesehen, obwohl sie private Räume sind und auf einer anderen Ebene als der Straßenebene auftauchen. Dieses Prinzip führt zu einer dreidimensionalen Annäherung an die Stadt, in der die Begegnung zwischen Straße (Grundriss) und Gebäude (Schnitt und Aufriss) zeigt, dass das Städtische nicht nur im Erdgeschoss, sondern in verschiedenen Stockwerken erfahrbar ist.[10] Durch die Forschung, die das Reflexive Entwerfen einbezieht, kann überdacht werden, wie aus Architekturprojekten resultierende Aneignungsweisen gefördert oder eingeschränkt werden können. Um Eingriffe zu ermöglichen, die sich stärker auf die Umgebung beziehen, wird Entwerfen als Verschmelzung des architektonischen Projekts mit den Aneignungen der Nutzenden betrachtet. In diesem Sinne ist es notwendig, die Untersuchung durch die verschiedenen Teile des Entwurfsprozesses hindurch zu führen: die Beobachtungen des Vorhandenen vor Ort und deren Synthese. Es wird mit der Analyse formaler Elemente begonnen wie architektonischen Komponenten (Türen, Fenster, Balkone), der Fassadentypologie und des Maßstabs. Sie ermöglichen, Kombinationen vorherzusagen, welche die stärkste Dynamik in der Stadt erzeugen. Dann werden die informellen Elemente dargestellt, wie z.B. Aneignungen, die Teil der Stadtlandschaft sind. Durch die Einbindung des Entwurfsprozesses in die Untersuchung versuchen wir, für die formellen und informellen Elemente, die beide im Stadtraum sichtbar sind, einen gemeinsamen Ansatz anzuwenden.

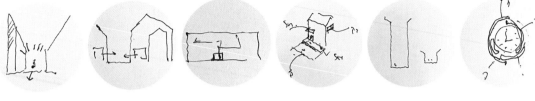

6 | Criteria of analysis

as the fusion of the architectural project with the appropriations of the user. In this sense, it is necessary to conduct the investigation through parts of the design process: the observation of the existing on site and its synthesis. We start by analysing formal elements, such as architectural components (doors, windows, balconies), typology of façades and the scale, which will allow us to predict the combinations that create the most dynamics in the city. We then represent the informal elements, such as appropriations, that are part of the urban landscape. So, by using the design process in the investigation we seek to apply a common approach to the formal and informal elements because both are visible in the urban space.

FORMAL ELEMENTS WHICH ENCOURAGE OR INHIBIT APPROPRIATIONS
There are several reasons which originate the appropriations. In this sense, a look to European medium-sized cities as case studies elucidates that it is necessary to approach the place by understanding what already exists. Thus, six initial criteria associated with formal elements are stipulated (fig 6).[11] The limits of the street, such as walls, vegetation or permeable space influence the way people move. An example of this is the plan of Rome in 1748 by Giambattista Nolli, where the city is represented by the limits of what we walk along instead of the limits of the public space. Other criteria are the programme and/ or the ground floor, as the function existing in each building relates directly to stopping points in the street (fig. 7). The typology of the façade is the criteria which allows the relating of the formal elements of architecture such as the constructive elements (like balconies and doors) and the materiality with the appropriations. It is at this point that one seeks to understand the architectural project and the aesthetics allied to the functionality which are responsible for changing the dynamics of a place (fig. 8).[12] The transition is associated to the intervals: it qualifies the relationship between the public and private spaces through the depth, the thickness, which represents a moment of adaptation to what is on the other side, and is also associated to the principle of atmospheres.[13] The relation of the building scale and the human scale is a formal element to analyse as it is related to our perception and experience, capable of giving us a sense of comfort or discomfort. The last criterion is time, which – through the decay of a building or through the course of the day – influences the urban experience (fig. 9). Often associated with the programme, time changes the configuration of the street boundaries, for example, when stores are open or closed. These criteria are not complete, they are correlated to each other and allow us to create the axes of analysis for an urban reading from the

7 | Storefront Braga 2021   8 | Stairs Valencia 2022

FORMALE ELEMENTE, DIE ANEIGNUNGEN FÖRDERN ODER VERHINDERN
Es gibt mehrere Gründe, die Aneignungen bedingen. In dieser Hinsicht verdeutlicht
der Blick auf die europäischen Mittelstädte als Fallstudien, dass es notwendig ist, sich
dem Ort mittels eines Verständnisses des Bestehenden zu nähern. Daher werden sechs
grundlegende Kriterien für formale Elemente etabliert (Abb. 6).[11] Die Begrenzungen
der Straße wie Mauern, Vegetation oder durchlässige Räume beeinflussen die Art und
Weise, wie sich Menschen bewegen. Ein Beispiel dafür ist der Plan von Rom aus dem Jahr
1748 von Giambattista Nolli, in dem die Stadt durch die Grenzen dessen repräsentiert
wird, woran wir entlanggehen, anstatt durch die Grenzen des öffentlichen Raums. Ein
weiteres Kriterium ist das Programm und/oder das Erdgeschoss, da sich die in jedem
Gebäude vorhandene Funktion als Haltepunkt in der Straße auswirken kann (Abb. 7).
Die Typologie der Fassade ist ein Kriterium, das es erlaubt, die formalen Elemente der
Architektur wie die konstruktiven Elemente (etwa Balkone und Türen) und die Materialität mit den Aneignungen in Beziehung zu setzen. An diesem Punkt wird versucht,
das architektonische Projekt und die mit der Funktionalität in Zusammenhang stehende
Ästhetik zu verstehen, welche für die Veränderung der Dynamik eines Ortes verantwortlich sind (Abb. 8).[12] Der Übergang ist mit Intervallen verbunden. Er qualifiziert die
Beziehung zwischen öffentlichen und privaten Räumen durch die Tiefe – die Dicke –,
die eine Anpassung ermöglicht an das, was sich auf der anderen Seite befindet und
auch mit dem Prinzip von Atmosphären verbunden ist.[13] Die Beziehung des Gebäude-
maßstabs zum menschlichen Maßstab ist ein formales Element, das es zu analysieren
gilt, da es sich auf unsere Wahrnehmung und Erfahrung bezieht und imstande ist, uns
ein Gefühl von Wohl- oder aber Unbehagen zu vermitteln. Das letzte Kriterium ist die
Zeit, die durch den Verfall eines Gebäudes oder den Tagesverlauf das urbane Erleben
beeinflusst (Abb. 9). Oft auch in Verbindung zum Programm, ändert die Zeit die Konfiguration der Straßengrenzen, beispielsweise wenn der Handel geöffnet oder geschlossen ist.

147

9 | Collage: Abandoned with uses Spain and India 2022

scale of the path to the scale of the street and the neighbourhood. It allows us to understand what influence the formal elements have in promoting or inhibiting appropriations, and also to identify what type of informal dynamics derive from the formal elements.

REPRESENTING INFORMALITY   It is after determining the criteria to observe, that the way to represent and synthesise the existent and its dynamics is defined. Through drawing, the elements are decomposed and graphically explored, demonstrating visually what is experienced in the place. Drawing as a form of observing is used since it is a tool of both architecture and urbanism, capable of communicating in both disciplines and thus feeding dialogue. Starting from the general to the particular, from the concrete to the speculative (associated to the urban experience), different modes of representation are used (fig. 10–11). Intrinsic tools of the architectural project, such as the section, the plan, the elevation and the axonometries allow 'to relate very distinct parts in the large scale and in the proximity scale', demonstrating the built elements and their uses.[14] In our study, this goes from the metric of the elevations of the street to the decomposition of these in components (windows, doors, stairs) and to the constructive detail. After this analysis it will be possible to reflect on the impact of these elements and identify what kind of appropriations they produce. In short, this analysis will allow us to understand combinations of formal components in the production of a certain effect/informality. As a consequence of informality arises the representation and synthesis of appropriations that are represented through schemes, maps and drawings inspired by the synthesis of urban experience in 'Walkscapes', Queneau's personal experiences of travelling or Rothuizen's cartography of Amsterdam (fig. 12).[15] It is through artistic reproductions and representations from other disciplinary fields that an image of ambiguity and personal experience is made possible in the attempt to portrait the atmospheres and the movements that exist in the relation between the façade and the enveloping uses.[16]

10–11 | Appropriation Oporto 2022

Diese Kriterien sind nicht abgeschlossen, sie korrelieren miteinander und erlauben, die Analyseachsen für eine urbane Lesart vom Maßstab des Weges bis zum Straßen- und Quartiersmaßstab zu erstellen. Dies ermöglicht uns zu verstehen, welchen Einfluss die formalen Elemente auf die Förderung oder Hemmung von Aneignungen haben, und auch zu identifizieren, welche Art von informeller Dynamik von den formalen Elementen ausgeht.

REPRÄSENTATION VON INFORMALITÄT   Nach der Festlegung der zu beachtenden Kriterien wird die Weise definiert, wie das Existierende und seine Dynamik dargestellt und synthetisiert werden können. Durch Zeichnen werden die Elemente zerlegt und grafisch untersucht, wodurch visuell demonstriert wird, was an dem Ort erlebt wird. Das Zeichnen als Beobachtungsform wird verwendet, da es ein Werkzeug sowohl der Architektur als auch des Urbanismus ist, das in der Lage ist, in beiden Disziplinen zu kommunizieren und so den Dialog zu nähren. Ausgehend vom Allgemeinen zum Besonderen, vom Konkreten zum Spekulativen (verbunden mit der urbanen Erfahrung), werden unterschiedliche Darstellungsweisen verwendet (Abb. 10–11). Intrinsische Werkzeuge der Architekturdarstellung wie der Schnitt, der Plan, der Aufriss und die Axonometrien ermöglichen es, „sehr unterschiedliche Teile im großen Maßstab und im Nahmaßstab in Beziehung zu setzen", wodurch die gebauten Elemente und ihre Verwendung demonstriert werden.[14] In unserer Studie wird dies von der Metrik der Straßenansichten über die Zerlegung dieser in Bauteile (Fenster, Türen, Treppen) bis hin zum konstruktiven Detail durchgeführt. Nach dieser Analyse wird es möglich sein, über die Auswirkungen dieser Elemente nachzudenken und festzustellen, welche Arten von Mitteln durch sie produziert werden. Kurz gesagt, diese Analyse ermöglicht, Kombinationen formaler Komponenten bei der Erzeugung einer bestimmten Wirkung/Informalität zu verstehen. Als Folge der Informalität entstehen die Repräsentation und Synthese von Aneignungen, die durch Schemata, Karten und Zeichnungen gezeigt werden. Diese sind von der Synthese urbaner

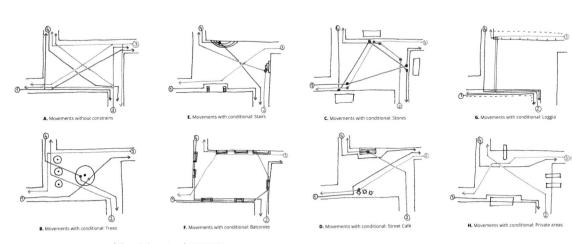

A. Movements without constrains

E. Movements with conditional: Stairs

C. Movements with conditional: Stores

G. Movements with conditional: Loggia

B. Movements with conditional: Trees

F. Movements with conditional: Balconies

D. Movements with conditional: Street Café

H. Movements with conditional: Private areas

12 | Formal elements and movements

FROM INFORMALITY BACK TO THE PROJECT   We are in a moment of change, of looking at what has already been done and redesigning a future that uses all the tools that technological evolution offers us, combined with the principles of society to improve the quality of life by promoting flexibility and diversity in cities. It is a time when the crossing between disciplines and the use of the resources we have for a better intervention are privileged. In this sense, the model presented does not give us a formula of how to intervene generically but enables urban reading tools and synthesises knowledge about the existing layers in the city by understanding the uses as an element that qualifies the urban, strengthening the relationship between the building and the city.

OUTLOOK   The engagement with 'Products' allowed to reinforce the presented approach, putting in question the product, in first place the configuration of the urban space that gives origin to this research and, consequently, the result of the research as a product. In other words, to think about the product that is analysed in the research (the merger of the architectural project + the appropriations) and the product that will come out of it. It allows rethinking the role of the architect/designer as the driver of dynamics and the user as the definer of the urban experience, being himself the one who, through his uses, rewrites the urban environment. So, how can the architect anticipate and stimulate uses and appropriations in design? With this in mind, can the reflection and representation of the design of uses be the product of this research or should the product be a formula for future interventions?

Erfahrungen in ‚Walkscapes', Queneaus persönlichen Reiseerfahrungen, oder Rothuizens Kartografie von Amsterdam inspiriert (Abb. 12).[15] Durch künstlerische Reproduktionen und Darstellungen aus anderen Disziplinen wird ein Bild der Mehrdeutigkeit und persönlichen Erfahrung ermöglicht, um die Atmosphären und Bewegungen darzustellen, die in der Beziehung zwischen der Fassade und den umhüllenden Nutzungen bestehen.

VON DER INFORMALITÄT ZURÜCK ZUM PROJEKT   Wir befinden uns in einem Wandlungsmoment: des Blicks auf das, was bereits getan wurde, und der Neugestaltung einer Zukunft, die alle Werkzeuge des technologischen Entwicklungsstandes nutzt und mit gesellschaftlichen Prinzipien kombiniert, um die Lebensqualität durch eine Förderung von Flexibilität und Vielfalt in Städten zu erhöhen. Hierbei werden für eine bessere Intervention die Transdisziplinarität sowie die Nutzung der Ressourcen bevorzugt, die wir haben. In diesem Sinne gibt uns das vorgestellte Modell keine universell einsetzbare Formel, sondern erzeugt Werkzeuge für Lesarten des Urbanen und synthetisiert Wissen über die bestehenden Schichten in der Stadt, indem es die Nutzungen als ein Element versteht, das das Städtische qualifiziert und die Beziehung zwischen Gebäude und Stadt stärkt.

AUSBLICK   Die Beschäftigung mit den Produkten hat es ermöglicht, den vorgestellten Ansatz zu stärken und das Produkt infrage zu stellen – in erster Linie die Konfiguration des städtischen Raums, die dieser Forschung und folglich dem Ergebnis der Forschung als Produkt entspringt. Mit anderen Worten, es ist ein Nachdenken über das Produkt, das in der Forschung analysiert wird (die Zusammenführung des Architekturprojekts + der Mittel), und das Produkt, das daraus hervorgehen wird. Es ermöglicht, die Rolle von Design- und Architekturschaffenden als Motor der Dynamik und die Rolle der Nutzenden als Definierende des urbanen Erlebnisses zu überdenken, da sie selbst diejenigen sind, die durch ihre Nutzungen die städtische Umgebung neu schreiben. Wie also können Architekturschaffende Nutzungen und Aneignungen im Entwurf antizipieren und anregen? Können vor diesem Hintergrund auch die Reflexion und Repräsentation der Nutzungsgestaltung Produkte dieser Forschung sein oder sollte das Produkt eine Formel für zukünftige Interventionen sein?

1 Cf. | Vgl. Ursula von der Leyen, State of the Union 2020, on: | auf: https://ec.europa.eu/commission/presscorner/detail/ov/SPEECH_20_1655, 20.06.2022   **2** Peter Zumthor, Atmosferas, Barcelona: Gustavo Gili, 2006, 16–17   **3** N.N., Anne Lacaton and Jean-Philippe Vassal receive the 2021 Pritzker Architecture Prize, on: | auf: https://www.pritzkerprize.com/laureates/anne-lacaton-and-jean-philippe-vassal, 20.06.2022   **4** Donald Winnicott, Transitional objects and transitional phenomena – A study of the first not-me possession, in: The international journal of psychoanalysis 34(1953), 89–97   **5** Cf. | Vgl. Michael Lazarin, Phenomenology of Japonese Architecture: En (edge, connection, destiny), Kyoto: Ryukoku University 2014, 138–140   **6** Cf. | Vgl. Junichiro Tanizaki, In praise of shadows, London: Vintage 2001, 32–34   **7** Cf. | Vgl. Margitta Buchert (ed.), Prozesse Reflexiven Entwerfens. Processes of Reflexive Design. Entwerfen und Forschen in Architektur und Landschaft. Design and research in architecture and landscape, Berlin: jovis, 2018   **8** Cf. | Vgl. N.N., Alternative mobility, on: | auf: https://ok.pontevedra.gal/en/alternative-mobility/, 04.07.2022   **9** Cf. | Vgl. Diana Gouveia Amaral, Rethinking collective spaces through the façade element: From formality to informality, (PhD in progress | PhD in Bearbeitung)   **10** Cf. on this also | Vgl. dazu auch Nicolas John Habraken/Jonathan Teicher (eds.), The structure of the ordinary: Forms and control in the built environment, Cambridge, MA: MIT Press 2000, 216   **11** Cf. | Vgl. ibid., 133–134   **12** Cf. | Vgl. Rem Koolhaas, Elements of architecture, Köln: Taschen 2018, 543–1225   **13** Nicolaas John Habraken/Jonathan Teicher (eds.) (2000), op. cit. (note | Anm. 10), 29, 137–139   **14** Manuel Solà-Morales, De cosas urbanas, in: Miradas sobre la ciudad, Barcelona: Acantilado 2021, 235   **15** Cf. | Vgl. Francesco Careri, Walkscapes: O caminhar como prática estética, Barcelona: Editorial Gustavo Gili 2014; Raymond Queneau, Exercícios de estilo, Lisbon: Edições Colibri 2000; Jan Rothuizen, The soft atlas of Amsterdam: Hand drawn perspectives from daily life, Amsterdam: Amsterdam University Press 2015   **16** Cf. | Vgl. Edward Hall, A dimensão oculta (The hidden dimension), Lisbon: Relógio d'Água Editores, 1986, 55–91

ONE. SOUND. SPACE

Susan Jebrini

If one asks about the formation, effect and meaning of products of reflexive design, it becomes clear that the field of research itself directs the scope of action within creative and knowledge-generating production processes. Because every reflexive movement and stance never happens in isolation, impulsively or unconditionally, but always sets an initial framework for a conscious consideration and an analysis of the intentions and products of creative effect processes. If one understands a product to be the combination of different parameters leading to a result, then product development can be understood within a scientific discussion, especially in reflexive design, as the development of approaches that oscillate between a theoretical study and a practical formation.

F O R M A T I O N   Given that the shaping of an intention and the elaboration of various parameters represent the basis of a method, a phenomenological-hermeneutical approach has been chosen for the research work presented in the following. The research design can be regarded as a first product of a necessary decision within an academic context (fig. 1). This necessary decision represents both the outward foundation for the communication, mediation and transparency of the research process and internally the effect of a continuity of a constant monitoring of the procedure within the further academic development and considerations.

At the centre of the research work 'One.Sound.Space. Approaches to an aesthetic perception theory of space and sound' – based on the example of contemporary opera and musical theatre – is the theory that contemporary music can only work to a limited extent in traditionally conceived spaces for musical theatre. This means that if the conception, message and form of contemporary music develop further, but the spatial corpus such

ONE. SOUND. SPACE

Susan Jebrini

Fragt man nach der Formation, Wirkung und Bedeutung von Produkten des Reflexiven Entwerfens, so wird deutlich erkennbar, dass das Forschungsfeld selbst den Handlungsspiel-
raum innerhalb kreativer und wissensgenerierender Produktionsprozesse steuert. Denn
jede reflexive Bewegung und Haltung geschieht niemals losgelöst, impulsiv oder bedin-
gungslos, sondern setzt stets eine erste Rahmung für eine bewusste Auseinandersetzung
und eine Analyse von Intentionen und Produkten kreativer Wirkungsprozesse. Versteht
man unter einem Produkt die Verknüpfung verschiedener Parameter zu einem Ergebnis, so
kann die Produktentwicklung innerhalb eines wissenschaftlichen Diskurses insbesondere
im Reflexiven Entwerfen als die Entwicklung von Ansätzen verstanden werden, die zwischen einer theoretischen Auseinandersetzung und einer praktischen Formation oszilliert.

FORMATION   Geht man davon aus, dass die Basis einer Methodik als Ausformung
einer Intention und Multiplikation verschiedener Parameter produzierend erscheint, so
wurde für die im weiteren vorgestellte Forschungsarbeit eine phänomenologisch-herme-
neutische Herangehensweise gewählt. Das Forschungsdesign kann als ein erstes Produkt
einer notwendigen Entscheidung innerhalb eines wissenschaftlichen Wirkungskontextes
betrachtet werden (Abb.1). Diese notwendige Entscheidung bildet sowohl den Grundstock
im Außen für die Kommunikation, Vermittlung und Transparenz des Forschungsprozesses
als auch im Inneren die Wirkung einer Kontinuität der steten Überprüfung der Vorgehens-
weise innerhalb der weiteren wissenschaftlichen Gestaltung bzw. Auseinandersetzung.

Im Zentrum der Forschungsarbeit ‚One.Sound.Space – Ansätze zu einer ästhetischen Wahr-
nehmungstheorie von Raum und Klang' – am Beispiel zeitgenössischer Oper und des Musiktheaters –, steht die These, dass zeitgenössische Musik in herkömmlich gedachten Räumen
für das Musiktheater nur eingeschränkt funktionieren kann. Das bedeutet, wenn sich die

PRACTISE A
postproject analyse

PRACTISE B
spatial experiment I

PRACTISE C
spatial experiment II

THEORIE

Perception of space
Perception of sound
Perception of space and sound

CASE STUDIES

1. space for a sound
2. sound for a space I
3. sound for a space I I

THEORIE

approaches to an
aesthetic perception
theory of space and
sound

design modules

1 | One.Sound.Space Research design

as an opera house remains the same in its form and function, then space and music can potentially collide (fig. 2). Already back in 1967, the statement by Pierre Boulez "Blow the opera houses up" in an interview in the German weekly magazine 'Der Spiegel' caused a big stir but remained unheeded.[1] Boulez advocated not performing modern operas in traditional opera houses, as these did not correspond to the requirements and criteria.[2]

Since the middle of the 20th century, a new compositional means developed in music theory and practice with the start of serial music that was intended for a real musical space.[3] The shaping materiality of this space is the positing of sound. The new criteria of formation in the fabric of space and sound are e.g. positioning, multilayeredness, temporal processes and sound movements. A distinction between architecture as spatial art and music or musical theatre as temporal art is thereby questioned for the first time.[4] Through a materialisation of sound away from an intended sound space notion, space becomes experienceable with the senses in both concerts and musical theatre, if the architectural-spatial structures do not prevent it. The space is subsequently much more than an objective shell that serves the acoustic development of musically arranged time. Answers regarding the significance and function of space in and for music remain open and largely not reflected on to date, especially regarding the architectural formation of a new type of concert hall and of the opera house, as well as a resulting new form of musical theatre and concert culture. The research work One.Sound.Space therefore examines whether the consciously discerning music experience, which is based largely on already gathered musical experiences, should make way for a sensory space and music experience. This leads to the key question of whether a new form of music should be combined with a new type of spatial thinking.

2 | The dissolution of music as pure contemporary art 'Space experiment C', November der Wissenschaft 2010

zeitgenössische Musik in ihrer Konzeption, ihrer Aussage und in ihrer Form weiterentwickelt, der räumliche Korpus wie ein Opernhaus aber in seiner Form und Funktion gleichbleibt, dann wirken Raum und Musik potenziell gegeneinander und kollidieren (Abb. 2). Schon 1967 führte Pierre Boulez' Aussage „Sprengt die Opernhäuser in die Luft" in einem Interview in der deutschen Wochenzeitschrift ‚Der Spiegel' zu großem Aufsehen und zu Aufruhr und führte doch ins Leere.[1] Boulez sprach sich dafür aus, moderne Opern nicht in traditionellen Opernhäusern aufzuführen, da diese den Anforderungen und Kriterien nicht entsprechen.[2]

Seit Mitte des 20. Jahrhunderts entwickelte sich mit Beginn der seriellen Musik ein neues kompositorisches Mittel in der Musiktheorie und Praxis, welches einen realen musikalischen Raum intendiert.[3] Die formgebende Materialität dieses Raumes ist die Setzung des Klanges. Die neuen Kriterien der Formgebung im Gefüge von Raum und Klang sind zum Beispie Verortungen, Vielschichtigkeit, zeitliche Prozesse und Klangbewegungen. Eine Unterscheidung der Architektur als Raumkunst und der Musik bzw. des Musiktheaters als Zeitkunst wird dadurch zum ersten Mal infrage gestellt.[4] Durch eine Materialisierung des Klanges weg von einer intendierten Klangraumvorstellung wird Raum sowohl im Konzert als auch im Musiktheater sinnlich erfahrbar, wenn die architektonisch-räumlichen Strukturen es nicht verhindern. Der Raum ist folglich vielmehr als eine objektive Hülle, die zur akustischen Entwicklung musikalisch angeordneter Zeit dient. Antworten nach der Bedeutung und Funktion von Raum in und für Musik sind insbesondere im Bereich der architektonischen Ausformung eines neuen Typs des Konzertsaales und des Opernhauses sowie einer dadurch bedingten neuen Form von Musiktheater und Konzertkultur bis dato offen und weitgehend unreflektiert. Die Forschungsarbeit ‚One.Sound.Space' untersucht daher, ob das bewusst erkennende Musikerlebnis, welches zu einem großen Teil auf bereits gemachten musikalischen Erfahrungen beruht, für ein sinnliches Raum und Musikerleben Platz machen sollte. Daraus folgt als zentrale Fragestellung, ob eine neue Form der Musik mit einem neuen Typ des Raumgedankens verbunden werden sollte.

3 | The limits of an architectural space 'insideout'

INTERIM PRODUCTS / END PRODUCTS   In order to set out bases for the design of suitable performance spaces, the structure of the research work consists of an interplay of practical and theoretical units. Space and sound are thereby regarded as integrative and studied as mutually dependent units, as well as the relationship of the two to physical perception. Insights into the creative conceptualisation of new types of space for music were generated through three performative, experimental actions on the subject of space, sound and perception, carried out in the form of a post-project analysis and the implementation, documentation and analysis of two spatial experiments, as well as a review of theories from the field of architecture and music science about the link between space and music. The experiments form interim products as important leading units of the research process. In addition, preliminary end products are developed as 'design building blocks', addressing the question of the added value of space and music as a proposal of a holistic physical perception of contemporary music. The interim products created within the theoretical and practical considerations in the form of spatial experiments not only serve to answer questions but also to keep asking new ones.

With the help of spatial experiments that build on each other, which do not signify conclusive results but merely long-term indicators for further spatial experiments, one can achieve an accompanying ongoing review of the theory in specific points, as well as practice-related results. The American architecture theorist Linda Groat presents experimental work in connection with architecture research in her article 'Experimental and Quasi-Experimental Research'. She discusses precisely controlled laboratory situations, as well as field studies that are less determinable. The derived findings can range from exact physical parameters such as the air temperature to more descriptive results such as the behaviour of test persons (fig. 3).[5] These spatial experiments provide a contribution to more differentiated insights than theoretical considerations alone would allow, through the inclusion of real people such as musicians and visitors, their actions and reactions, their subsequent reflections in discussions and statements on questionnaires, as well as through participatory observation and the individual experience of space.

ZWISCHENPRODUKTE / ENDPRODUKTE   Um hierzu Grundlagen
für das Entwerfen adäquater Darbietungsräume zu entwickeln, besteht der Aufbau der Forschungsarbeit aus einer wechselseitigen Beziehung zwischen praktischen und theoretischen
Einheiten. Raum und Klang werden dabei als integrativ betrachtet und als voneinander
abhängige Einheiten untersucht ebenso wie das Verhältnis der Einheit beider zur körperlichen
Wahrnehmung. Über drei performative, experimentelle Aktionen zum Thema Raum, Klang
und Wahrnehmung, die in Form einer Postprojektanalyse und der Durchführung, Dokumentation und Analyse von zwei Raumexperimenten erfolgten, sowie durch eine Aufarbeitung
der Theorien aus dem Bereich der Architektur und der Musikwissenschaft zum Zusammenhang von Raum und Musik wurden Erkenntnisse zur entwerferischen Konzeptualisierung von
neuen Raumtypen für Musik generiert. Die Experimente bilden Zwischenprodukte als wichtige erkenntnisleitende Einheiten des Forschungsprozesses. Zudem werden vorläufige Endprodukte, ‚Entwurfsbausteine', entwickelt, die sich der Fragestellung nach einem Mehrwert
von Raum und Musik als einem Entwurf zu einer ganzheitlichen körperlichen Wahrnehmung
zeitgenössischer Musik annähern. Die Zwischenprodukte, welche innerhalb der theoretischen wie praktischen Auseinandersetzung in Form von Raumexperimenten entstehen, dienen dabei nicht nur dazu, Fragen zu beantworten, sondern auch dazu, stets neue zu stellen.

Mithilfe der aufeinander aufbauenden Raumexperimente, welche keine abschließenden
Ergebnisse, sondern lediglich langfristige Richtungskorrekturen für weitere Raumexperimente bedeuten, lässt sich eine begleitende immerwährende Überprüfung der Theorie in
konkreten Punkten erreichen und praxisbezogene Ergebnisse können erzielt werden. Die
amerikanische Architekturtheoretikerin Linda Groat stellt hierzu in ihrem Artikel ‚Experimental and Quasi-Experimental Research' experimentelles Arbeiten in den Zusammenhang
mit Architekturforschung. Sie diskutiert genau kontrollierte Laborsituationen wie auch
weniger vorbestimmbare Feldstudien. Die daraus zu gewinnenden Erkenntnissen können
demnach von präzisen physikalischen Parametern wie etwa der Lufttemperatur bis hin zu
eher beschreibenden Ergebnissen wie dem Verhalten von Proband:innen reichen (Abb. 3).[5]
Diese Raumexperimente ermöglichen, durch die Einbeziehung von realen Menschen wie
Musiker:innen und Besucher:innen, ihrer Aktionen und Reaktionen, ihrer anschließenden
Reflexionen in Gesprächen und Äußerungen in Fragebögen sowie durch teilnehmende
Beobachtung und das eigene Erleben des Raumes zu differenzierteren Erkenntnis-
sen beizutragen, als es eine theoretische Auseinandersetzung allein vermögen würde.

PERFORMATIVE EINHEITEN   Die Postprojektanalyse sowie auch
die zwei Raumexperimente sind in enger Zusammenarbeit mit dem Architekten und
Musiker Dipl.-Ing. Leif Thomsen entworfen, entwickelt und durchgeführt worden.

4–5 | Sound gate 'Animating Braunschweig' 2004

PERFORMATIVE UNITS   The post-project analysis, as well as two spatial experiments, were conceived, developed and carried out in close cooperation with
architect and musician Dipl. Ing. Leif Thomsen.

POST-PROJECT ANALYSIS ('ANIMATING BRAUNSCHWEIG')
As part of the 'Festliche Tage Neuer Musik in Braunschweig' 2004 ('Festive Days of New
Music in Braunschweig'), two designs for the Braunschweig State Theatre were drawn
up, based on the theatre's task of animating the urban space with New Music.[6] In order
to realise the encounter between passers-by and New Music within the urban space, two
different intervention concepts were developed in our project: the 'sound gate' and the
'sound barrier'. The choice of location for the 'sound gate' was the main entrance to the
mostly vibrant pedestrian zone from the cathedral square, where every summer several
open-air theatre performances are held (fig. 4). The 'sound barrier', on the other hand, was
positioned in the middle of a courtyard situation, which blocked a shortcut between two
parts of the pedestrian zone (fig. 5). The question guiding the design was what reactions
are triggered by space and sound through this direct and unexpected overwhelming
moment. The passers-by get into the situation, quite in contrast to a concert, without
expectations. This everyday situation leads to a sudden confrontation and also to a direct
physical reaction, as a design intention. It was studied in particular how the persons
position themselves within the space and what happens to their movement and direction
of attention, in order to gain an impression of the spatial requirements and preferences
of the recipients, as a place of sojourn that has the greatest possible effect on the
recipients. A significant finding was that the spatial and musical interior space created by
the structural intervention within the urban space must be contained within a designed
exterior space that has a strong influence on the receptive behaviour of the recipients.

6–7 | 'Spatial experiment B' Entrance and exit, Layering of space LUH 2007

POSTPROJEKTANALYSE ‚BRAUNSCHWEIG BESPIELEN'
Im Rahmen der ‚Festlichen Tage Neuer Musik in Braunschweig' 2004 sind zwei Entwürfe
für das Staatstheater Braunschweig entstanden, ausgehend von der Aufgabenstellung des
Theaters, den Stadtraum mit Neuer Musik zu bespielen.[6] Um die Begegnung zwischen Passant
:innen und Neuer Musik im städtischen Raum umzusetzen, wurden in unserem Projekt zwei
unterschiedliche Interventionskonzepte entwickelt: die ‚Klangschleuse' und die ‚Klangsperre'.
Die Wahl des Ortes fiel für die ‚Klangschleuse' auf den Haupteingang zur meist belebten Fußgängerzone vom Domplatz aus, auf dem im Sommer stets mehrere Open-Air-Aufführungen
des Theaters stattfinden (Abb. 4). Die ‚Klangsperre' hingegen wurde mitten in eine Hofsituation
platziert, wodurch eine Abkürzung zwischen zwei Teilen der Fußgängerzone versperrt wurde
(Abb. 5). Die entwurfsleitende Fragestellung war hierbei, welche Reaktionen über diesen
unmittelbaren und unerwarteten Überwältigungsmoment durch Raum und Klang ausgelöst
werden. Die Passant:innen geraten in die Situation, ganz im Gegensatz zum Konzert, ohne eine
Erwartungshaltung. Diese alltägliche Situation führt zu einer plötzlichen Auseinandersetzung
und in der Entwurfsintention auch zu einer unmittelbaren körperlichen Reaktion. Es wurde
insbesondere untersucht, wie sich die Personen innerhalb des Raumes positionieren, und was
mit ihrer Bewegung und ihren Blickrichtungen passiert, um einen Eindruck von den räumlichen
Bedürfnissen und Präferenzen der Rezipient:innen in Bezug auf den Aufenthaltsort zu bekom-
men, der eine größtmögliche Wirkung bei den Rezipient:innen hervorruft. Eine wesentliche
Feststellung war dabei, dass der durch die bauliche Intervention innerhalb des Stadtraumes
räumlich und musikalisch entstehende Innenraum durch einen gestalteten Außenraum gefasst
werden muss, der einen großen Einfluss auf das Rezeptionsverhalten der Rezipient:innen hat.

RAUMEXPERIMENT ‚KLANGRAUM'   Der zweite Entwurf war ein
Raumexperiment in Form eines 150 Quadratmeter großen gebauten Raumes im Foyer der
Fakultät für Architektur und Landschaft der Leibniz Universität Hannover in 2007. Ausge-
hend von der Postprojektanalyse sollte hier aufgrund einer differenzierteren theoretischen

8 | 'Spatial experiment B' Different layers of the spatial experiment LUH 2007

SPATIAL EXPERIMENT 'SOUND SPACE'   The second design was a spatial experiment in the form of a 150m² built space in the foyer of the Faculty of Architecture and Landscape at Leibniz University Hannover in 2007. Based on the post-project analysis, a space-within-a-space was to be created here based on a differentiate theoretical consideration of the perception of space and music. It was intended to provide the possibility of assuming a variety of spatial-musical scenarios, as well as to be able to function in itself as a space for music without additional installations. At the heart of the considerations was a space for New Music which – contrary to the intervention in urban space – offers a form of encounter within an enclosed space. With an elementary geometry of four freestanding, rectangular wall panels, an outwardly confined form was created with four narrow entrances and exits (fig. 6). This space was designed to question or even dissolve the standard conventions of a concert hall or opera house, as well as the separation of stage and spectator space, accustomed behaviours such as applause and silence, as well as movement patterns such as quiet sitting during a performance (fig. 7). The architectural theory approach was initially through a consideration of the human body as a space in the sense of a thinking model. This personal space consists of one's own body as an interior space and the surrounding world as an exterior space. There are transitional zones between the two spaces. As a starting point for this spatial experiment, the aim was to seek or create transitional zones in spaces for music also in practice.[7] A significant finding of the study consists in generating the physical and mental freedom of movement of the audience and thereby offering the possibility of entering the musical works and experiencing them holistically.

SPATIAL EXPERIMENT 'SPATIAL SOUND'   The third design 'Spatial Sound' was a spatial experiment as part of the November of Science Hanover in 2010 in the theatre hall of the University of Music, Drama and Media in Hannover. An existing spatial order was to be reinterpreted and animated in relation to space and sound, in

Auseinandersetzung mit der Wahrnehmung von Raum und Musik ein Raum im Raum geschaffen werden. Dieser sollte die Möglichkeit bieten, verschiedene räumlich-musikalische Inszenierungen in sich aufzunehmen. Er sollte aber auch für sich selbst als Raum für Musik ohne zusätzliche Einbauten funktionieren können. Im Zentrum der Überlegung stand ein Raum für Neue Musik, welcher – im Gegensatz zur Intervention im Stadtraum – eine Form der Begegnung innerhalb eines geschlossenen Raumes bietet. Es wurde mit einer elementaren Geometrie aus vier frei stehenden rechteckigen Wandscheiben eine in sich bzw. nach außen geschlossene Form mit vier schmalen Ein-und Ausgängen gebildet (Abb. 6). Dieser Raum sollte die gängigen Konventionen eines Konzertsaals oder Opernhauses wie das Gegenüber von Bühne und Zuschauerraum, die eingeübten Verhaltensweisen wie Applaus und Ruhe und Bewegungsmuster wie das ruhige Sitzen während einer Aufführung hinterfragen oder gegebenenfalls auflösen (Abb. 7). Die architekturtheoretische Annäherung erfolgte zunächst über eine Auseinandersetzung mit dem menschlichen Körper als Raum im Sinne eines Denkmodells. Dieser eigene Raum besteht aus einem Innenraum, dem eigenen Körper, und einem Außenraum, die uns umgebende Welt. Zwischen beiden Räumen gibt es Übergangszonen. Als ein Ausgangspunkt für dieses Raumexperiment war es das Ziel, auch in der Praxis in Räumen für Musik Übergangszonen zu suchen oder aber zu schaffen.[7] Eine wesentliche Erkenntnis in der Untersuchung besteht darin, eine physische und psychische Bewegungsfreiheit des Publikums zu generieren, und somit die Möglichkeit zu bieten, die musikalischen Werke betreten und ganzheitlich erleben zu können.

RAUMEXPERIMENT ‚RAUMKLANG'   Der dritte Entwurf, ‚Raumklang', war ein Raumexperiment im Rahmen des Novembers der Wissenschaft Hannover in 2010 im Theatersaal der Hochschule für Musik, Theater und Medien in Hannover. Eine bestehende räumliche Ordnung sollte in Bezug auf Raum und Klang neu interpretiert und bespielt werden, um Verhaltensmuster der Rezipient:innen im Raum zu erforschen (Abb. 8). Innerhalb eines bestehenden Konzertsaals führten die Erkenntnisse dieses Raumexperiments zu der Frage, wie sich in dieser konventionellen Raumkonstellation, bestehend aus Bühne, Vorbühne bzw. Orchestergraben und Zuschauerraum, eine Diffusion eines Orchesters auf die bestehende Ordnung des Raumes auswirkt und inwieweit sich aus den vorhandenen Verhaltensmustern und räumlichen Zuordnungen, beispielsweise Abstandsflächen des Publikums zur Musik, Grenzen der Neuordnung ergeben. Die Rolle der Rezipierenden als ein eigenständiger Teil innerhalb eines Werkes und nicht als beobachtende Masse erfordert aufgrund der anderen daraus resultierenden Wertigkeit der Rezipierenden als Akteur:innen im Raum auch grundlegend andere Überlegungen bezüglich der räumlichen Bedürfnisse im Zusammenhang mit der Begegnung mit Raum und Musik.[8]

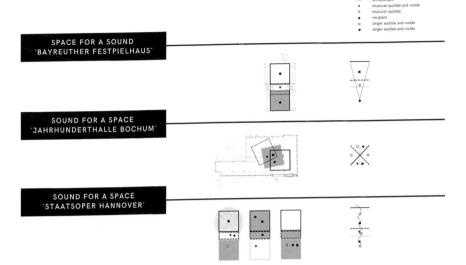

order to research the behavioural patterns of the recipients within the space (fig. 8). Within an existing concert hall, the insights of this spatial experiment led to the question of how, in this conventional spatial constellation consisting of a stage, proscenium, orchestra pit and spectator area, a diffusion of an orchestra affects the existing arrangement of the space and to what extent existing behavioural patterns and spatial arrangements, such as distances between the audience and the music, lead to redefining boundaries. The role of the recipient as an independent entity within a work and not as an observing mass requires fundamentally different considerations regarding spatial requirements in connection with the encounter with space and music, due to the resulting different status of the recipients as actors within the space.[8]

CASE STUDIES   Beyond the spatial experiments, three case study analyses with the research focus 'opera house building typology' form a further main theoretical unit. This involved studies of traditional opera houses and modern playhouses, as well as of musical theatre staging, with regard to the possibilities of a holistic physical perception of space and sound. In relation to this, the scientific research task consists in particular of the consideration of how the visitors perceive or could potentially perceive a work in the respective space, whereas in research literature the focus hitherto has been especially on 'what' can be perceived on stage (fig. 9). In the first case study 'Space for a sound – based on the example of the Bayreuth Festival Theatre' by Otto Bruckwald, it was about examining Richard Wagner's views of space and sound in relation to his own compositions and the presentation of his own music and its physical perception. He used his architectural concept as a mediating platform to evoke, according to his theory, a process of dissolution of the recipients in their real presence when watching and listening to the work of art.[9] The focus of the analysis is therefore on the aesthetic relationship between the spectators, stage and orchestra through the specifications and possibilities of

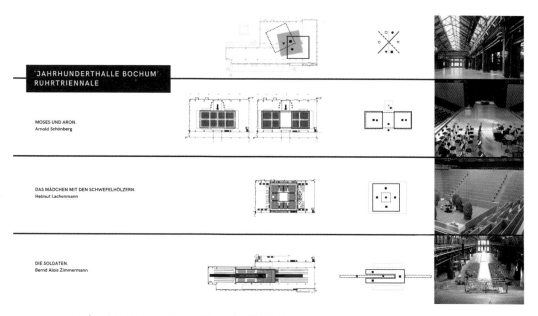

10 | Analytical drawings on three spatial concepts of the Ruhrtriennale

CASE STUDIES   Über die Raumexperimente hinaus bilden drei Case-Study-Analysen zum Forschungsschwerpunkt ‚Bautypus Opernhaus' eine weitere theoretische Haupteinheit aus. Dabei erfolgten Untersuchungen sowohl von traditionellen Opernhäusern und modernen Spielstätten als auch von Inszenierungen des Musiktheaters in Hinblick auf Gegebenheiten und Möglichkeiten der ganzheitlichen körperlichen Wahrnehmung von Raum und Klang. In diesem Zusammenhang besteht der wissenschaftliche Forschungsbedarf insbesondere in der Auseinandersetzung mit der Art, wie die Besucher:innen ein Werk in dem jeweiligen Raum wahrnehmen oder potenziell wahrnehmen könnten, während in der Forschungsliteratur bisher der Schwerpunkt vor allem darauf fokussierte, ‚was' auf der Bühne wahrgenommen werden kann (Abb. 9). Bei der ersten Case Study, ‚Raum für einen Klang - am Beispiel des Festspielhauses Bayreuth' von Otto Bruckwald, ging es darum, Richard Wagners Ansichten von Raum und Klang im Zusammenhang mit seinen eigenen Kompositionen bzw. die Darstellung seiner eigenen Musik und deren körperlicher Wahrnehmung zu untersuchen. Sein architektonisches Konzept setzte er als vermittelnde Ebene ein, um seiner Theorie nach einen Prozess der Auflösung der Rezipient:innen in ihrer realen Anwesenheit beim Betrachten und Hören des Kunstwerks in diesem selbst zu evozieren.[9] Der Fokus der Analyse liegt damit auf dem rezeptionsästhetischen Verhältnis von Zuschauer:innen, Bühne und Orchester durch die Vorgaben und Möglichkeiten des Raumes sowie der relevanten architektonischen Mittel. Die angestrebten Erkenntnisziele bei der Untersuchung dieses Bauwerkes liegen im konzeptionellen Umgang mit dem Verhältnis zwischen Zuschauer:innen, Bühne und Orchester sowie in der Frage, warum Wagners Werke bis heute in dem von ihm dafür konzipierten Opernhaus anders wirken als in anderen Opernhäusern der vergangenen und auch der heutigen Zeit, um neue Erkenntnisse für die Konzeption neuer Räume für die Oper zu generieren.

the space and the relevant architectural means. The aim of studying this building is insights into the conceptual handling of the relationship between the spectators, stage and orchestra, as well as the question of why Wagner's works up until today have a different effect in the opera house he conceived than in other opera houses of the past and today, in order to generate new insights for the conception of new spaces for opera.

In the second case study 'Sound for a space – aesthetic performance concepts for New Music in existing buildings', the Jahrhunderthalle Bochum (Century Hall), which was converted in 2002 by the architects Karl-Heinz Petzinka and Thomas Pink from Dusseldorf into an assembly hall for art, was examined closer by means of on-site studies and participatory observation.[10] It was chosen because, on the one hand, the topic of the repurposing of an industrial hall as a flexibly usable space for music was addressed here and, on the other hand, the art festival 'Ruhr Triennial' primarily held here is among the worldwide leading events for contemporary opera and all other art sectors.[11] In this building, a space-within-a-space is newly conceived and realised for each staging, so that three performances with their respective spatial concepts were studied within the Century Hall (fig. 10).[12] This provided insights about the handling of spatial concepts within an existing building as an external framework with a relatively open layout, in which the positioning of stage, orchestra and audience could potentially be rethought for each performance by means of an individual concept of space and sound.

In the third case study 'Sound for a space – contemporary performance concepts in a traditional opera house', the building form of a traditional opera house is considered with the Hanover State Opera in combination with three performances with new spatial concepts.[13] It shows, contrary to the special status of the Century Hall with its spatial possibilities, artistic 'everyday life' dealing with contemporary works and their interpretation of space and music within a building in which traditional concepts of space and music must also work. Through the observed performances, possibilities and limits were examined of the ways in which the relationship between the singers, orchestra and visitors, as well as their perception of space and music, could be redefined through new spatial concepts.

In der zweiten Case Study, ,Klang für einen Raum – Ästhetische Aufführungskonzepte Neuer Musik im Bestand', wurde die Jahrhunderthalle Bochum, die 2002 von den Architekten Karl-Heinz Petzinka und Thomas Pink aus Düsseldorf zu einer Montagehalle für Kunst umgebaut wurde, durch Vor-Ort-Studien sowie teilnehmende Beobachtung näher untersucht.[10] Sie wurde ausgewählt, da hier zum einen das Thema der Umnutzung einer Industriehalle in einen flexibel nutzbaren Raum für Musik bearbeitet wurde, und zum anderen, weil das primär dort stattfindende Kunstfest ,Die Ruhrtriennale' zu einer der weltweit führenden Veranstaltungen für zeitgenössische Oper und allen weiteren Sparten der Kunst gehört.[11] In diesem Gebäude wird ein Raum im Raum für jede Inszenierung neu konzipiert und realisiert, sodass drei Inszenierungen mit den jeweiligen Raumkonzepten innerhalb der Jahrhunderthalle untersucht wurden (Abb. 10).[12] Dadurch konnten Erkenntnisse über den Umgang mit Raumkonzepten innerhalb eines bestehenden Gebäudes als äußerer Rahmen mit einem relativ offenen Grundriss gewonnen werden, bei denen die Positionierung von Bühne, Orchester und Publikum bei jeder Inszenierung mittels eines individuellen Konzeptes von Raum und Klang potenziell neu gedacht werden könnte.

In der dritten Case Study, ,Klang für einen Raum – Zeitgenössische Aufführungskonzepte in einem traditionellen Opernhaus', wird mit der Staatsoper Hannover in Kombination mit drei Inszenierungen mit neuen Raumkonzepten die Bauform eines traditionellen Opernhauses betrachtet.[13] Sie zeigt im Gegensatz zur besonderen Stellung der Jahrhunderthalle mit ihren räumlichen Möglichkeiten den künstlerischen ,Alltag' im Umgang mit zeitgenössischen Werken und ihrer Interpretation von Raum und Musik innerhalb eines Gebäudes, in dem gleichzeitig auch traditionelle Konzepte von Raum und Musik funktionieren müssen. Es wurden Möglichkeiten und Grenzen der Weisen untersucht, wie durch die betrachteten Inszenierungen das Verhältnis zwischen Sänger:innen, Orchester und Besucher:innen sowie deren Wahrnehmung von Raum und Musik mittels neuer Raumkonzepte neu definiert werden konnten.

11 | Aesthetic processes of effect 'Spatial experiment B' LUH 2007

EFFECT. SIGNIFICANCE   To more closely consider the effects and significance of products, interim products and end products in this context, a clear context
is required, as well as a distinction of the formation from 'aesthetic effect processes'. Aesthetics in the interplay of space and music is understood within this work as a perception
of phenomena. In an analysis of Kant's understanding of aesthetic, for example, the cultural
scientist Gundula Felten writes in her thesis: "Kant's aim [...] is the explanation of a scientific
aesthetic, because it is only such an aesthetic that makes verifiable statements that can
be called philosophical aesthetic. [...] It especially becomes necessary to justify the general
validity of the aesthetic verdicts on beauty, because this verdict is not factual but appears
in the first instance to be purely subjective, as a judgement by a subject's feelings with
regard to something beautiful."[14] The studies represent an attempt to use the 'aesthetic
potential' especially in the observation of artistic design processes, as a theory of perception
in the sense of an orientation towards a systematic naming and research of the triggers of
sensory perception and awareness, by taking an analogy to hermeneutical processes as an
approach.[15] According to the philosopher Hans-Georg Gadamer, one not only possesses the
art of interpretation but also knows how to justify it theoretically.[16] These interpretations are
intended to help increase the clarity and appropriateness of the experience of the work of art.

In summary, one can say that the continuous structuring and modification of design parameters thus carried out with the help of the systematisation of existing own projects and by
means of creative processes for new projects in the form of spatial experiments, along with
carrying out case studies, can offer getting closer to a 'design production' that is not fully
scientifically tangible. The continuous structuring and modification can be understood as
a product of a previous intention and shapes the deeper explanation, justification, modification and further development of this intention and, in the best case, provides clarification. The aim is a product that can become visible and readable in a scientific context. At
the end and at the centre of the research there is always the creation of a holistic physical
perception of space and sound as a product of seemingly intuitive experience (fig. 11).

WIRKUNG. BEDEUTUNG   Um die Wirkungen und die Bedeutung von Produkten, Zwischenprodukten und Endprodukten in diesem Zusammenhang näher herauszustellen, bedarf es einer klaren Einbettung sowie einer Abgrenzung der Formation zu ‚ästhetischen Wirkungsprozessen'. Ästhetik im Zusammenspiel von Raum und Musik wird im Zusammenhang dieser Arbeit als eine Wahrnehmung von Phänomenen verstanden. In einer Analyse von Kants Verständnis von Ästhetik zum Beispiel schreibt die Kulturwissenschaftlerin Gundula Felten in ihrer Promotion: „Kants Anliegen [...] ist die Begründung einer wissenschaftlichen Ästhetik, denn erst solch eine Ästhetik, die zu überprüfbaren Aussagen kommt, kann philosophische Ästhetik genannt werden. [...] Notwendig wird die besondere Begründung der Allgemeingültigkeit der ästhetischen Urteile über das Schöne, weil dieses Urteil kein Erkenntnisurteil ist, sondern in der Beurteilung des Gefühls des Subjekts angesichts etwas Schönem zunächst rein subjektiv zu sein scheint."[14] In Zusammenhang der Studien soll versucht werden, die ‚Fähigkeit der Ästhetik' als Lehre von der Wahrnehmung im Sinne der Ausrichtung für eine systematische Benennung und Erforschung der Auslöser sinnlicher Wahrnehmung und Erkenntnis, insbesondere in der Beobachtung von künstlerischen Gestaltungsprozessen, einzusetzen, indem sich über eine Analogie zu hermeneutischen Prozessen angenähert wird.[15] Man besitzt, dem Philosophen Hans-Georg Gadamer folgend, nicht nur die Kunst der Auslegung, sondern weiß, dieselbe theoretisch zu rechtfertigen.[16] Diese Auslegungen sollen der Erfahrung des Kunstwerkes zu gesteigerter Klarheit und Angemessenheit verhelfen.

Zusammenfassend lässt sich sagen, dass die so durchgeführte kontinuierliche Strukturierung und Modifizierung von Entwurfsparametern mithilfe der Systematisierung bestehender eigener Projekte und mittels kreativer Prozesse für neue Projekte in Form von Raumexperimenten sowie die Durchführung von Case Studies eine immer weiterführende Annäherung an ein nicht vollständig wissenschaftlich greifbares ‚Entwurfsproduzieren' bieten können. Die kontinuierliche Strukturierung und Modifizierung lässt sich als Produkt einer vorangegangenen Intention verstehen, und wirkt formgebend dafür, diese Intention tiefer zu ergründen, zu begründen, zu verändern, weiterzuentwickeln und, im besten Falle, klärend wirksam werden zu lassen. Ziel ist ein Produkt, das in einem wissenschaftlichen Kontext sichtbar und lesbar werden kann. Am Ende sowie im Mittelpunkt der Forschungen steht stets das Hervorbringen einer ganzheitlichen körperlichen Wahrnehmung von Raum und Klang als ein Produkt scheinbar intuitiven Erlebens (Abb. 11).

1 Pierre Boulez/Jürgen Hohmeyer/Felix Schmidt, Sprengt die Opernhäuser on die Luft!, Gespräch in: DER SPIEGEL 40 (1967) 172   **2** Cf. | Vgl. ibid.   **3** Cf. | Vgl. Gisela Nauck, Musik im Raum – Raum in der Musik. Ein Beitrag zur Geschichte der seriellen Musik (Archiv für Musikwissenschaft. Beihefte, Band 38), Stuttgart: Franz Steiner 1997, 19   **4** Cf. | Vgl. ibid.   **5** Cf. | Vgl. Linda Groat/David Wang, Architectural research methods, New York: John Wiley & Sons 2002, 263–264   **6** Cf. | Vgl. Marc-Philip Reichwald/Peter-Karsten Schulz, Bakenfelder, Programmheftbeitrag, in: Staatstheater Braunschweig (ed.), FESTLICHE TAGE NEUER MUSIK, Braunschweig 2004, 6   **7** Prof. Jonas Schoen composed a five-part 'Jazz suite for jazz orchestra and space' (2007) especially for this room, other works included the 'Drum quartet for four large drums' (2002) by Benjamin Lang and 'Darkened for alto solo' (1992) by Aribert Reimann. | Eigens für diesen Raum wurde von Prof. Jonas Schoen eine fünfteilige ‚Jazzsuite für Jazzorchester und Raum' (2007) komponiert, weitere Werke waren das ‚Trommelquartett für vier große Trommeln' (2002) von Benjamin Lang und ‚Eingedunkelt für Altsolo' (1992) von Aribert Reimann.   **8** For the room experiment, a large commissioned musical composition 'Room 3' (2010) by Prof. Jonas Schoen was premiered. Embedded in this work was 'Solo for Voice' (1958) by John Cage. | Für das Raumexperiment wurde eine große musikalische Auftragskomposition ‚Raum 3' (2010) von Prof. Jonas Schoen uraufgeführt. In dieses Werk eingebettet war

‚Solo for Voice' (1958) von John Cage.   **9** Cf. | Vgl. Richard Wagner, Das Kunstwerk der Zukunft, Schutterwald, Baden: Dr. Klaus Fischer 2010, 155–157   **10** Cf. | Vgl. Kultur Ruhr GmbH (ed.), Jahrhunderthalle Bochum Montagehalle für Kunst, Wuppertal: Müller+Bußmann 2003, 6   **11** Cf. | Vgl. ibid., 9   **12** The following three room concepts from the productions 'The soldiers' (Alois Zimmermann) by David Pountney, 2006, 'Moses and Aron' (Arnold Schönberg) by Willy Decker, 2009, 'The match girl' (Helmut Lachenmann) by Robert Wilson, 2013, were selected. | Ausgewählt wurden folgende drei Raumkonzepte der Inszenierungen ‚Die Soldaten' (Alois Zimmermann) von David Pountney, 2006, ‚Moses und Aron' (Arnold Schönberg) von Willy Decker, 2009, ‚Das Mädchen mit den Schwefelhölzern' (Helmut Lachenmann) von Robert Wilson, 2013.   **13** The following three spatial concepts by Katrin Wittig from the productions by Benedikt von Peter 'Intolleranza 1960' (Luigi Nono), 2010, 'La Traviata' (Guiseppe Verdi), 2011, and 'Don Giovanni' (Wolfgang Amadeus Mozart), 2014, were selected. | Ausgewählt wurden folgende drei Raumkonzepte von Katrin Wittig der Inszenierungen von Benedikt von Peter ‚Intolleranza 1960' (Luigi Nono), 2010, ‚La Traviata' (Guiseppe Verdi), 2011 und ‚Don Giovanni' (Wolfgang Amadeus Mozart), 2014.   **14** Gundula Felten, Die Funktion des Sensus communis in Kants Theorie des ästhetischen Urteils, München: Brill/Fink 2004, 14   **15** Cf. | Vgl. ibid.   **16** Hans-Georg Gadamer, Hermeneutik. Wahrheit und Analyse, Tübingen: Mohr 1993, 93

"Universes of worlds, like worlds themselves, can be built in many ways."

„Universen von Welten, ebenso wie Welten selbst, können auf viele Weisen erbaut werden."

Nelson Goodman

ZUKUNFTSENTWÜRFE
FUTURE DESIGNS

Speculative procedures do not appear unusual at first glance, as the spatial design disciplines always work 'with a view to the future'.[1] Speculative procedures as conscious work methods of design through research and research through design differ in the gradation of the targeted unfolding of ideal, factual and social suggestions and effects that can be associated with the journey into possible futures. Questioning and envisioning are combined in proactive reflexivity. The specific synthesising features, as well as the media of architectural, urban and landscape design can become critical and constructive moments of the study. They then act as thinking tools and tools for bringing forth alternatives and possibilities for achieving them. They therefore also harbour the potential of generating knowledge.[2] Apart from pragmatic solutions, many contemporary tasks require the aim of changing outdated ways of thinking, values, stances and behaviour.[3] The anticipations offered in the design articulation invite one to extend existing notions through new, unprecedented perspectives based on experience. Speculative designs can contribute to this by showing possibilities, stimulating rethinking, prompting discussions and inspiring further imagination.[4]

Spekulative Verfahren scheinen auf den ersten Blick nicht ungewöhnlich, da die raumentwerfenden Disziplinen immer ,in die Zukunft gerichtet' arbeiten.[1] Spekulative Verfahren als bewusste Arbeitsmittel forschenden Entwerfens und entwerfenden Forschens unterscheiden sich in der Gradation der gezielten Entfaltung von ideellen, gegenständlichen und gesellschaftlichen Vorschlägen und Wirkungen, die mit der Reise in eine mögliche Zukunft verbunden sein können. In der proaktiven Reflexivität verbinden sich Befragen und Vorausschauen. Die spezifischen synthetisierenden Eigenschaften wie auch die Medien des Entwerfens von Architektur, Städtebau und Landschaftsarchitektur können zu kritischen und konstruktiven Momenten der Untersuchung werden. Sie fungieren dann als Denkinstrumente und Instrumente des Hervorbringens von Alternativen und von Möglichkeiten, wie man diese erreichen kann. Somit bergen sie auch das Potenzial zur Erzeugung von Wissen.[2] Viele der zeitgenössischen Aufgaben benötigen neben pragmatischen Lösungen das Ziel, überkommene Denkweisen, Werte, Haltungen und Verhaltensweisen zu ändern.[3] Die in der entwerferischen Artikulation dargebotenen Antizipationen laden dazu ein, ausgehend von Erfahrungen bestehende Vorstellungen durch neue, ungeahnte Perspektiven zu erweitern. Spekulative Entwürfe können dazu beitragen, indem sie Möglichkeitsräume aufzeigen, das Überdenken stimulieren, Diskussion anregen und weitere Imaginationen inspirieren.[4]

Products in this field of reflexive design are, on the one hand, the individual, collaborative or collective future designs associated with specific themes, which can further contribute to gaining a better understanding of the present, and, on the other hand, the physical manifestations of these designs. Furthermore, they show positions on the role of design and emphasise the relevance of creative aspects for the mastering of complex tasks. The capacity of anticipatory moments to enable new structuring and perception orders also has the potential of stimulating the revision and redefining of practices. They also form approaches to and trials of new productive research and design strategies. This does not exclude adaptive reuse, in which the unknown is sought through analogy, based on the known.[5] What is conceivable relatively consistently and what remains uncertain are the two poles between which the suggestions and proposals move. Ultimately it is also about widening the individual and collective repertoire as a resource for future designs. The contributions by Martin Prominski, Sarah Wehmeyer and Tom Bieling thematise these speculative moments in design and research in different ways, starting with the pragmatic anchoring in established facts for the complex handling of tasks, to the development of alternatives that opens up possibilities, through to the critical imagination that shows various fictive realities in order to raise questions, break down narrow notions, prejudices and situations and initiate thought processes.

Produkte in diesem Feld des Reflexiven Entwerfens sind einerseits die mit spezifischen Themen verbundenen individuellen, kollaborativen oder kollektiven Zukunftsentwürfe, die zudem dazu beitragen können, die Gegenwart besser zu verstehen, und andererseits die physischen Manifestationen dieser Entwürfe. Darüber hinaus zeigen sie Positionen zur Rolle des Entwerfens auf und lassen die Relevanz schöpferischer Aspekte für die Bewältigung komplexer Aufgaben hervortreten. Die Kapazität der antizipatorischen Momente, neue Strukturierungs- und Wahrnehmungsordnungen zu ermöglichen, hat nicht zuletzt auch das Potenzial, die Revision und Neuausprägung von Praktiken zu stimulieren. So bilden sie auch Annäherungen an und Proben von neuen produktiven Forschungs- und Entwurfsstrategien. Das schließt die adaptive Wiederverwendung nicht aus, bei der vom Bekannten ausgehend das Unbekannte durch Analogie gesucht wird.[5] Das, was relativ widerspruchsfrei denkbar ist, und das, was im Ungewissen bleibt, sind die beiden Pole, zwischen denen sich die Vorschläge und Angebote bewegen. Letztlich geht es auch darum, das individuelle und kollektive Repertoire als Ressource für Zukunftsentwürfe zu vergrößern. Die Beiträge von Martin Prominski, Sarah Wehmeyer und Tom Bieling thematisieren diese spekulativen Momente im Forschen und Entwerfen in unterschiedlicher Weise, ausgehend von der pragmatischen Verankerung in ermittelten Fakten für die komplexe Aufgabenbewältigung, über die Alternativbildung, die Möglichkeitsräume öffnet, bis hin zur kritischen Imagination, die verschiedene fiktive Wirklichkeiten erstmal aufzeigt, um Fragen aufzuwerfen, enge Vorstellungen, Vorurteile und Gegebenheiten zu öffnen und Denkprozesse anzustoßen.

In his contribution, Martin Prominski explores how solutions can be worked out in interdisciplinary groups for the major challenges of our time, such as population growth, water shortages or climate change, reflecting on the special role and relevance of designers in such collective research tasks. This is presented exemplarily based on the example of coastal protection in Lower Saxony. An active interdisciplinary process generates by interacting – also with civil society actors – information about the situatedness of the task, about conditions, aims and possibilities which, even if they are ultimately incomplete, can form starting points for what is presumed probable. In the interests of instrumental knowledge, in combination with anticipatory experience values in the design procedure they enable the creative production of syntheses and insights. Products are models or scenarios as a type of guidance and operative work model, which go far beyond quantifiable aspects. For complex tasks for which there are not yet any model solutions, the scenarios that envisage possible future developments provide excellent means of communication that at the same time transfer knowledge.[6] They can be compared and evaluated and to a certain extent also allow the prediction of medium-term and long-term effects. Conscious action and reflecting on the knowledge continuously interpenetrate in the constituting and designing activity. In this context, reflection can also be understood as an intellectually reintegrating trial action.[7]

In seinem Beitrag vermittelt Martin Prominski, wie jenseits bestehender Möglichkeiten Lösungen für die großen Herausforderungen der Gegenwart wie Bevölkerungswachstum, Wasserknappheit oder Klimawandel in interdisziplinären Kooperationen bearbeitet werden können, und reflektiert die besondere Rolle und Relevanz der Entwerfenden in solchen kollektiven Forschungsaufgaben. Am Beispiel des Wasserschutzes an Küsten Niedersachsens wird dies exemplarisch ausgeführt. Aus einem aktiven interdisziplinären Analyseprozess werden im Austausch Informationen über die Situiertheit der Aufgabe erzeugt, über Bedingungen, Ziele und Möglichkeiten, die, auch wenn sie letztlich unvollständig sind, Ausgangspunkte für ein als wahrscheinlich Vermutetes bilden können. Im Sinne instrumentellen Wissens ermöglichen sie im Verbund mit antizipatorischen Erfahrungswerten im entwerferischen Vorgehen das kreative Hervorbringen von Synthesen und von Erkenntnissen. Produkte sind Modelle bzw. Szenarien als eine Art Anleitung und operative Werkgestalt, die über quantifizierbare Aspekte weit hinausreichen. Für komplexe Aufgaben, für die es bislang keine modellhaften Lösungen gibt, bilden die mögliche Zukunftsentwicklungen veranschaulichenden Szenarien hervorragende Kommunikationsmittel, die gleichzeitig Wissen transferieren.[6] Sie können bewertet werden und in gewisser Weise auch mittel- und langfristige Wirkungen prognostizieren lassen. Bewusstes Handeln und Reflektieren des Wissens durchdringen sich in der konstituierenden und entwerfenden Tätigkeit stetig. In diesem Kontext kann Reflexion auch als ein denkerisch re-integrierendes Probehandeln verstanden werden.[7]

A questioning of the role of images in research contexts as well as unexpected suggestions for a contemporary building task are at the centre of Sarah Wehmeyer's contribution. She presents a research and design project created by means of collages and text components. With the aim of conceiving urban refuges in the city as building blocks of habitats of the future through the creative reinterpretation of large complexes such as prisons, a visual discourse is developed, accompanied only by reduced text. Originated as a study as part of the dissertation, the potential of the collage as an instrument of thought, as a knowledge-generating medium and as an artistically created manifestation is conveyed. It also explains how these text-image discourses stimulate the imagination and can help architects in design related research to consolidate unfamiliar ideas, to gain new knowledge for potential future spatial and architectural developments and to formulate new alternatives and possibilities. Through a formally direct application of analogies, quite specific spatial figurations were developed and newly composed. They form unprecedented scenarios and aids to imagination.[8] It is through the possibilities of layering and juxtaposition inherent in collaging, with unfamiliar linking of the known, unknown and voids, that patterns can be transformed in these reflexive procedures and new innovative formations, perspectives and appropriations are mentally stimulated.[9] The anticipations presented in the image-text discourse and fostered by it can lead to new insights that also encourage the thinking and actions of others and make them productive.

Eine Befragung der Rolle des Bildlichen in Forschungskontexten ebenso wie unerwartete Vorschläge für eine zeitgenössische Bauaufgabe stehen im Zentrum des Beitrags von Sarah Wehmeyer. Sie stellt ein mittels Collagen und Textbausteinen entstandenes Forschungs- und Entwurfsprojekt vor. Mit dem Ziel, durch kreative Reinterpretation von Großkomplexen, beispielsweise Gefängnissen, urbane Refugien in der Stadt als Bausteine von Habitaten der Zukunft zu konzipieren, wird ein bildlicher nur von reduziertem Text begleiteter Diskurs entwickelt. Entstanden als Studie im Rahmen der Dissertation wird dabei das Potenzial der Collage als Denkinstrument, als wissenserzeugendes Medium und als künstlerisch geschaffene Manifestation vermittelt. Ausgeführt wird zudem, wie diese Text-Bild-Diskurse Imaginationen stimulieren und Architekt:innen beim forschenden Entwerfen helfen können, unvertraute Ideen zu fixieren, für potenzielle zukünftige baulich-räumliche Entwicklungen neues Wissen zu gewinnen sowie neue Alternativen und Möglichkeiten zu formulieren. Durch eine formell direkte Anwendung von Analogien wurden dabei ganz spezifische räumliche Figurationen entwickelt und neu komponiert. Sie bilden unvorhergesehene Szenarien und Imaginationshilfen.[8] Gerade mit den dem Collagieren eigenen Möglichkeiten der Schichtung und des Zusammenstoßes, mit unvertrauten Verknüpfungen von Bekanntem, Unbekanntem und Leerstellen können in diesen reflexiven Verfahren Schemata transformiert werden und neue innovative Formationen, Anschauungen und Aneignungen mental stimuliert werden.[9] Die im Bild-Text-Diskurs dargebotenen und durch ihn angeregten Antizipationen können zu neuen Einsichten führen, die auch das Denken und Handeln anderer ermuntern und produktiv werden lassen.

In another way still, Tom Bieling's contribution exemplifies how fictions can change perceptions, in allusions to familiar worlds, through decomposition and reforming, but nevertheless recognisable, in order to evoke progress in understanding.[10] Building on analyses and a personal catalogue of criteria, experiences of time and temporality and layering are created and articulated in graphic representations with visual narratives, miniature stories about the urban fabric and the presumed spatial events through the intertwining of historical images and contemporary representations that show urban development and architectural features, supplemented by current and cultural history information. Through gestures of allusion, ambiguities, contradictions and multiple references, interpretations are stimulated that exceed narrow notions of the city, in order to reveal their multifacetedness and human significances, as well as to incorporate socio-cultural relations.[11] The layering is aimed at creating different levels of coherence through associations. This can therefore also work as speculative thinking about urban peculiarities, from which other notions of reality potentially result and knowledge can develop.[12] At the same time, a utopian potential is inherent to it in the sense of Thomas Morus's concept.[13] Through the imaginative design presented in the images, a better possibility is added to an imperfect reality. At the same time, there is an attempt to develop strategies that can make the invisible perceptible in combination with the visible. MB

In noch anderer Weise exemplifiziert Tom Bielings Beitrag, wie Fiktionen in Anspielung auf vertraute Welten durch Zerlegung und Umformung, aber doch wiedererkennbar Wahrnehmungen verändern können, um Fortschritte des Verstehens zu evozieren.[10] Auf Analysen und einem persönlichen Kriterienkatalog aufbauend werden in zeichnerischen Darstellungen mit visuellen Narrativen, Miniaturgeschichten zum urbanen Gewebe und zum vermuteten Raumgeschehen, durch Verschränkung historischer Ansichten und zeitgenössischer Darstellungen, die städtebauliche und architektonische Eigenschaften zeigen, sowie ergänzt durch aktuelle und kulturgeschichtliche Informationen Erfahrungen von Zeiten und Zeitlichkeit sowie Überlagerungen kreiert und artikuliert. Durch Gesten des Andeutens, Mehrdeutigkeiten, Widersprüche und multiple Referenzen werden hier Interpretationen angeregt, die enge Vorstellungen der Stadt überschreiten, um deren Vielschichtigkeit und humane Bedeutungen zu entbergen sowie soziokulturelle Relationen einzubeziehen.[11] Die Überlagerungen sind darauf ausgerichtet, über Assoziationsleistungen unterschiedliche Ebenen der Kohärenz zu erzeugen. So kann dies auch als ein spekulatives Nachdenken über die städtische Eigenart wirken, aus der potenziell andere Wirklichkeitsvorstellungen resultieren und Wissen entfaltet werden kann.[12] Gleichzeitig wohnt dem ein utopisches Potenzial inne im Sinne des Konzepts von Thomas Morus.[13] Mittels des in den Bildern dargebotenen imaginativen Entwurfs wird einer unvollkommenen Wirklichkeit die bessere Möglichkeit hinzugefügt. Gleichzeitig wird versucht, dabei Strategien zu entwickeln, die das Unsichtbare in Verbindung mit dem Sichtbaren wahrnehmbar machen können. MB

1 Cf. on this e.g. | Vgl. dazu beispielsweise Rem Koolhaas, in: Brett Steele, Supercritical. Peter Eisenman and Rem Koolhaas, London: AA publications 2010, 13; Werner Oechslin, Der Architekt als Theoretiker, in: Winfried Nerdinger (ed.), Der Architekt. Geschichte und Gegenwart eines Berufsstandes, München: Prestel 2012, 576–601, 584 and | und passim.   **2** Cf. on this | Vgl. hierzu Nelson Goodman, Weisen der Welterzeugung, Frankfurt a. M.: Suhrkamp 1984, 124–130   **3** Cf. | Vgl. Anthony Dunne/Fiona Raby, Speculative everything. Design, fiction and social dreaming, Cambridge, MA: MIT 2013, 2–6   **4** Cf. | Vgl. Arjun Appadurai, The future as cultural fact. Essays on the global condition, London et al.: Verso 2013, 285–286 and | und 298   **5** Cf. on this also | Vgl. dazu auch Catherine Abell, Fiction. A philosophical analysis, Oxford: Oxford University Press 2020, 14, 187 and | und passim   **6** Cf. on this | Vgl. hierzu Christian Salewski, Zukunftsbilder, in: Trans 25(2014) 80–83, 83   **7** Cf. on this also | Vgl. dazu auch Hans Ulrich Reck, Theorie durch Theoriemangel. Episteme und Verfahren in Kunst und Design, auch zu verstehen als Erörterung ästhetischen Urteilens, in: Hans Zitko (ed.), Theorien ästhetischer Praxis, Köln: Böhlau 2014, 19–34, 19–20   **8** Cf. on this also | Vgl. hierzu auch Albena Yaneva/Bruno Latour, Give me a gun and I make buildings move: An ANT's view of architecture, in: Ardeth 1(2017) 103–111, 106–107   **9** Cf. on this also | Vgl. hierzu auch Isabelle Stengers, Another science is possible, A manifesto for slow science, Cambridge, UK: Polity 2018, 126   **10** Cf. | Vgl. Nelson Goodman (1984), op. cit. (note | Anm. 2), 130   **11** Cf. on this also | Vgl. hierzu auch Kendall L. Walton, Mimesis and make-believe. On the foundations of the representational arts, Cambridge, MA: Harvard University Press 1990, 4 and | und 75   **12** Cf. on this also | Vgl. dazu auch Karin Knorr-Cetina, Wissenskulturen, Frankfurt a. M.: Suhrkamp 2002, 342–343   **13** Thomas More, Utopia, Oxford et al.: Oxford University Press 1999

THE ROLE OF DESIGN PRODUCTS WITHIN DESIGN RESEARCH

Martin Prominski

INTRODUCTION   When designing in architecture and landscape architecture, in my opinion there are two fundamentally different types of products: on the one hand, there is the projective product that represents the design digitally or analogously, on the other hand is the realised product that manifests the spatial realisation of the design. The projective product is a necessary part of the design process because designing is always the projection of something that does not yet exist in reality but has to be somehow represented and communicated. A product is therefore required, and in most design disciplines these projective communication products are sketches and models. A design is therefore both a project and a product. As soon as a design is no longer a future projection but has become part of the present, for example through the making of a chair, building or park, then it is no longer a design but a realised product. For the design, it only becomes relevant again if it is reflected on as a reference for future projects in the design process. In the following, I am focusing on the first type of product – the projective product – and ask what role designs play as projective products in the knowledge generation of transdisciplinary research projects. This is also intended as a contribution to the topic of 'Research through Design' (RtD) in which designs become an essential part of the research process.

DESIGN PRODUCTS IN TRANSDISCIPLINARY RESEARCH PROJECTS
Transdisciplinary design has become an increasingly common research type in recent years, in which not only various sciences conduct interdisciplinary research, but parties from civil society or administration are involved in the research process. The research

DIE ROLLE VON ENTWURFSPRODUKTEN IN DER ENTWURFSFORSCHUNG

Martin Prominski

EINLEITUNG   Beim Entwerfen in Architektur und Landschaftsarchitektur gibt es aus meiner Sicht zwei grundsätzlich verschiedene Arten von Produkten: Es gibt zum einen das projektive Produkt, das den Entwurf digital oder analog darstellt, zum anderen das realisierte Produkt, das die räumliche Umsetzung des Entwurfes manifestiert. Das projektive Produkt ist notwendiger Bestandteil des Entwurfsprozesses, denn Entwerfen ist immer die Projektion von etwas real noch nicht Existentem, das aber gleichzeitig irgendwie dargestellt und kommuniziert werden muss. Es braucht also ein Produkt, und in den meisten Entwurfsdisziplinen sind diese projektiven Kommunikationsprodukte Zeichnungen und Modelle. Ein Entwurf ist damit sowohl ein Projekt als auch ein Produkt. Sobald ein Entwurf keine Zukunftsprojektion mehr ist, sondern in der Gegenwart angekommen ist, also beispielsweise ein Stuhl, Gebäude oder Park hergestellt worden ist, dann ist es kein Entwurf mehr, sondern ein realisiertes Produkt. Für das Entwerfen wird es erst wieder relevant, wenn es als Referenz für zukünftige Projekte im Entwurfsprozess reflektiert wird. Ich fokussiere mich im Folgenden auf den ersten Produkttypus – das projektive Produkt –, und frage, welche Rolle Entwürfe als projektive Produkte in der Wissensgenerierung transdisziplinärer Forschungsprojekte spielen. Damit soll auch ein Beitrag zum Thema ‚Research through Design‘ (RtD) geleistet werden, bei dem Entwürfe zum essenziellen Teil des Forschungsprozesses werden.

ENTWURSPRODUKTE IN TRANSDISZIPLINÄREN FORSCHUNGSPROJEKTEN
Transdisziplinäre Forschung ist ein in den letzten Jahren zunehmender Forschungstypus, bei dem nicht nur verschiedene Wissenschaften interdisziplinär forschen, sondern darüber hinaus zivilgesellschaftliche Akteure aus Verwaltung oder Gesellschaft in den Forschungsprozess involviert werden. Die Forschung findet meist in realen räumlichen Kontexten statt,

191

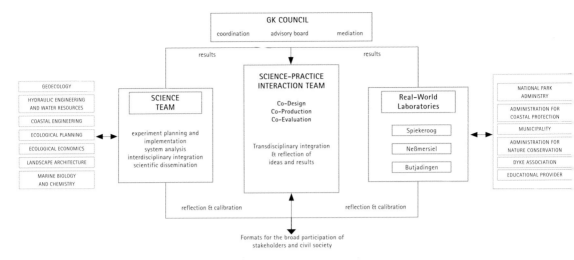

GK COUNCIL

coordination   advisory board   mediation

results   results

GEOECOLOGY

HYDRAULIC ENGINEERING
AND WATER RESOURCES

COASTAL ENGINEERING

ECOLOGICAL PLANNING

ECOLOGICAL ECONOMICS

LANDSCAPE ARCHITECTURE

MARINE BIOLOGY
AND CHEMISTRY

SCIENCE TEAM

experiment planning and
implementation
system analysis
interdisciplinary integration
scientific dissemination

SCIENCE-PRACTICE INTERACTION TEAM

Co-Design
Co-Production
Co-Evaluation

Transdisciplinary integration
& reflection of
ideas and results

Real-World Laboratories

Spiekeroog

Neßmersiel

Butjadingen

NATIONAL PARK
ADMINISTRY

ADMINISTRATION FOR
COASTAL PROTECTION

MUNICIPALITY

ADMINISTRATION FOR
NATURE CONSERVATION

DYKE ASSOCIATION

EDUCATIONAL PROVIDER

reflection & calibration   reflection & calibration

Formats for the broad participation of
stakeholders and civil society

1 | 'Gute Küste Niedersachsen' Design of the transdisciplinary research programme

mostly takes place in real spatial contexts, which is why in Germany there is often a mention of "Real-World Laboratories" in transdisciplinary design (in an international context, the term 'Living Labs' is predominant).[1] If transdisciplinary research is to succeed, then it is necessary to develop the new knowledge in the living labs on three levels, together with the scientific disciplines and parties from civil society: the entire research project including the research questions should be developed from the outset as a 'co-design', the research work should take place as 'co-production' and the subsequent reflection on the results as 'co-evaluation'.[2] With this approach, transdisciplinary research should be able to meet the complex social challenges better than conventional, more descriptive scientific approaches.[3] And two factors of transdisciplinary research – the concrete spatial relation and the incorporation of social actors – open the gateway wide for bringing the design into the research process, because contrary to traditional scientists, designers have significant experience with this. I have already theoretically outlined in detail this potential of design in transdisciplinary research; now, since 2020 there is the possibility to apply it practically.[4]

GUTE KÜSTE NIEDERSACHSEN   The research project 'Gute Küste Niedersachsen' (2020–2024, 'Good Coast Lower Saxony') was specifically applied for as a real-world laboratory. It has a budget of 5 million euros and is directed by three coastal engineers at three Lower Saxony universities. In total, the transdisciplinary organisation involves seven institutes with 25 scientists, as well as many actors from society and administration (fig. 1). At the centre of the joint project are the two research questions of (1) how robust, multifunctional and especially ecosystem-reinforcing coastal protection measures work in the long term and (2) at the same time how they are taken account of in reliable planning and authorisation by the responsible state organisations and find acceptance in civil society. These questions are to be studied at the three real-world laboratory sites of Spiekeroog, Neßmersiel and Butjadingen, which all lie on the North Sea coast of Lower Saxony. Our landscape architecture group consists of two doctoral

weshalb in Deutschland bei transdisziplinärer Forschung häufig von Reallaboren gesprochen wird (im internationalen Kontext überwiegt der Begriff ‚Living Labs').[1] Wenn transdisziplinäre Forschung gelingen soll, dann wird gefordert, dass in den Reallaboren das neue Wissen auf drei Ebenen gemeinsam von den Wissenschaftsdisziplinen und den zivilgesellschaftlichen Akteuren entwickelt wird: Das gesamte Forschungsprojekt inklusive der Forschungsfragen soll von Beginn an in einem ‚Co-Design' entwickelt werden, die Forschungsarbeiten sollen in ‚Co-Produktion' stattfinden, und auch die abschließende Ergebnisreflexion soll in ‚Co-Evaluation' stattfinden.[2] Mit diesem Ansatz soll sich transdisziplinäre Forschung den komplexen gesellschaftlichen Herausforderungen besser stellen können als gewöhnliche, eher beschreibende wissenschaftliche Ansätze.[3] Und zwei Faktoren der transdisziplinären Forschung – der konkrete räumliche Bezug sowie das Einbeziehen gesellschaftlicher Akteure – öffnen die Tore weit für das Hereinholen des Entwerfens in den Forschungsprozess, denn damit haben Entwerfende im Gegensatz zu traditionellen Wissenschaftler:innen große Erfahrung. Dieses Potential des Entwerfens in transdisziplinärer Forschung habe ich theoretisch schon ausführlich skizziert, seit 2020 besteht nun die Möglichkeit, es praktisch anzuwenden.[4]

GUTE KÜSTE NIEDERSACHSEN   Das Forschungsprojekt ‚Gute Küste Niedersachsen' (2020–2024) ist dezidiert als Reallabor beantragt worden. Es hat ein Budget von 5 Millionen Euro und wird geleitet von drei Küstenbauingenieuren an drei niedersächsischen Universitäten, insgesamt sind an der interdisziplinären Aufstellung sieben Institute mit 25 Wissenschaftler:innen beteiligt sowie zahlreiche gesellschaftliche Akteur:innen (Abb. 1). Im Zentrum des Verbundvorhabens stehen die beiden Forschungsfragen, wie (1) robuste, multifunktionale und insbesondere ökosystemstärkende Küstenschutzmaßnahmen auf lange Sicht funktionieren und (2) diese gleichzeitig in der zuverlässigen Planung und Genehmigung durch die zuständigen Landesbetriebe Berücksichtigung sowie in der Zivilgesellschaft Akzeptanz finden.

Diese Fragen sollen an den drei Reallaborstandorten Spiekeroog, Neßmersiel und Butjadingen, die alle an der niedersächsischen Nordseeküste liegen, untersucht werden. Unsere Landschaftsarchitekturgruppe besteht aus zwei Doktorand:innen mit Landschaftsarchitekturausbildung sowie meiner Person, und wir sind die einzigen Mitglieder des Forschungskonsortiums mit einem Entwurfshintergrund. Unsere Hauptaufgabe ist es, die verschiedenen disziplinären und gesellschaftlichen Beiträge innerhalb des Konsortiums zu komplexen Landschaftsszenarien für die Reallaborstandorte zu synthetisieren, die einen ökosystemstärkenden Küstenschutz angesichts des Meeresspiegelanstiegs aufzeigen sollen. Im zweiten von fünf Projektjahren initiierten wir im Rahmen des Masterstudiengangs Landschaftsarchitektur

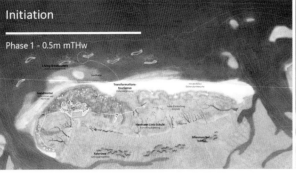
Initiation

Phase 1 - 0.5m mTHw

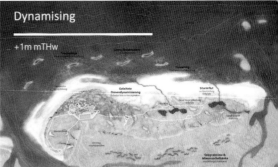
Dynamising

+1m mTHw

2 | Four scenarios of the design product 'Scapeshifter'

students with landscape architecture education, as well as myself, and we are the only members of the research consortium with a design background. Our main task is to synthesise the various disciplinary and social contributions within the consortium into complex landscape scenarios for the real-world labororatory sites, intended to show coastal protection that strengthens the ecosystem in view of the rise in sea level. In the second of five project years, as part of the Master's degree course in landscape architecture, we initiated a design studio that drew up future scenarios for the island of Spiekeroog, one of the three real-world labororatory sites.[5] These projections by the students are design products in the aforementioned sense and represent test runs for the designs that we will compile towards the end of the research project. During the semester, other researchers from "Good Coast Lower Saxony" regularly visited the design studio and gave advice pertaining to their specific background, such as coastal sediment movement, seaweed proliferation or salt marsh processes. Overall, four groups of two worked at the design studio. The design product of one of the four groups is to be presented in the following.

DESIGN PRODUCT 'SCAPELIFTER'   The two students Eva Liebig and Dag-Ole Ziebell understand Spiekeroog as a complex area that must grow and change with the rise in sea level in order to remain preserved.[6] They propagate an 'actantivism' that choreographs suitable actants in order to enable a sediment growth on the island and establish dynamic coastal protection.[7] Four phases of actantivism are outlined, ranging from the current sea level to a rise of five metres (fig. 2). The first phase, 'initiating', is based on the current sea level and builds up the conditions to prepare the island for the rise in sea level. A sand motor and artificially set up oyster reefs are supposed to protect the north side of the island, while on the south side artificially initiated mussel banks and seaweed meadows are intended to let the tidal flat grow. Human actors are incorporated through transformation tourism, which aims to contribute to the rejuvenation of the dunes through actively controlled interventions by the tourists. In the second phase, 'dynamising', which assumes a rise in sea level of one metre, the state of the island can be kept stable through the nature-based measures established in the initial phase, with the development of the first little dune breakthroughs and lagoons. From a 1.5-metre rise in sea level, modest coastal protection measures are no longer sufficient. In the 'adapting'

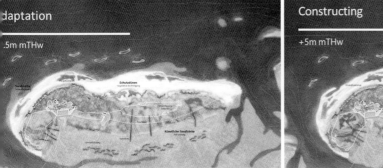
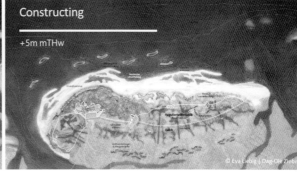

ein Entwurfsstudio, das Zukunftsszenarien für die Insel Spiekeroog, einen der drei Reallaborstandorte, erarbeitete.[5] Diese Projektionen der Studierenden sind Entwurfsprodukte im oben genannten Sinne und stellen Testläufe für die Entwürfe dar, die wir gegen Ende des Forschungsprojekts erstellen werden. Während des Semesters besuchten andere Forscher:innen von ‚Gute Küste Niedersachsen' regelmäßig das Entwurfsstudio und gaben Ratschläge aus ihrem spezifischen Hintergrund, wie Küstensedimentbewegung, Seegrasansiedlung oder Salzwiesenprozesse. Insgesamt arbeiteten in dem Entwurfsstudio vier Zweiergruppen, das Entwurfsprodukt von einer der vier Gruppen soll im Folgenden vorgestellt werden.

ENTWURFSPRODUKT ‚SCAPELIFTER'   Die beiden Studierenden Eva Liebig und Dag-Ole Ziebell verstehen Spiekeroog als einen komplexen Raum, der mit dem Meeresspiegelanstieg (MSA) mitwachsen und sich wandeln muss, um erhalten zu bleiben.[6] Sie propagieren einen ‚Aktantivismus', der die passenden Aktanten choreografiert, um einen Sedimentaufwuchs der Insel zu ermöglichen und einen dynamischen Küstenschutz zu etablieren.[7] Es werden vier Phasen des Aktantivismus skizziert, die vom aktuellen Meeresspiegelstand bis hin zu einem Anstieg von 5 Metern gehen (Abb. 2). Die erste Phase, ‚Initiieren', geht vom aktuellen Meeresspiegelstand aus und baut die Voraussetzungen auf, um die Insel für den MSA zu präparieren. Ein Sandmotor und künstlich angelegte Austernriffe sollen die Nordseite der Insel schützen, während auf der Südseite künstlich initiierte Miesmuschelbänke und Seegraswiesen das Watt mitwachsen lassen sollen. Menschliche Akteur:innen werden durch einen Transformationstourismus einbezogen, der durch aktiv gesteuerte Störungen der Dünen durch die Touristen zur Dünenverjüngung beitragen soll. In der zweiten Phase, ‚Dynamisieren', die einen MSA von 1 Meter annimmt, kann der Zustand der Insel durch die in der Initialphase etablierten naturbasierten Maßnahmen stabil gehalten werden, es entwickeln sich erste kleine Dünendurchbrüche und Lagunen. Ab 1,5 Meter MSA reichen weiche Küstenschutzmaßnahmen nicht mehr aus. Im Szenario ‚Adaptieren' wird daher auf der Südseite ein Deich gebaut, in dessen Vorland durch Sandspülungen neue Salzwiesen entstehen, die die Wellenkraft abpuffern sollen. Auf der Nordseite soll die stabile Dünenkette durch Transformationstourismus mit Aufpflanzungen weiter gestärkt werden. Das Extremszenario ‚Konstruieren' nimmt 5 Meter MSA an und verlangt weitere harte Baumaßnahmen wie Sperrwerke im Deich, die die

scenario, therefore, an embankment is built on the south side, in whose foreshore new salt marshes develop through the washing up of sand, intended to buffer the force of the waves. On the north side, the stable chain of dunes is to be strengthened further through transformation tourism with planting. The extreme scenario of 'constructing' assumes a 5-metre rise in sea level and requires further stringent building measures such as barrages in the embankment that guide the approaching water into the middle of the island, creating new and regulated wetlands there. These attractive, biodiverse habitats become part of a new system of walkways on which tourists can experience the dynamic island processes.

With the help of this and the three further design products of the student project group, for the first time in the research project many strands of the ongoing disciplinary works came together in a coherent spatial design for one of the real-world laboratory sites. We presented these design products to both the local research participants and the public (fig. 3) at an exhibition at the National Park House in Spiekeroog. The feedback that we received made it clear that the designs bring together the various aspects of the ecosystem-reinforcing coastal protection and allow a better understanding of their relations to each other. Furthermore, they enable reflection on possible future measures by drawing up various scenarios. The projective character of designing becomes a real benefit here, because only few other scientific methods are capable of integrating a complex bundle of spatial, social and ecological parameters into a coherent product that is understandable both for academics and for laypersons.

Based on the example of the future scenarios for Spiekeroog, the role of design products in the research process was now described. This description makes it clear that design products or 'Research through Design' are not the research in themselves but have to be

3 | Exhibition 'NEWISLANDLAND. Landscape architectural scenarios about the sea level rise in Spiekeroog' 2022

Wasserzufuhr in die Inselmitte steuern und dort neue, regulierte Feuchtgebiete entstehen lassen. Diese attraktiven, artenreichen Habitate werden Teil eines neuen Stegerschließungssystems, auf dem die Touristen die dynamischen Inselprozesse erfahren können.

Mithilfe dieses und der drei weiteren Entwurfsprodukte der studentischen Projektgruppe kamen zum ersten Mal in dem Forschungsprojekt viele Stränge der laufenden disziplinären Arbeiten in einem kohärenten räumlichen Entwurf für einen der Reallaborstandorte zusammen. In einer Ausstellung im Nationalparkhaus auf Spiekeroog haben wir diese Entwurfsprodukte sowohl den lokalen Forschungsakteur:innen als auch der Öffentlichkeit vorgestellt (Abb. 3). Die Rückmeldungen, die wir erhielten, machten deutlich, dass die Entwürfe die verschiedenen Aspekte des ökosystemstärkenden Küstenschutzes zusammenführen und ein besseres Verständnis der Zusammenhänge untereinander ermöglichen. Darüber hinaus ermöglichen sie eine Reflexion möglicher zukünftiger Maßnahmen durch den Entwurf verschiedener Szenarien. Hier wird der projektive Charakter des Entwerfens zu einem echten Gewinn, denn nur wenige andere wissenschaftliche Methoden sind in der Lage, ein komplexes Bündel räumlicher, sozialer und ökologischer Parameter in ein kohärentes Produkt zu integrieren, das sowohl für Akademiker:innen als auch für Laien verständlich ist.

Am Beispiel der Zukunftsszenarien für Spiekeroog wurde nun die Rolle von Entwurfsprodukten im Forschungsprozess beschrieben. Aus dieser Beschreibung wird schon deutlich, dass Entwurfsprodukte bzw. ‚Research through Design' für sich genommen nicht schon die Forschung sind, sondern sie müssen mit anderen Momenten des Forschungsprozesses verbunden werden. Diese Bemerkung ist mir wichtig, weil es eine wichtige Phase der Entwurfsforschung gab, in der ‚Research through Design' als eigenständig neben ‚Research about Design' und ‚Research for Design' definiert wurde.[8] Diese Unterscheidung war aber

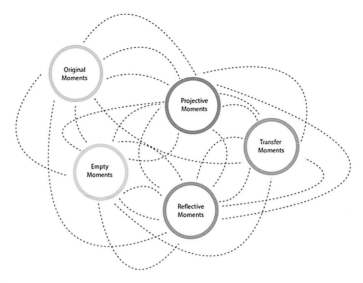

4 | Non-linear interplay of five moments

combined with other moments of the research process. This comment is important to me, because there was an important phase in the design research in which 'Research through Design' was defined independently alongside 'Research about Design' and 'Research for Design'.[8] This differentiation was not productive, however, because in the articles there were few convincing examples of pure 'Research through Design'. The question is now: how can the embedding of design products in the research process be meaningfully described theoretically? For this purpose, I would like to start with the very general criteria for research, as formulated for example by the Deutsche Forschungsgemeinschaft (German Research Society) or the Arts and Humanities Research Council (AHRC). For example, the AHRC requires from the research proposals: "Our primary concern is to ensure that the research we fund addresses clearly articulated research questions, issues or problems, set in a clear context of other research in that area, and using appropriate research methods and/or approaches. [...] The outcomes of the research may only benefit other researchers and influence future research, but consideration must be given to potential opportunities for the transfer of knowledge into new contexts where the research could have an impact."[9]

In summary one can say that each research project poses a novel research question, reflects on the scientific context, uses appropriate methods and strives for knowledge transfer. All research proposals, including those that contain design products, should fulfil this list of criteria. Against this background, I made a suggestion with "Design research as the non-linear interplay of five moments"[10] (fig. 4). I refer to the design products as projective moments, because what is special about the method of the design is to show conditions that are currently not yet in existence. Alain Findeli expresses it like this: "Design researchers consider [the world] as a project (of design). Their epistemological stance may thus be characterised as projective".[11] In these projective moments, designing itself becomes an essential part of the research process in line with 'Research through Design'. But these projective moments need the interplay with four other moments:[12] (1) Original moments that comprise research questions that are novel and ensure the originality of the research.

nicht produktiv, denn es gab in den Artikeln wenig überzeugende Beispiele von reinem ‚Research through Design'. Die Frage ist nun: Wie kann die Einbettung von Entwurfsprodukten in den Forschungsprozess theoretisch sinnvoll beschrieben werden? Dafür möchte ich mit den ganz allgemeinen Kriterien für Forschung beginnen, wie sie beispielsweise die Deutsche Forschungsgemeinschaft oder das Arts and Humanities Research Council (AHRC) formulieren. Das AHRC verlangt beispielsweise von den Forschungsanträgen: „Our primary concern is to ensure that the research we fund addresses clearly-articulated research questions, issues or problems, set in a clear context of other research in that area, and using appropriate research methods and/or approaches. [...] The outcomes of the research may only benefit other researchers and influence future research, but consideration must be given to potential opportunities for the transfer of knowledge into new contexts where the research could have an impact."[9]

Es lässt sich zusammenfassen, dass jede Forschung eine neuartige Forschungsfrage stellt, den wissenschaftlichen Kontext reflektiert, angemessene Methoden benutzt und einen Wissenstransfer anstrebt. Diese Kriterienliste sollten alle Forschungsanträge inklusive denen, die Entwurfsprodukte enthalten, erfüllen. Vor diesem Hintergrund habe ich mit der „Entwurfsforschung als nicht-lineares Zusammenspiel von fünf Momenten" einen Vorschlag gemacht (Abb. 4).[10] Die Entwurfsprodukte bezeichne ich als projektive Momente, denn das Besondere der Methode des Entwerfens ist es, Zustände zu zeigen, die es aktuell noch nicht gibt. Alain Findeli drückt es so aus: „Design researchers consider [the world] as a project (of design). Their epistemological stance may thus be characterized as projective".[11] In diesen projektiven Momenten wird das Entwerfen selbst im Sinne des ‚Research through Design' zum essenziellen Teil des Forschungsprozesses. Aber diese projektiven Momente brauchen das Zusammenspiel mit vier anderen Momenten: (1) Originale Momente, die Forschungsfragen umfassen, die neuartig sind und die die Originalität der Forschung sicherstellen. (2) Reflektierende Momente, in denen der Stand der Forschung erkundet wird und die die Einbettung in die jeweiligen wissenschaftlichen Kontexte herstellen. (3) Leere Momente, eine zugegeben spezielle Kategorie, die ausdrückt, dass Forschung (fast) immer durch Phasen der Leere, der Verzweiflung oder des Abschweifens geht, die nicht negativ zu bewerten sind, sondern positive Effekte haben, wie sich in Gesprächen mit zahlreichen Forschenden gezeigt hat. (4) Transfermomente, die gerade in der Entwurfsforschung sicherstellen, dass das generierte Wissen über den spezifischen Entwurfsfall hinaus auch für andere Kontexte nutzbar gemacht bzw. verallgemeinert wird.[12]

(2) Reflective moments in which the status of the research is considered and that establish the embedding into the respective scientific contexts. (3) Empty moments, an admittedly special category that expresses that research (almost) always goes through phases of emptiness, frustration or digression, which are not to be viewed negatively but have positive effects, as has been evident in discussions with many researchers. (4) Transfer moments that ensure, particularly in design research, that the generated knowledge is also made usable in other contexts and generalised beyond the specific design case.

For our research contribution in GKN, this means that our design products of landscape scenarios (projective moments) must always relate to the research questions (original moments) already developed early on. As the interplay of five moments is non-linear, it can by all means happen that findings from the projective moments relate in such a way to the original moments that the research question has to be adapted. We should study both the disciplinary findings on landscape scenarios and the findings of the other involved disciplines and of the civil society actors (reflective moments), and after running through some empty moments attain transferable knowledge (transfer moments) at the end. This means in the case of GKN that we derive typical models for an ecosystem-reinforcing coastal protection that can be used beyond our real-world laboratories. The role of design products in design research can therefore be summarised such that they represent a decisive contribution that no other method can provide but which are also always just part of many other moments of design research. It is only through their interplay that a research result emerges that is acceptable in the science landscape.

SUMMARY AND OUTLOOK   In the GKN project, it was already evident early on that future scenarios for the island of Spiekeroog have a high value for the transdisciplinary research process as design products. They have the unique potential to bundle the various strands of disciplinary research in the form of complex spatial scenarios. No other method in the research project has such a strong synthesising and projecting power as design! In many other disciplines, this potential of design products or of 'Research through Design' for transdisciplinary research has not yet taken hold, and design researchers should communicate this value confidently. Should we even go as far as Wolfgang Jonas who suggests "that RTD has the potential to act as the epistemological paradigm for transdisciplinary studies"?[13] I am not so sure about this. 'Research through Design' is undoubtedly an important moment in transdisciplinary research, but a non-hierarchical interplay with other epistemological paradigms seems to me to correspond more to the multidimensional character of research processes and gives designers a modest grounding that is necessary for transdisciplinary research.

Für unseren Forschungsbeitrag in GKN bedeutet das, dass unsere Entwurfsprodukte der Landschaftsszenarien (projektive Momente) immer auf die schon früh entwickelten Forschungsfragen (originalen Momente) bezogen sein müssen. Da das Zusammenspiel der fünf Momente nicht linear ist, kann es durchaus sein, dass Erkenntnisse aus den projektiven Momenten so auf die originalen Momente zurückspielen, dass die Forschungsfrage angepasst werden muss. Wir sollten sowohl die disziplinären Erkenntnisse zu Landschaftsszenarien als auch die Erkenntnisse der anderen beteiligten Disziplinen sowie der zivilgesellschaftlichen Akteure studieren (reflektierende Momente), und nach dem Durchlaufen einiger leerer Momente am Ende zu übertragbarem Wissen (Transfermomente) gelangen. Das bedeutet im Fall von GKN, dass wir typische Muster für einen ökosystemstärkenden Küstenschutz ableiten, die über unsere Reallabore hinaus anwendbar sind. Die Rolle von Entwurfsprodukten in der Entwurfsforschung kann damit so zusammengefasst werden, dass sie einen entscheidenden Beitrag darstellen, den keine andere Methode leisten kann, aber immer auch nur Teil vieler anderer Momente der Entwurfsforschung sind. Nur in deren Zusammenspiel entsteht eine in der Wissenschaftslandschaft akzeptable Forschungsleistung.

ZUSAMMENFASSUNG UND AUSBLICK   Im Projekt GKN hat sich schon zu einem frühen Zeitpunkt gezeigt, dass Zukunftsszenarien für die Insel Spiekeroog als Entwurfsprodukte einen hohen Wert für den transdisziplinären Forschungsprozess haben. Sie haben ein einzigartiges Potenzial, die verschiedenen Stränge der disziplinären Forschung in Form komplexer räumlicher Szenarien zu bündeln. Keine andere Methode im Forschungsprojekt hat eine so starke synthetisierende und projizierende Kraft wie das Entwerfen! Bei vielen anderen Disziplinen ist dieses Potenzial von Entwurfsprodukten bzw. ‚Research through Design' für transdisziplinäre Forschung noch nicht angekommen und die Entwurfsforschenden sollten diesen Wert selbstbewusst kommunizieren. Sollen wir sogar so weit gehen wie Wolfgang Jonas, der vorschlägt, „that RTD has the potential to act as the epistemological paradigm for transdisciplinary studies"?[13] Hier bin ich mir nicht so sicher. ‚Research through Design' ist zweifellos ein wichtiges Moment transdisziplinärer Forschung, aber ein nicht hierarchisches Zusammenspiel mit anderen epistemologischen Paradigmen scheint mir eher dem multidimensionalen Charakter von Forschungsprozessen zu entsprechen und gibt den Entwerfenden eine bescheidene Bodenhaftung, die für transdisziplinäre Forschung notwendig ist.

* Acknowledgements This article was written with the support of Felix Brennecke and David Kreis, research assistants at the Institute for Open Space Development at Leibniz Universität Hannover within the research project 'Gute Küste Niedersachsen'. | Dieser Artikel entstand mit Unterstützung von Felix Brennecke und David Kreis, wiss. Mitarbeiter im Institut für Freiraumentwicklung der Leibniz Universität Hannover innerhalb des Forschungsprojektes 'Gute Küste Niedersachsen'. **1** Cf. e.g. | Vgl. z.B. Richard Beecroft et al., Reallabore als Rahmen transformativer und transdisziplinärer Forschung: Ziele und Designprinzipien, in: Rico Defila/Antonietta Di Giulio (eds.) Transdisziplinär und transformativ forschen, Wiesbaden: Springer VS 2018, 75–100; Yuliya Voytenko et al., Urban living labs for sustainability and low carbon cities in Europe: Towards a research agenda, in: Journal of cleaner production 123(2016), 45–54 **2** Mathias Wanner et al., Towards a cyclical concept of real-world laboratories, in: disP. The Planning Review 54,2 (2018), 94–114 **3** Uwe Schneidewind/Mandy Singer-Brodowski/Karoline Augenstein/Franziska Stelzer, Pledge for a transformative science: A conceptual framework, Wuppertal Papers 191, Wuppertal: Institute for climate, environment and energy 2016 **4** Martin Prominski, Design research as non-linear interplay of five moments, in: Martin Prominski/Hille von Seggern (eds.), Design research for urban landscapes. Theories and methods, London: Routledge 2019, 44–46 **5** NEWISLANDLAND. Landscape architecture scenarios for sea level rise on Spiekeroog. Heads: Martin Prominski and David Kreis, winter semester 2021/22 | NEUINSELLAND. Landschaftsarchitektonische Szenarien zum Meeresspiegelanstieg auf Spiekeroog.

Leitung: Martin Prominski und David Kreis, Wintersemester 2021/22   **6** Eva Liebig/Dag-Ole Ziebell, Scapeshifter, in: Institut für Freiraumentwicklung (ed.), NEUINSELLAND. Landschaftsarchitektonische Szenarien zum Meeresspiegelanstieg auf Spiekeroog, Leibniz Universität Hannover: Projektbericht 2022, 159   **7** Ibid.; In the sense of Bruno Latour, actants include not only human but also non-human actors such as animals, plants, water or sand. | Als Aktanten werden im Sinne Bruno Latours neben menschlichen auch nicht-menschliche Agierende wie Tiere, Pflanzen, Wasser oder Sand verstanden.   **8** Cf. | Vgl. Christopher Frayling, Research in art and design, in: Royal College of Art Research Paper 1(1993); Henk Borgdorff, The debate on research in the arts, in: Focus on Artistic Research and development, no. 02, 2007; Wolfgang Jonas, Exploring the swampy ground, in: Simon Grand/Wolfgang Jonas (eds.), Mapping design research, Basel: Birkhäuser 2012, 11–41   **9** Arts and humanities research council, Definition of 'research', on: | Definition von ‚Forschung' auf: www.ahrc.ac.uk/funding/research/researchfundingguide/definitionofresearch 2015, 13.11.2015   **10** Martin Prominski (2019), op. cit. (note | Anm. 4)   **11** Alain Findeli, Searching for design research questions: Some conceptual clarifications, in: Rosan Chow/Wolfgang Jonas/Gesche Joost (eds.) Questions, hypotheses & conjectures: Discussions on projects by early stage and senior design researchers, New York-Bloomington, NY: iUniverse 2010, 286–302   **12** Martin Prominski (2019), op. cit. (note | Anm. 4)   **13** Wolfgang Jonas, Research through design is more than just a new form of disseminating design outcomes, in: Constructivist Foundations 11,1(2015), 35

PRODUCTIVE IMAGES

Sarah Wehmeyer

The collage is experiencing an (apparent) comeback as a presentation medium in the contemporary architecture discipline. A profusion of representations can be found under this term in online magazines and on social networks. Designers digitally imitate the manually created, layered character of a collage in order to produce images that convey not an idealised but more of an 'authentic' architecture that is easily accessible to people. It remains questionable to what extent these representations can be referred to as collage. At first glance, they have nothing in common with the original artistic technique of layering and sticking on real paper and material fragments, as well as photographic reproductions that feature in cubism, Dadaism and pop art – nor with the intention of artists to criticise the accessibility of their own discipline through collage and to depart from traditional representation and perception patterns.

However, there are also exceptions. Beyond the purely representational, contemporary firms such as Tatiana Bilbao Estudio, Dogma or OFFICE Kersten Geers David van Severen are characterised by various forms of collage associated with the aim of producing 'good' designs and design-related knowledge. From the architects' point of view, these two 'products' of architecture are required in order to design high-quality contemporary and future living spaces. It does not appear adequate to them when designing to strive merely for the object and its realisation. Consequently, they combine the search for creative ideas – the design – with the search for design-related insights – the research. In what way the researching designers use collages in this as a thinking and communication medium,

PRODUKTIVE BILDER

Sarah Wehmeyer

Die Collage erlebt in der gegenwärtigen Architekturdisziplin ein (scheinbares) Comeback als Präsentationsmedium. Es gibt eine Überfülle an Darstellungen, die unter dem Begriff in Online-Magazinen und den sozialen Netzwerken zu finden sind. Entwerfende imitieren digital den händisch hergestellten Schichtcharakter einer Collage, um auf diese Weise Bilder zu produzieren, die keine idealisierte, vielmehr eine ‚ehrliche' und für den Menschen leicht zugängliche Architektur vermitteln sollen. Inwieweit diese Darstellungen als Collage zu bezeichnen sind, bleibt fragwürdig. Mit der ursprünglich künstlerischen Technik des Überlagerns und Klebens von realen Papier- und Materialfragmenten sowie fotografischen Reproduktionen, wie man es aus dem Kubismus, dem Dadaismus und der Pop-Art kennt, haben sie auf den ersten Blick keine Gemeinsamkeiten – ebenso wenig wie mit der Intention der Kunstschaffenden, die eigene Disziplin über die Collage in ihrer Zugänglichkeit zu kritisieren und mit tradierten Darstellungs- und Wahrnehmungsmustern zu brechen.

Doch es gibt auch Ausnahmen. Über das rein Darstellerische hinaus zeichnen sich zeitgenössische Büros wie Tatiana Bilbao Estudio, Dogma oder auch OFFICE Kersten Geers David van Severen durch unterschiedliche Collageformen aus, verbunden mit dem Ziel, qualitätsvolle Entwürfe und entwurfsbezogenes Wissen hervorzubringen. In den Augen der Architekturschaffenden braucht es eben diese zwei ‚Produkte' des Architekturschaffens, um qualitätsvolle Lebensräume der Gegenwart und Zukunft zu gestalten. Im Entwerfen lediglich das zu gestaltende Objekt und dessen Realisierung anzustreben, erscheint ihnen nicht ausreichend. Folglich verknüpfen sie die Suche nach gestalterischen Ideen – das Entwerfen – mit der Suche nach entwurfsbezogenen Erkenntnissen – dem Forschen. Auf welche Weise die forschend Entwerfenden hierbei Collagen als Denk- und Kommunikationsmedium einsetzen,

1 | OFFICE Oasis Sharjah (Arab Emirates) 2013   2 | Tatiana Bilbao Estudio Botanical Garden Culiacán (Mexico) since 2007

define them as a stance and/or as the actual end product is investigated by the author with the help of literature and image analyses, visits to exhibitions, interviews and her own collaging. 'Urban Refugium' is the title of the collage-based design study that was developed as part of the scientific research and is the focus of this article. It also pursues the question of what type of 'products' the outcome of a research activity in architecture can comprise.

URBAN REFUGIUM. A DESIGN STUDY...   consists, on the one hand, of digitally composed collages that envisage places of longing in contemporary urban society and, on the other hand, of a collection of potential design sites with aerial photographs, explanatory pictograms and text modules for the compartments. What prompted the study initiated in 2019 was the hypothesis that inner-city 'refuges' will increasingly disappear due to the changing of our city centres, while the yearning for peace and reclusion will be intensified. The wish is growing in society to escape urban everyday life, to slow down and recharge one's batteries. The pandemic has strengthened these longings further. Allotment gardens have become a luxury asset in the city, the lonesome cabin in the forest and the converted van a residential ideal, gaining appeal alongside a second home in the countryside. For various reasons, these developments are not very desirable.[1] In light of this, it seems to be important for architects to focus their attention once again on the city itself, looking for potential spaces for individual retreat and (re)designing them. It remains to be questioned to what extent historical and religious models such as the monastery are being used as a reference, or whether a refuge is necessarily to be thought of as a green oasis. Outdoor spaces on different scales and with varying degrees of publicness are at least currently being discussed in architecture and landscape architecture as urban retreats.[2] However, the greatest challenge no doubt remains the question of 'where'. Where does the city still have space for places where we can celebrate being alone or even boredom?

'Urban Refugium' sees such possible spaces in large inner-city structures, such as in historical prison architectures that still exist in many European cities: panoptic systems, star-shaped or as a rotunda, built between the 19th and 20th century, whose usage as

als Haltung definieren und/oder als das eigentliche Endprodukt anstreben, erforscht die Autorin mithilfe von Literatur- und Bildanalysen, Ausstellungsbesuchen, Interviews ebenso wie über das eigene Collagieren. ‚Urban Refugium' lautet der Titel der collagenbasierten Entwurfsstudie, die als Teil der wissenschaftlichen Forschung entwickelt wurde und im Fokus dieses Beitrages steht. Es wird damit auch der Frage nachgegangen, welche Art von ‚Produkten' der Outcome einer forschenden Tätigkeit in der Architektur umfassen kann.

URBAN REFUGIUM. EINE ENTWURFSSTUDIE besteht zum einen aus digital komponierten Collagen, in denen Sehnsuchtsorte der zeitgenössischen Stadtgesellschaft imaginiert werden und zum anderen aus einer Sammlung von potenziellen Entwurfsgrundstücken mit Luftbildaufnahmen, erklärenden Piktogrammen sowie Textbausteinen zu den benannten Kompartimenten. Der Anlass der 2019 initiierten Studie gründet in der These, dass innerstädtische ‚Refugien' angesichts der Veränderung unserer Innenstädte zunehmend schwinden werden, während das Bedürfnis nach Ruhe und Zurückgezogenheit stärker werden wird. In der Gesellschaft wächst der Wunsch, dem städtischen Alltag zu entfliehen, um sich selbst zu entschleunigen und neue Kraft zu tanken. Die Pandemie hat diese Sehnsüchte zusätzlich vorangetrieben. Schrebergärten sind mittlerweile ein Luxusgut in der Stadt, die einsame Hütte im Wald und der selbstausgebaute Camper als ein Wohnideal sowie auch der Zweitwohnsitz im ruralen Raum gewinnen an Attraktivität – aus unterschiedlichen Gründen sind dies wenig wünschenswerte Entwicklungen.[1] Vor diesem Hintergrund erscheint es umso wichtiger, dass Architekturschaffende ihren Blick wieder auf die Stadt selbst richten und hier nach potenziellen Räumen für den individuellen Rückzug suchen und diese (neu) gestalten. Inwieweit man sich hierbei an historischen und religiösen Modellen wie der Klosteranlage orientiert oder das Refugium zwingend als grüne Oase zu denken ist, bleibt zu hinterfragen. Freiräume unterschiedlicher Maßstäbe und Öffentlichkeit werden zumindest gegenwärtig als urbane Rückzugsorte in der Architektur und Landschaftsarchitektur diskutiert.[2] Die wohl größte Herausforderung bleibt jedoch vorerst die Frage nach dem Wo. Wo bietet die Stadt noch Platz für Orte, an denen wir das Alleinsein oder auch die Langeweile zelebrieren können?

‚Urban Refugium' sieht derartige Möglichkeitsräume in innerstädtischen Großstrukturen, beispielsweise in den historischen Gefängnisarchitekturen, wie es sie noch in zahlreichen europäischen Städten gibt: panoptische Systeme in Sternform oder als Rotunde, erbaut zwischen dem 19. und 20. Jahrhundert, bei denen abzusehen ist, dass ihre Nutzung aufgrund unzureichender Sicherheitskonzepte und Platzangebote zukünftig verlagert werden muss.[3] Was zurückbleiben wird, sind leer stehende enklavenartige Großstrukturen inmitten der Stadt,

1. Münster Innenstadt Gartenstraße, 1848
denkmalgeschützt, in Teilen geschlossen ◉

2. Berlin Alt-Moabit 12a 1881
denkmalgeschützt, sanierungsbedürftig ◉

4. Freiburg Hermann-Herder-Str. 8, 1878
denkmalgeschützt, vollständig saniert ◉

3. Halle Am Kirchtor 20, 1842
denkmalgeschützt?, geplante Schließung 2015 ◉

3. Naumburg Am Salztor 3, 1859
geschlossen, teils zum Abriss freigegeben ◉◉

3. Hamburg Innenstadt Holstenglacis 3, 1881
denkmalgeschützt, teilsaniert ◉

Eine Sammlung panoptischer Systeme im urbanen Raum lässt den Suchenden in fast jeder größeren Stadt fündig werden. Gefängnisse stehen in Teilen bereits leer und sind geschlossen, warten auf ihren Verkauf oder zeigen einen dringenden Renovierungsbedarf, der auf Grund des Denkmalschutzes unnötig hohe Kosten verursachen würde. Zudem mehren sich die kritischen Diskurse um die Wirksamkeit und Zukunftsfähigkeit der Institution des Gefängnisses an und für sich. Wie kann Isolation zur Resozialisierung beitragen?

3 | Sarah Wehmeyer Urban Refugium Collection of panoptic systems

a prison will have to be relocated in future due to inadequate security concepts and availability of space.[3] What will remain are empty, enclave-like big structures in the middle of the city, which will be lacking a function and accessibility. The Münster Penal Institution (JVA) is the first study object of the series of studies. The municipal planning office, the heritage protection authority and North Rhine-Westphalian architects have already been discussing alternative usages of this special but derelict building shell since 2015. The future of the complex remains uncertain. There is even talk of demolition.[4] The fact that JVA Münster is not an isolated case is underlined by the collection of eighteen panoptic systems in Germany and Europe (fig. 3). These are sorted according to their context, their cell structure, their current usage and the building substance. Further building complexes were identified in the research and could extend the collection, but even this selection makes it clear that existing historical prisons have scarcely been accorded design attention as a building task.

It is only the Dutch architecture scene that forms an exception. Many prison closures in recent years have led to transformations also of more recent prison architectures, such as the Amsterdam Bijlmerbaje quarter.[5] OMA, who won the associated competition in 2017, recognise the emblematic function of the six prison high-rises for the periphery of Amsterdam. They preserve the island character of the prison, supplement pedestrian and bicycle bridge connections, and implement a mixed programme of housing and urban farming within the 1970s architecture. Koolhaas's fascination with the urban potential of prison structures is already evident in earlier projects. In the renovation studies for the panopticon in Arnheim (1980), he compares this in relation to the communally used and popular ground floor, framed by circulating balconies, with the Milan Galleria Vittorio Emanuele (fig. 4).[6] In 'Exodus' (1972), Koolhaas together with Madelon

4 | OMA Study on renovation of Arnhem prison (NL) 1980   5 | Exodus, or the Voluntary Prisoners of Architecture: The Strip 1972

denen es an Funktion und Zugänglichkeit fehlen wird. Die Justizvollzugsanstalt (JVA) Münster ist das erste Untersuchungsobjekt der Studienreihe. Bereits seit 2015 diskutieren der Stadtbaurat, der Denkmalschutz und nordrheinwestfälische Architekturschaffende über alternative Nutzungen dieses besonderen, jedoch baufälligen Gebäuderohlings. Die Zukunft des Komplexes ist weiterhin ungewiss. Selbst von Abriss ist die Rede.[4] Dass die JVA Münster diesbezüglich kein Einzelfall ist, unterstreicht die angelegte Sammlung von 18 panoptischen Systemen aus dem deutschen wie auch aus dem europäischen Raum (Abb. 3). Sortiert sind diese entsprechend ihres Kontextes, ihrer Zellenstruktur, ihres aktuellen Programms und ihrer Bausubstanz. Weitere Gebäudekomplexe wurden in der Recherche identifiziert und könnten die Sammlung erweitern, doch bereits diese Auswahl verdeutlicht, dass historischen Gefängnissen als Bauaufgabe (im Bestand) bislang kaum gestalterische Aufmerksamkeit zukommt.

Eine Ausnahme bildet lediglich die niederländische Architekturszene. Zahlreiche Gefängnisschließungen in den letzten Jahren führten zu Transformationen auch jüngerer Gefängnisarchitekturen, beispielsweise dem Amsterdamer Bijlmerbaje-Quartier.[5] OMA, die 2017 den dazugehörigen Wettbewerb gewonnen haben, erkennen die Wahrzeichenfunktion der sechs Gefängnishochhäuser für die Peripherie von Amsterdam. Sie erhalten den Inselcharakter des von Mauern umschlossenen Gefängnisses, ergänzen Verbindungen aus Fußgänger- und Fahrradbrücken und implementieren der 1970er-Jahre-Architektur einen Programmmix aus Wohnen und Urban Farming. Koolhaas' Faszination für die urbanen Potenziale von Gefängnisstrukturen wird bereits in früheren Projekten deutlich. In den Renovierungsstudien zum Panoptikum in Arnheim (1980) verglich er dieses in Bezug auf das gemeinschaftlich belebte und beliebte Erdgeschoss, gerahmt von umlaufenden Balkonen, mit der Mailänder Galleria Vittorio Emanuele (Abb. 4).[6] In ,Exodus' (1972) entwickelte Koolhaas mit Madelon Vriesendorp, Elia und Zoe Zenghelis eine großmaßstäbliche lineare Gefängnisstruktur, welche die Bürger:innen vor dem chaotischen Stadtleben und -wachstum in London beschützen soll (Abb. 5).[7]

6 | Sarah Wehmeyer Urban Refugium Pair of collages

Vriesendorp, Elia and Zoe Zenghelis develops a large-scale, linear prison structure intended to protect the citizens against chaotic urban life and growth in London (fig. 5).[7] 'Urban Refugium' pursues similar ideals, also intending to activate the previously neglected urban potential of prison architectures and create a counterbalance to the city. In the words of Foucault, panoptic systems serve the purpose of monitoring and punishing but also of individual reflection on one's own deeds, free from external influences.[8] Encounters with strangers who are unavoidable outside of the private cell can, however, also be defined as a quality. The internal organisation of a prison is also to be taken into consideration. As a self-enclosed, almost autarchic enclave in the city with a range of functions and communal (outdoor) spaces, a prison already has certain urban dynamics – even if these remain hidden behind the walls.

With regard to the media that are used, there are decisive differences. 'Exodus' is characterised by verbal descriptions that promise paradisal circumstances and collages that surrealistically communicate daunting scenes from the inside of the newly designed enclave. Between verbal enticement and visual shock, the readers or viewers are brought to the limits of the rationally comprehensible. However, the actual intentions of the design therefore remain largely unclear. 'Urban Refugium', on the other hand, pursues the aim of overwriting various existing prison structures with positive projections and presenting them as high-quality living spaces (for a time). Furthermore, the study is associated with the intention of reviewing and deepening knowledge of the architecture-specific use of collages gained through traditional research methods. Collage-specific particularities that contemporary architects make use of for designing and researching are reproduced, reinterpreted and developed further in 'Urban Refugium'. Examples worth mentioning are the framing function, the state of drifting between reality and fiction, the evident layering of already available image resources and an ambiguity created in a targeted manner through empty spaces.

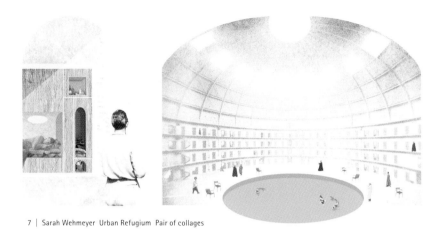

7 | Sarah Wehmeyer Urban Refugium Pair of collages

‚Urban Refugium' verfolgt ähnliche Ideale. Auch hier sollen bislang verkannte urbane Potenziale von Gefängnisarchitekturen aktiviert und soll damit ein Ausgleichsventil zur Stadt geschaffen werden. Mit den Worten von Foucault dienen panoptische Systeme dem Überwachen und Strafen, jedoch ebenso dem individuellen Reflektieren über das eigene Handeln, befreit von äußeren Einflüssen.[8] Begegnungen mit fremden Mitmenschen, die außerhalb der privaten Zelle unausweichlich sind, können jedoch auch als Qualität definiert werden. Ebenso zu berücksichtigen ist die innere Organisation eines Gefängnisses. Als in sich funktionierende, fast autarke Enklave in der Stadt mit unterschiedlichsten Programmbausteinen und gemeinschaftlichen (Frei-)Räumen verfügt ein Gefängnis bereits über gewisse urbane Dynamiken – wenngleich diese hinter den Mauern verborgen bleiben.

In Bezug auf die verwendeten Medien gibt es hingegen entscheidende Unterschiede. ‚Exodus' ist gekennzeichnet durch verbale Beschreibungen, die paradiesische Zustände versprechen und Collagen, die in surrealistischer Manier abschreckende Szenen aus dem Inneren der neu entworfenen Enklave kommunizieren. Zwischen verbaler Verführung und visuellem Schock werden die Lesenden bzw. Betrachtenden an die Grenzen des rational Nachvollziehbaren gebracht. Die tatsächlichen Absichten des Entwurfes bleiben dadurch weitgehend unklar. ‚Urban Refugium' hingegen verfolgt das Ziel, unterschiedliche vorhandene Gefängnisstrukturen mit positiven Vorstellungsbildern zu überlagern und als qualitätsvolle Lebensräume (auf Zeit) sichtbar zu machen. Darüber hinaus ist die Studie mit der Intention verbunden, das mittels traditioneller Forschungsmethoden gewonnene Wissen über die architekturspezifische Verwendung von Collagen zu überprüfen und zu vertiefen. Collagenspezifische Eigenarten, derer sich zeitgenössische Architekturschaffende bedienen, um zu entwerfen und zu forschen, werden hierzu in ‚Urban Refugium' reproduziert, reinterpretiert und weiterentwickelt. Beispielhaft zu nennen sind die rahmende Funktion, der Schwebezustand zwischen Wirklichkeit und Fiktion, das offensichtliche Schichten von bereits vorhandenen Bildressourcen sowie eine durch Leerstellen gezielt hervorgerufene Mehrdeutigkeit.

211

THE COLLAGES   The possibilities of knowledge genesis and communication associated with these particularities are explored and considered further in six
collages or three pairs of collages. The first pair of collages is about the simultaneous
perception of indoor and outdoor space, the past and the present of an urban refuge
(fig. 6). The viewers are situated, on the one hand, at the intersection between the
reinterpreted cell structure and the jungle-like garden along the prison wall. On the
other hand, they are part of the urban context and perceive the dome as a distinctive
form or as a foreign body in the growing city. The second pair of collages provides
intimate glimpses of the prison interior, with the viewers becoming observers (fig. 7).
Standing at the threshold, their eyes are drawn towards a sleeping cell inmate. From
one of the upper balconies in the panopticon, they watch the pacing and meditating
people. However, as these are scaled down and in relation to the domed room flooded
with light, they also escape from view. The architecture is the protagonist. Finally, the
third collage duo is again dedicated to the outdoors (fig. 8). The viewers find themselves in a nighttime scenario that emphasises the mysterious and sinister sides of the
prison context. A moment later, they are standing on the edge of a pool with a view
of a beach occupied by colourful parasols: holiday feelings in the middle of the city.

Photographic originals of prisons in Münster, Haarlem, Berlin and Halle serve as a
background and orientation in the structuring of the image. However, it is not of any
significance what place the collages are ultimately about. Instead, the linking of the
collages is intended to create the impression of one big urban refuge. This is supported
by recurring compositional means. These include a male staffage with his back turned
towards the viewers, thereby directing their gaze and making them part of the collage. There is also a consistent use of white areas in order to emphasise particularities
of the prison typology – cell, panopticon, wall, window openings. The white area in
some cases replaces the elements and makes them look cut out. In other cases, the
white area hides certain parts of the building to focus attention on something else.

FRAMING   In what way can these collages enrich the design, research and
communication of the future? Architects can use collages to frame the complexity of
everyday life, to offer themselves and others an alternative, often simplified perspective
on topics that are difficult to grasp. OFFICE, for example, use the collage in this respect
to break away from customary perception patterns in order to achieve new insights into
everyday and commonplace architectures of the urban periphery (fig. 9).[9] The framing is

8 | Sarah Wehmeyer Urban Refugium Pair of collages

DIE COLLAGEN   Die mit diesen Eigenarten verbundenen Möglichkeiten der
Wissensgenese und -kommunikation werden in sechs Collagen bzw. drei Collagenpaaren
erprobt und weitergedacht. Im ersten Collagenpaar geht es um das simultane Wahrnehmen von Innenraum und Außenraum, Vergangenheit und Gegenwart eines urbanen
Refugiums (Abb. 6). Die Betrachtenden befinden sich zum einen an der Schnittstelle
zwischen der neu interpretierten Zellenstruktur und dem dschungelartigen Garten entlang
der Gefängnismauer. Zum anderen sind sie Teil des städtischen Kontextes und nehmen
die Kuppel als markante Form oder auch als Fremdkörper in der wachsenden Stadt wahr.
Es folgen mit dem zweiten Collagenpaar intime Einblicke in das Gefängnisinnere, wobei
die Betrachtenden zu Beobachtenden werden (Abb. 7). Auf der Türschwelle stehend, fällt
ihr Blick auf einen schlafenden Zellengenossen. Von einem der oberen Balkone im Panoptikum beobachten sie die umherschreitenden und meditierenden Menschen. Aufs Kleinste
skaliert und im Verhältnis zum lichtdurchfluteten Kuppelraum entziehen sich diese jedoch
gleichsam dem Blick. Die Architektur ist die Protagonistin. Das dritte Collagenduo widmet
sich schließlich erneut dem Außenbereich (Abb. 8). Die Betrachtenden befinden sich in
einer nächtlichen Szenerie, die das Geheimnisvolle und Düstere des Gefängniskontextes
betont. Im nächsten Moment stehen sie am Rande eines Pools mit Blick auf einen von
bunten Sonnenschirmen eingenommenen Strand: Urlaubsgefühle inmitten der Stadt.

Als Hintergrund und Orientierung im Bildaufbau dienen fotografische Originale der Gefängnisse aus Münster, Haarlem, Berlin und Halle. Um welchen Ort es sich in den Collagen
schlussendlich handelt, ist jedoch nicht von Bedeutung. Vielmehr soll in der Verknüpfung
der Collagen der Eindruck entstehen, dass es sich um ein großes urbanes Refugium handelt.
Unterstützt wird dies durch wiederkehrende Kompositionsmittel. Dazu gehört unter anderem eine männliche Staffage, die den Betrachtenden den Rücken zuwendet, ihnen dadurch
die Richtung des Schauens vorgibt und sie zum Teil der Collage werden lässt. Ebenfalls
konstant eingesetzt werden weiße Flächen, um Eigenarten der Gefängnistypologie – Zelle,
Panoptikum, Mauer, Fensteröffnungen – zu betonen. Teils ersetzt die weiße Fläche die
Elemente und lässt sie wie ausgeschnitten erscheinen. Teils werden mit der weißen Fläche bestimmte Gebäudeteile ausgeblendet, um den Blick auf anderes zu fokussieren.

9 | OFFICE 117 Dryhall 2013

by no means collage-specific, however. It is a feature that fundamentally characterises the ways of working and products of artists – whether it is paintings, photographs, sculptures or installations.[10] What is special about a collage, though, is that by making use of available and contemporary image material, there is a search for a direct relation to the present. The collage thereby inevitably documents a certain time, its society, needs and problems. The recourse to documentations of the time is often associated with criticism of existing situations.[11] 'Urban Refugium' also makes use of this possibility. Contrary to artistic collages, new design proposals are developed beyond the critical mode..

HYPOTHESES   The collage not only allows aspects of reality to be presented in an alternative manner. If it is treated as a potential excerpt of the world, where there is experimentation according to its own rules and aims, then it also offers research potential. It then enables the formulation and composition of visual hypotheses, as well as a study thereof on paper. Fictive and even dystopian future scenarios can be developed that take up existing discussions or initiate new ones. The collage rhetoric of the Brussels firm Dogma serves as an example here for 'Urban Refugium'. The duo develops extreme, in some cases not very desirable high-rise typologies as potential walls of a city in order to promote and delineate urban dynamics (fig. 10).[12] The intervening in the pictorial reality, initially detached from reality, appears to encourage the architects to venture not only feasible but also experimental ways of thinking. The varying degrees of reality of a collage, created by abstract areas of colour combined with photographic picture elements, ensure the necessary relation to reality. In communication with third parties, the use of everyday image media that depict reality can also make the experimental appear familiar and realistic. Contrary to renderings, such as those used by OMA for the new Bijlmerbaje quarter, the collages of the study presented here are not intended to appear deceptively real. With their layered character, they celebrate the 'pictorial' and retain a certain degree of abstraction.[13]

10 | Dogma Stop City 2007

R A H M U N G E N   Auf welche Weise können diese Collagen das Entwerfen, Erforschen und Kommunizieren von Zukunft bereichern? Collagen können den Architekturschaffenden dazu dienen, die Komplexität des Alltags zu rahmen, um sich selbst wie auch anderen eine alternative, oftmals vereinfachte Sichtweise auf schwer greifbare Themen zu offerieren. OFFICE beispielsweise nutzen die Collage in dieser Hinsicht, um sich von gewohnten Wahrnehmungsschemata loszulösen und dadurch zu neuen Erkenntnissen über alltägliche und banale Architekturen der Stadtperipherie vorzudringen (Abb. 9).[9] Das Rahmende ist jedoch keineswegs collagenspezifisch. Es handelt sich um eine Eigenschaft, die Arbeitsweisen und Produkte von Kunstschaffenden grundlegend kennzeichnet – seien es Gemälde, Fotografien, Skulpturen oder Installationen.[10] Das Besondere einer Collage ist jedoch, dass durch den Rückgriff auf vorhandenes und zeitgenössisches Bildmaterial der unmittelbare Bezug zur Gegenwart gesucht wird. Dadurch dokumentiert die Collage unweigerlich eine bestimmte Zeit, ihre Gesellschaft, Bedürfnisse und Problemstellungen. Mit dem Rückgriff auf Zeitdokumente oftmals verbunden ist eine Kritik an bestehenden Situationen.[11] Dieser Möglichkeit bedient sich auch ‚Urban Refugium'. Im Gegensatz zu künstlerischen Collagen werden jedoch über den kritischen Modus hinausgehend ebenso neue Gestaltungsvorschläge entwickelt.

H Y P O T H E S E N   Die Collage ermöglicht es nicht nur, Aspekte der Wirklichkeit auf alternative Art und Weise darzustellen. Wird sie wie ein potenzieller Ausschnitt der Welt behandelt, in dem nach eigenen Regeln und Zielsetzungen experimentiert wird, offeriert sie ebenfalls forschendes Potenzial. Dann ermöglicht sie das Formulieren bzw. Komponieren von visuellen Hypothesen sowie deren Untersuchung auf dem Papier. Es können fiktive, mitunter dystopische Zukunftsszenarien entwickelt werden, die bestehende Diskussionen aufgreifen oder aber neue initiieren. Die Collagenrhetorik des Brüsseler Büros Dogma dient ‚Urban Refugium' hier diesbezüglich als Vorbild. Das Duo entwickelt extreme, teils wenig wünschenswerte Hochhaustypologien als potenzielle Wände einer Stadt, um urbane

11 | Tatiana Bilbao Estudio Hunters Point Los Angeles Reference collage 2016

A U T H O R S H I P   The collages are intended to remain open to being reflected on further and appropriated by third parties. White areas, which are to be filled in by the viewers, are the most obvious evidence of this intention behind the image. Even staffage elements, such as the unknown man, allow the viewers to participate in the imagination of the urban refuges. The collage is therefore also an expression of a certain attitude. It shows that it is not the individual creative genius that is significant. Instead, the knowledge and imaginative strengths of others – also non-designers – are to be appreciated. This type of criticism of one's own discipline is inherent in collage art.[14] In contemporary architecture, collage is associated with similar intentions. Tatiana Bilbao, who defines the city as a communal vision, carries out collective collage practices (fig. 11).[15] With white building panels, Dogma calls on viewers to become aware once again of the ordering and structuring responsibility of urban architecture.[16] OFFICE, who worked with Dogma for the first time in 2005, share this view. In their collages, architecture is veritably monumentalised independently of programme and context through the choice of perspective and lighting atmospheres.[17] In order to relativise their own importance as the authors of these architectures, they place the collages at exhibitions or in publications in a targeted manner in relation to their photographic and artistic references. This makes thematic and compositional associations become directly evident (fig.12).

12 | OFFICE Article: Architecture without Content Domus 964 (2012)

Dynamiken zu fördern und zu begrenzen (Abb.10).[12] Das Intervenieren in der Bildrealität, vorerst losgelöst von der Wirklichkeit, scheint die Architekturschaffenden dabei zu ermutigen, nicht nur machbare, sondern auch experimentelle Denkansätze zu wagen. Die unterschiedlichen Realitätsgrade einer Collage, hervorgerufen durch abstrakte Farbflächen kombiniert mit fotografischen Bildbestandteilen, sichern dabei den notwendigen Wirklichkeitsbezug. In der Kommunikation mit Dritten kann die Verwendung alltäglicher und realitätsabbildender Bildmedien zudem erwirken, dass das Experimentelle vertraut und realistisch erscheint. Im Gegensatz zu Renderings, wie sie OMA für das neue Bijlmerbaje-Quartier einsetzte, sollen die Collagen der hier vorgestellten Studie dabei nicht täuschend echt wirken. Mit ihrem Schichtcharakter zelebrieren sie das ‚Bildliche' und bewahren sich einen gewissen Abstraktionsgrad.[13]

AUTORSCHAFT   Die Collagen sollen offen bleiben für ein Weiterdenken und Aneignen durch Dritte. Weiße Flächen, die seitens der Betrachtenden zu vervollständigen sind, sind das offensichtlichste Zeugnis dieser Intention hinter dem Bild. Doch auch Staffageelemente wie der unbekannte Mann lassen die Betrachtenden an der Imagination der urbanen Refugien teilhaben. Die Collage ist damit zugleich Ausdruck einer bestimmten Haltung. Sie verdeutlicht, dass nicht das einzelne kreative Genie von Bedeutung ist. Vielmehr sollten das Wissen und die imaginativen Kräfte der anderen – auch Nicht-Entwerfenden – wertgeschätzt werden. Diese Art der Kritik an der eigenen Disziplin ist der Collagenkunst inhärent.[14] In der zeitgenössischen Architektur wird die Collage mit ähnlichen Intentionen verknüpft. Tatiana Bilbao, welche die Stadt als Gemeinschaftsvision definiert, praktiziert kollektive Collagepraktiken (Abb. 11).[15] Dogma appelliert mit weißen Gebäudescheiben an die Betrachtenden, sich der ordnenden und gestaltgebenden Verantwortung urbaner Architekturen wieder bewusst zu werden.[16] OFFICE, die 2005 erstmals mit Dogma zusammenarbeiten, teilen diese Auffassung. In ihren Collagen wird die Architektur unabhängig von Programm und Kontext durch Perspektivwahl und

RE-PRODUCTIONS   OFFICE teach their students that such re-producing is based on an intensive study of the references and can also encourage it. Collaging therefore serves at the start of the semester as a kind of portraying of reference objects in order to analyse their architectural qualities. The students should not lapse into stupid copying but design based on the newly acquired insights.[18] Tatiana Bilbao uses so-called refence collages with comparable intentions. As concept images, these are pasted together in early design phases from representations of her own architectures and photographs of her architectural role models.[19] It is also evident at OFFICE that re-production can also comprise one's own work as a reflexive approach to design. The Belgians understand the reuse of their own design strategies as well as the establishment of an office-specific image rhetoric as a mirror image of a promoted, time-saving and cost-saving design that may not end in repetition devoid of creativity.[20] 'Urban Refugium' sees re-production as a possibility to gain a better understanding of the collage techniques of other architects. Furthermore, it is about the cementing of one's own basic concept as a central knowledge segment. Published and unpublished collages of the Master's thesis (2015) in which JVA Münster was already programmatically and creatively transformed, are reworked and recombined for this. It is a retrospective confrontation with representations perceived as accomplished or failed, which shows how important it is to become more aware of the available resources, even if these – such as the prison or the selected representation – appear useless at first glance. Collages whose existence and quality are determined by what already exists strengthen this design thinking.

The fact that architects and their 'products' – their designs and their knowledge – contribute to shaping present and future living environments can be described at the same time as a challenge, a responsibility and a privilege. Aiming in a targeted manner for the reflexive while designing describes a way of not allowing one's creativity to be inhibited when facing this immense task but instead of thinking responsibly as well as freely and developing something new. Collages can strengthen, initiate and express the reflexive in design in a variety of ways, as the examples thematised here have shown.

Lichtstimmungen regelrecht monumentalisiert.[17] Um die eigene Bedeutung als Urheber dieser Architekturen zu relativieren, setzen sie die Collagen in Ausstellungen oder Publikationen gezielt in Bezug zu ihren fotografischen und künstlerischen Referenzen. Thematische und kompositorische Anleihen werden dadurch unmittelbar deutlich (Abb.12).

RE - PRODUKTIONEN   Ihren Studierenden lehren OFFICE, dass ein derartiges Re-Produzieren das intensive Studium der Referenzen voraussetzt und auch fördern kann. So dient das Collagieren zu Semesterbeginn als eine Art Porträtieren von Bezugsobjekten, um deren architektonische Qualitäten zu analysieren. Die Studierenden sollen nicht in ein stupides Kopieren verfallen, sondern auf Grundlage der neu gewonnenen Erkenntnisse entwerfen.[18] Mit vergleichbaren Absichten verwendet Tatiana Bilbao sogenannte Referenzcollagen. Als Konzeptbilder werden diese in frühen Entwurfsphasen aus Darstellungen eigener Architekturen und Fotografien ihrer architektonischen Vorbilder zusammengeklebt.[19] Dass das Reproduzieren als eine reflexive Annäherung an das Entwerfen ebenso eigene Arbeiten umfassen kann, zeigt sich auch bei OFFICE. Die Belgier verstehen das Wiederverwenden eigener Entwurfsstrategien wie auch das Etablieren einer bürospezifischen Bildrhetorik als Spiegelbild eines vermehrt geforderten, zeit- und kostensparenden Entwerfens, das nicht in der kreativitätsarmen Wiederholung enden darf.[20] ‚Urban Refugium' nun sieht das Re-Produzieren als Möglichkeit, die Collagentechniken anderer Architekturschaffender besser zu verstehen. Darüber hinaus geht es um die Festigung der eigenen Grundkonzeption als zentrales Wissenssegment. Veröffentlichte und unveröffentlichte Collagen der Masterthesis (2015), in der die JVA Münster bereits programmatisch und gestalterisch transformiert wurde, werden hierzu überarbeitet und neu kombiniert. Es ist eine rückblickende Konfrontation mit gelungenen wie gescheitert geglaubten Darstellungen, die erkennen lässt, wie bedeutend es ist, den Blick für die vorhandenen Ressourcen zu schärfen, auch wenn diese – wie das Gefängnis oder die aussortierte Darstellung – auf den ersten Blick nutzlos erscheinen. Collagen, deren Existenz und Qualität durch das bereits Bestehende bedingt werden, bestärken eben dieses Entwurfsdenken.

Als Herausforderung, Verantwortung und Privileg zugleich kann der besondere Umstand beschrieben werden, dass Architekturschaffende mit ihren ‚Produkten' – ihren Entwürfen und ihrem Wissen – gegenwärtige wie auch zukünftige Lebenswelten mitgestalten. Das Reflexive im Entwerfen gezielt anzuvisieren, beschreibt eine Möglichkeit, um sich von dieser immensen Aufgabe in seiner Kreativität nicht hemmen zu lassen, vielmehr verantwortungsvoll, aber auch befreit zu denken und Neues zu entwickeln. Collagen können das Reflexive im Entwerfen auf vielfältige Weise verstärken, initiieren und zum Ausdruck bringen, wie die hier thematisierten Beispiele gezeigt haben.

1 On the relevance of the topic 'retreat' in architecture cf. | Zur Aktualität des Themas ‚Rückzug' in der Architektur vgl. Archithese 2(2019)/Jun-Aug: Rückzug; cf. esp. | vgl. insbesondere Jørg Himmelreich, Editorial in: ibid., 3; on the negative sides cf. | zu den negativen Seiten vgl. Eleonore Harmel et al., Ländliche Verheissung, in: ibid., 8–17   **2** Cf. | Vgl. Tom Avermaete im Gespräch mit Jørg Himmelreich, Rückzug nach innen, in: ibid. 18–27   **3** Cf. | Vgl. Katja Fennel Gefängnisarchitektur und Strafvollzugsgesetz. Anspruch und Wirklichkeit am Beispiel des hessischen Vollzugs, Würzburg: Universität Würzburg 2006   **4** Fachtagung 2. November 2015, Denkmalzukunft JVA Münster; Martin Kalitschke, Droht der JVA Münster nun der Abriss? on: | auf: https://www.wn.de/muenster/muenster-jva-abriss-denkmalschutz-2554038?pid=true, 07.04.2022   **5** Building closures in the Netherlands are due to declining crime rates and the legalization of cannabis. Cf. on this | Gebäudeschließungen in den Niederlanden sind bedingt durch eine rückläufige Zahl an Straftaten und die Legalisierung von Cannabis. Vgl. hierzu https://www.positive.news/society/the-empty-prisons-being-put-to-good-use-in-the-netherlands/, 25.07.2022; on Bijlmerbaje District cf. as well as on the following: | zum Bijlmerbaje Quartier vgl. sowie zum Folgenden: https://www.oma.com/projects/bajes-kwartier, 25.07.2022; for further conversions cf. e.g. the British School of Amsterdam by Atelier Pro on: | zu weiteren Umnutzungen vgl. z. B. die British School of Amsterdam von Atelier Pro auf: https://www.atelierpro.nl/en/projects/223/35, 25.07.2022   **6** https://www.oma.com/projects/koepel-panopticon-prison, 29.07.2022   **7** To the project cf. e.g. | Zum Projekt vgl. z. B. Rem Koolhaas et al., Exodus oder Die freiwilligen Gefangenen der Architektur, in: ARCHplus 209(2012), 32–47   **8** Cf. | Vgl. Michel Foucault, Überwachen und Strafen. Die Geburt des Gefängnisses, 17. ed., Frankfurt a. M.: Suhrkamp 1993, 183–184, 302–305   **9** Kersten Geers himself examines architectural representations and specifically collage as a form of dealing with complexity, using the example of Donato Bramante and the illustrator Saul Steinberg, among others. Cf. on this | Kersten Geers selbst untersucht Architekturdarstellungen und im Spezifischen die Collage als eine Form der Komplexitätsbewältigung u.a. am Beispiel von Donato Bramante und dem Illustrator Saul Steinberg. Vgl. hierzu Kersten Geers, Looking elsewhere, in: San Rocco 11(2015), 105–110; Kersten Geers, Everything and nothing, in: Kersten Geers, Without content, Köln: Walther König 2021, 99–104; on the importance of box-like architectures at OFFICE cf. e.g. | zur Bedeutung der kistenartigen Architekturen bei OFFICE vgl. z. B. OFFICE Kersten Geers David van Severen, Architecture without content, in: Domus, 964(2012), 1–4   **10** On the knowledge-generating potential of an artistic work that ‚frames' complex phenomena or alternatively presents them cf. | Zum erkenntnisgenerierenden Potenzial eines künstlerischen Werkes, das komplexe Phänomene ‚rahmt', bzw. alternativ dargestellt vgl. Hans-Georg Gadamer, Bildkunst und Wortkunst, in: Gottfried Boehm (ed.), Was ist ein Bild?, München: Brill | Fink 2006, 99; cf. on this also | vgl. hierzu auch Margitta Buchert, Anderswohnen, in: id./Carl Zillich (eds.), Performativ. Architektur und Kunst, Berlin: Jovis 2007, 40–49 ,48; Margitta Buchert, Reflexives Entwerfen?. Topologien eines Forschungsfeldes, in: id. (ed.), Reflexives Entwerfen, Berlin: Jovis 2004, 24–49, 45; on the frame as a central characteristic of an image cf. | zum Rahmen als zentraler Eigenart eines Bildes vgl. übergreifend Michael Polanyi, Was ist ein Bild?, in: Gottfried Boehm (2006), op. cit. (Anm. 10), 154–155   **11** Regarding the critical intentions behind the collage cf. e.g. | In Bezug auf die kritischen Intentionen hinter der Collage vgl. z.B. Petrus Schaesberg, Konzept der Collage. Paradigmenwechsel in der Entwicklung

der Collage von Pablo Picasso bis Edward Ruscha, München: LMU 2004, 206   **12** As examples the projects 'City Walls' (2005), 'Stop City' (2007) and 'Locomotiva 3' (2010) can be named. Cf. on this e.g. | Beispielhaft zu nennen sind die Projekte ‚City Walls' (2005), ‚Stop City' (2007) und ‚Locomotiva 3' (2010). Vgl. hierzu z.B. Pier Vittorio Aureli/Martino Tattara, A limit to the urban: Notes on large scale design, in: Architectural Association (ed.), Dogma: 11 Projects, London: AA Publications 2013, 42–45; ids., Is this a city?, in: Kersten Geers/David van Severen et al. (eds.), Office Kersten Geers David Van Severen, Vol. 1, Buchhandlung Walther König 2017, 61, 61; on the typology of the 'building-as-wall' cf. | zur Typologie des ‚building-as-wall' vgl. Giovanna Borasi, Hunting for the present in the past, in: ibid., 12; for a detailed analysis cf. as well | für eine ausführliche Analyse vgl. ebenso Sarah Wehmeyer, Collagen Interaktionen. Eine spezifische Form entwerfender und forschender Prozesse, in: Margitta Buchert (ed.), Prozesse Reflexiven Entwerfens, Berlin: Jovis 2018, 124–14   **13** On layer character cf. | Zum Schichtcharakter vgl. Petrus Schaesberg, Das aufgehobene Bild: Collage als Modus der Malerei von Pablo Picasso bis Richard Prince, München: Brill/Fink 2007, 199   **14** On collage as a plea for togetherness cf. | Zur Collage als Plädoyer für das Miteinander vgl. ibid.   **15** Exhibition informations, cf. on this |Ausstellungsinformationen, vgl. hierzu Tatiana Bilbao Estudio. Werkschau im Louisiana Museum, Kopenhagen, 2019; on Bilbao's view on the 'others' in design cf. | zu Bilbaos Sicht auf die ‚Anderen' im Entwerfen vgl. Brigitte Labs-Ehlert/Andrea de Meo-Arbore, Entwerfen als Prozess der Verwandlung, in: FSB (ed.), Die Architektur der Anderen, Brakel: FSB 2018, 19 and | und 31   **16** For the white area at Dogma cf. e.g. | Zur weißen Fläche bei Dogma vgl. z.B. Pier Vittorio Aureli (ed.), Architecture after liberalism: Towards the form of the European capital city, in: Pier Vittorio Aureli/Martino Tattara et al. (eds.), Brüssel: A Manifesto towards the Capital of Europe, Rotterdam: nai010 2007, 201 and | und 203; Pier Vittorio Aureli/Martino Tattara (2017), op. cit. (note | Anm. 12)   **17** For monumentalization and Ed Rusch aas a reference in this regard, cf. | Zur Monumentalisierung sowie Ed Ruscha als Referenz diesbezüglich vgl. Ellis Woodman, Tools and territory, in: Kersten Geers/David van Severen et al. (eds.), Office Kersten Geers David Van Severen, Vol. 3, Buchhandlung Walther König 2017, 11–12; on collaboration cf. | zur Zusammenarbeit vgl. z.B. Christophe Van Gerrewey, Order, disorder. Ten choices and contradictions in the work of OFFICE, in: Kersten Geers/David van Severen et al. (eds.), Office Kersten Geers David Van Severen, Vol. 2, Buchhandlung Walther König 2017, 13–14; Sarah Wehmeyer (2018), op. cit. (note | Anm. 12)   **18** On the teaching content cf. | Zu den Lehrinhalten vgl. Atelier OFFICE Kersten Geers/David van Severen/Carola Daldoss/Andrea Zanderigo, Architecture without content II. Presentation booklet, arch.usi.ch, 2011 on: | auf : https://issuu.com/brunodealmeida/docs/architecture_without_content_presen, 31.08.2021; Kersten Geers, Necessary architecture, in: Architecture without content 1–5, 4, London: Koenig Book 2015, 2   **19** Cf. | Vgl. Brigitte Labs-Ehlert/Andrea de Meo-Arbore (2018), op. cit. (note | Anm. 15) 29; Sarah Wehmeyer, Collage, in: Margitta Buchert (ed.), Entwerfen gestalten. Shaping design. Medien der Architekturkonzeption. Media of architectural conception, Berlin: jovis 2020, 202–218   **20** Their former professors Ábalos & Herreros serve as a role model for OFFICE. Cf. on this | Als Vorbild dienen OFFICE hierbei ihre ehemaligen Professoren Ábalos & Herreros. Vgl. hierzu Kersten Geers und David van Severen, March 2015, in: Giovanna Borasi (eds.), AP164: Ábalos & Herreros, Zürich: Park Books 2016, 91–92, 95; Kersten Geers/David van Severen, Industrial Architecture, in: ibid., 73

EPISTEMIC IMAGERY
IN ARCHITECTURAL RESEARCH

Tom Bieling

P R O D U C T S   A S   K N O W L E D G E   P R O D U C T I O N   Models can do (or be) a lot: they act as a reference object for what is existent or not yet existent, they serve clarification purposes, they are haptic or visual, detailed or abstract. We speak of models in connection with theoretical concepts and we are familiar with practical models in the form of architecture models. The 'model' has always been, not only for designers, a useful aid and planning means in order to cast a light on possible futures – or pasts – and make them comprehensible and tangible. In design-relevant disciplines, the model serves for example as a storage medium or as a tool for formation and concept development. It can be a tool for insights and at the same time harbours didactic and communicative potential, i.e. it can therefore serve the distribution of knowledge.[1]

The dimension of experience and comprehensibility plays a significant role in this, if one assumes that different forms of knowledge are inherent in the generated, explored, analysed artefacts. They are conveyed on their part through the artefact, which in turn requires different forms of deciphering.[2] The many design and perception practices in the context of architecture and design therefore place a focus on research that "combines aesthetic with epistemic practices and shows how sensory insight can be used as a productive way of exploring the world".[3] Because researching design and designing research generate and structure products equally and are inextricably bound up with the question of how the knowledge they are based on is created and can be brought to light, and what forms of agency are inherent in them.[4] The 'product' presents itself therefore less as something that is completed and definitive but more as something unfinished and fluid. We have known for a long time that what is known and done can only be snapshots. The most exciting dimension of the productive is therefore no doubt what is processual: the product as knowledge production.

EPISTEMISCHE BILDWELTEN
IN DER ARCHITEKTURFORSCHUNG

Tom Bieling

PRODUKTE ALS WISSENSPRODUKTION   Modelle können vieles (sein): Sie fungieren als Referenzobjekt für Bestehendes oder noch nicht Existentes, sie dienen der Veranschaulichung, sind haptisch oder visuell, detailgenau oder abstrakt. Wir sprechen von Modellen im Zusammenhang mit theoretischen Konzepten und wir kennen praktische Modelle in Form von Architekturmodellen. Das Modell ist seit jeher, nicht nur für Gestalter:innen, ein nutzenbringendes Hilfs- und Planungsmittel, um mögliche Zukünfte – oder auch Vergangenheiten – in die Gegenwart zu befördern und dort (be-)greifbar zu machen. In gestaltungsrelevanten Disziplinen dient das Modell beispielsweise als Speichermedium oder als Instrument zur Formfindung und Konzeptentwicklung. Es kann dabei Erkenntniswerkzeug sein und birgt zugleich didaktisches und kommunikatives Potenzial, kann also der Distribution von Wissen dienen.[1]

Die Dimension der Erfahrung und Begreifbarkeit spielt dabei eine wesentliche Rolle, geht man davon aus, dass in den generierten, explorierten, analysierten Artefakten unterschiedliche Formen des Wissens eingeschrieben sind. Sie werden ihrerseits durch das Artefakt vermittelt, was wiederum unterschiedliche Formen der Dechiffrierung erfordert.[2] Die vielfältigen Gestaltungs- und Perzeptionspraktiken im Kontext von Architektur und Design legen somit den Fokus auf ein Forschen, das „ästhetische mit epistemischen Praktiken vermengt und zeigt, wie sinnliche Erkenntnis als produktive Weise der Welterschließung eingesetzt werden kann".[3] Denn forschendes Entwerfen und entwerfendes Forschen generieren und strukturieren Produkte gleichermaßen und sind unweigerlich mit der Frage verbunden, wie das ihnen zugrundeliegende Wissen hergestellt und zutage befördert werden kann und welche Formen der Handlungsmacht in sie eingeschrieben sind.[4] Das Produkt stellt sich uns demnach weniger als etwas Abgeschlossenes, Definitives, sondern eher als etwas Unfertiges, Fluides dar. Längst wissen wir, dass Gewusstes und Gemachtes lediglich Momentaufnahmen sein können. Die spannendste Dimension des Produktiven ist daher sicherlich die des Prozesshaften: das Produkt als Wissensproduktion.

OTHERWORLDLINESS AND DESIGN OF URBAN IMAGINARY WORLDS
The knowledge producing component can be regarded as especially challenging and at the same time fruitful in connection with the unexplained that is difficult to grasp from a rational point of view. Aspects of mysticism, the occult, rituals or transcendency, for example. In this contribution, the 'spectral' is examined as a metaphor for urban subjectivity, recollection and history. The main focus is on the variety of potential of design and architecture, especially with regard to the overlap of image, narration, im/materiality, spectrality, history, trauma and future. The starting point is the experimental, interdisciplinary research project 'Old City, New Futures'*, a partial project of the superordinate research project 'Speculative Space'.[5] 'Old City...' is concerned with various approaches to temporal implications of the spectral and ghostly in urbanity, which not least take effect through the medium of space and are narrated and perceived in the space and therefore exist.

The old town of Sanaa, the capital of Yemen which is a UNESCO World Cultural Heritage Site, has a distinctive architectural character expressed especially by multi-storey buildings. Over the course of time, however, external factors such as civil war, water damage and rapid population growth have been strongly detrimental to the area. Restoration programmes on the one hand and ongoing threats on the other keep presenting new challenges to the evocative function of social and cultural value categories of the region.[6] In the project, this tension is examined in the form of (speculative and specific) architecture drawings and visual narratives, which take a look at the sometimes abstract, not least architectural spectral areas from the point of view of an embodiment of temporality and permanence. Based on miniatures, the story of the urban fabric is told, showing how 'space' (as a sphere of memory) and 'time' are connected to material, structural and aesthetic characteristics. There is a focus on penetrating the effect of time, as well as on developing an understanding of architectural equivalents of temporality.[7]

SOCIOCULTURAL FUNCTIONS OF THE SPECTRAL   The spectral has historically always played an important role across cultures. Its representative and sociocultural functions, meanings and effects are at least as multifaceted as its representational forms and appearance – and are to be found for example in rituals, traditions, oral traditions or urban legends.[8] They are always associated with questions of the temporal and spatial localisation of history and tradition, as well as their effects on the possibilities of social change – for example if it is about aspects of the (individual or collective) memory or trauma and their effects on sociocultural processes.[9] Especially as part of the 'Spectral Turn' of the early 1990s, ghosts, haunting and spectrality found their way into the humanities and social science, for example when it comes to a culture of remembrance in relation to

SPUK UND GESTALTUNG URBANER VORSTELLUNGSWELTEN

Als besonders herausfordernd und zugleich fruchtbar kann die wissensproduktive Komponente im Zusammenhang mit Unerklärlichem, unter rationalen Gesichtspunkten schwer Greifbarem angesehen werden. Dinge der Mystik, des Okkulten, des Rituellen oder der Transzendenz zum Beispiel. In diesem Beitrag wird das ‚Geisterhafte' als Metapher für urbane Subjektivität, Erinnerung und Geschichte untersucht. Das Hauptaugenmerk liegt dabei auf verschiedenen Potenzialen von Design und Architektur, insbesondere mit Blick auf die Schnittmenge zwischen Bild, Narration, (Im-)Materialität, Spektralität, Geschichte, Trauma und Zukunft. Ausgangspunkt ist das experimentelle, interdisziplinäre Forschungsprojekt ‚Old City, New Futures', ein Teilprojekt des übergeordneten Forschungsprojekts ‚Speculative Space'.[5] ‚Old City, …' beschäftigt sich mit verschiedenen Ansätzen zu zeitlichen Implikationen des Spektralen, Spukhaften im Urbanen, die nicht zuletzt durch das Medium Raum wirken bzw. im Raum erzählt und wahrgenommen werden und somit existieren.

Die Altstadt von Sanaa, der Hauptstadt des Jemen, die zum UNESCO-Weltkulturerbe gehört, hat einen unverwechselbaren architektonischen Charakter, der sich vor allem in ihren mehrstöckigen Gebäuden ausdrückt. Im Laufe der Zeit haben jedoch äußere Faktoren wie Bürgerkrieg, Wasserschäden und schnelles Bevölkerungswachstum das Gebiet stark beeinträchtigt. Restaurierungsprogramme auf der einen Seite und anhaltende Bedrohungen auf der anderen fordern die Erinnerungsfunktion sozialer und kultureller Wertekategorien der Region immer wieder aufs Neue heraus.[6] Im Projekt wird dieses Spannungsverhältnis in Form von (spekulativen und spezifischen) Architekturzeichnungen und visuellen Erzählungen untersucht, die die mitunter abstrakten, nicht zuletzt architektonischen Spektralbereiche aus dem Blickwinkel einer Verkörperung von Zeitlichkeit und Permanenz in Augenschein nehmen. Anhand von Miniaturen wird die Geschichte des städtischen Gefüges erzählt und gezeigt, wie Raum (als Gedächtnisraum) und Zeit mit materiellen, strukturellen und ästhetischen Merkmalen zusammenhängen. Die Wirkung von Zeit zu durchdringen, steht dabei ebenso im Fokus, wie ein Verständnis architektonischer Äquivalenzen von Zeitlichkeit zu entwickeln.[7]

SOZIOKULTURELLE FUNKTIONEN DES GEISTERHAFTEN

Das Spukhafte hat historisch und kulturübergreifend immer eine wichtige Rolle gespielt. Seine repräsentativen und soziokulturellen Funktionen, Bedeutungen und Wirkungen sind mindestens so vielfältig wie seine Repräsentations- und Erscheinungsformen – und finden sich etwa in Ritualen, Traditionen, mündlichen Überlieferungen oder urbanen Legenden.[8] Sie sind dabei stets verbunden mit Fragen der zeitlichen und räumlichen Verortung von Geschichte und Tradition sowie deren Auswirkungen auf die Möglichkeiten eines sozialen Wandels – etwa wenn es um Aspekte des (individuellen oder kollektiven) Gedächtnisses

1 | Old City, New Futures 2021

the fleetingness of spaces and places. It is especially about considering cultural ways of interpretation of and assignments of meaning to the spectral that go "beyond the confines of the fictional and supernatural".[10] No doubt it is less about the paraphenomenal here and certainly not about the question of whether ghosts (really) exist, but more about aspects such as the consequences of suppression, of exclusion and 'othering' (such as in visual and narrative figures such as the witch, the alien, the monster).[11] As much as one would like to forget them, the 'ghosts' and 'spirits' are evidently called to mind all the more.[12] One of the central questions in this context: what does it mean to live with spirits? The ghost populates large parts of popular culture in a variety of figurations, emerges as a figure (of thought) in theoretical and artistic discourses and acts as a cypher of the socio-politically imaginary. This includes political as well as ethical and aesthetic potential.

To quote Maria Del Pilar Blanco and Esther Peeren: "The representational and socio-cultural functions, meanings, and effects (of ghosts and spectres) have been at least as manifold as their shapes – or non-shapes, as the case may be – and extend far beyond the rituals, traditions, ghost stories, folktales, and urban legends they populate."[13] Avery F. Gordon establishes in this regard that the ghost is "not simply a dead or missing person, but a social figure, and investigating it can lead to that dense site where history and subjectivity make social life."[14] 'Spectrality' can therefore be seen as a sociocultural phenomenon. Further central questions within the various areas of urban theory and practice can therefore be: how can architects identify, take up and address the phantom-like and ghostly; how do 'spectrality' and the uncanny transform or way of materialising futures, and how does this address questions of memory and responsibility in urban development?[15]

KEEPING IT (UN)REAL   Within and beyond research, we are sometimes moving in spheres that do not appear to be rationally explainable in a scientific sense. It is also possible that we are confronted with questions that are not asked by science, let alone answered. Precisely this could be a starting point for speculative architecture

oder ebensolcher Traumata und deren Auswirkungen auf soziokulturelle Prozesse geht.[9] Insbesondere im Zuge des ‚Spectral Turn‘ der frühen 1990er Jahre fanden Geister, Spuk und Spektralität Eingang in die Geistes- und Sozialwissenschaften, etwa in Bezug auf die Flüchtigkeit von Räumen und Orten, den Umgang mit Erinnerungskultur. Es geht dabei insbesondere um die Auseinandersetzung mit kulturellen Deutungsweisen und Bedeutungs-zuschreibungen des Spektralen, die „über die Grenzen des Fiktionalen und Übernatürlichen" hinausgehen.[10] Zweifellos geht es hier weniger um Paraphänomenales und schon gar nicht um die Frage, ob es Geister (wirklich) gibt, sondern vielmehr um Aspekte wie die Folgen von Verdrängung, von Ausgrenzung und ‚Othering‘ (etwa in visuellen und narrativen Figuren wie der Hexe, dem Alien, dem Monster).[11] So sehr man sie auch vergessen möchte, so sehr rufen sich die ‚Geister‘ und ‚Gespenster‘ offensichtlich in Erinnerung.[12] Eine der zentralen Fragen in diesem Zusammenhang: Was bedeutet es, mit Geistern zu leben? Das Gespenst bevöl-kert in vielfältigen Figurationen weite Teile der Populärkultur, taucht als (Denk-)Figur in theoretischen und künstlerischen Diskursen auf und fungiert als Chiffre des sozio-politisch Imaginären. Dies schließt sowohl politische als auch ethische und ästhetische Potenziale ein.

Um Maria Del Pilar Blanco und Esther Peeren zu zitieren: „Die repräsentativen und sozio-kulturellen Funktionen, Bedeutungen und Wirkungen (von Geistern und Gespenstern) sind mindestens so vielfältig wie ihre Formen – oder Nicht-Formen, je nachdem – und reichen weit über die Rituale, Traditionen, Geistergeschichten, Volksmärchen und urbane Legen-den hinaus, die sie bevölkern."[13] Avery F. Gordon stellt in diesem Zusammenhang fest, dass das Gespenst „nicht einfach eine tote oder vermisste Person, sondern eine soziale Figur [ist], deren Erforschung zu jenem dichten Ort führen kann, an dem Geschichte und Subjektivität das soziale Leben ausmachen."[14] Das Geisterhafte kann somit als ein soziokulturelles Phänomen betrachtet werden. Weitere zentrale Fragen innerhalb der ver-schiedenen Bereiche urbaner Theorie und Praxis könnten demnach lauten: Wie können Architekt:innen verschiedene Aspekte (und Effekte) des Phantomhaften und Gespens-tischen identifizieren, aufgreifen und adressieren? Wie transformieren ‚Spektralität‘ und das Unheimliche unsere Art und Weise, Zukünfte zu materialisieren? Und wie werden dadurch Fragen der Erinnerung und Verantwortung in der Stadtentwicklung angesprochen?[15]

(UN-)REALISTISCH BLEIBEN Dies- und jenseits der Forschung bewegen wir uns mitunter in Teilbereichen, die im wissenschaftlichen Sinne nicht rational erklärbar zu sein scheinen. Es ist auch möglich, dass wir mit Fragen konfrontiert werden, die von der Wissenschaft nicht gestellt, geschweige denn beantwortet werden. Genau das könnte ein Ansatzpunkt für spekulative Architektur innerhalb der Architekturforschung sein. Denn beide Ansätze haben das Potenzial, das Unverständliche verständlich und das Nicht-Existierende

within architectural research. Because both approaches have the potential to make the incomprehensible comprehensible and the non-existent tangible. In light of this, architecture and research make use of many techniques. For example, those of language, visualisation or materialisation (e.g. in the sense of prototyping). The boundary between thing and medium appears to be fluid: "We recognise our environment in some way. But not everything that surrounds is equivalent in this recognition. We not only recognise things [...] but we also often recognise a thing through something else...".[16] A fictional architectural practice therefore reveals the actual character of architecture: one can only speculate by withdrawing from the truth.[17] A paradox that Gerald Murnane could not have described more accurately: "Wanting to understand how the so-called actual and the so-called possible (what one did and what one only dreamt of doing) finally come to be indistinguishable in the sort of text that we call true fiction".[18]

(UN)KNOWING AND FICTION   From a strictly scientific point of view, the term 'fiction' is often associated with a connotation of the unserious. The self-understanding of many fields of science is based on the assumption that science is actually the opposite of speculation – an assumption that is not to be discussed further here.[19] But what architects do is in most cases somehow related to 'the future' and is therefore almost always speculative. Vilém Flusser's 'Philosophical Fiction' makes it clear that we, in order to be able to think about the world at all, have to invent it or try to reconstruct it with the help of various fictions. Science and architecture are also localised in this complex.[20]

Parallels can be found in the 'SF' approach developed by Donna Haraway.[21] According to this, thinking is constituted like a string game that links fiction and facts, invents new stories with open endings that can be linked further. Speculative architecture has a methodical set of tools with which alternative models and forms of knowledge can be explored and potentially legitimised, by creating worlds that are not or not yet based on socially normalised 'truths'. A form of trying out, sketching, prototyping, exploring and communicating ideas that allows us to "bridge imagination and materialisation by modelling, making things and telling stories through objects that are now, in a very real sense, actual objects of conversation".[22] In relation to this, SF stands both for Science Fiction and for Science Fact, for Speculative Feminism or for string games that connect various elements loosely together as points.

MATERIALISED METAPHORS   The term research occasionally appears diffuse in the context of architecture. The question arises as to which original methods of knowledge generation can be developed and applied in the architectural subdisciplines – and more importantly, out of them. This is not necessarily made easier by the fact that we work in areas there in which the subjective merges with the objective, the implicit with the explicit and the speculative with evidence-based and fact-based, "scientifically validated" knowledge. Even so, it is especially at this crossroads that possibly new, hybrid

SANA'A

YEMEN

With its architecture belonging to various cultures and periods, it bears the traces of many societies since its establishment.

II

The city of Sana'a is the capital of Yemen. Sana'a served as an urban center for the tribes around the region and a core of regional trade in southern Arabia.

I

III The civil war in 1969 and the proclamation of the newly established Republic of Yemen as the capital were the events that dealt the first blow to the architectural texture of Sana'a.

IV There was a rapid population growth in Sana'a, which was declared the capital city, and the people of Sana'a could not afford the maintenance of their buildings.

V Airstrikes by Saudi Arabia on the historical city in 2015 and 2016 caused serious damage to this world cultural heritage site.

VI With the disasters hunger, thirst and epidemic diseases started.

VII Many historical buildings were seriously damaged due to floods and storms that lasted for months in 2020.

2 | Sanaa External factors 2022

greifbar zu machen. Vor diesem Hintergrund bedienen sich Architektur und Forschung einer Vielzahl von Techniken, zum Beispiel der der Sprache, der Visualisierung oder der Materialisierung (z.B. im Sinne von Prototyping). Die Grenze zwischen Ding und Medium scheint fließend: „Wir erkennen unsere Umwelt in irgendeiner Weise. Aber nicht alles, was uns umgibt, ist für diese Erkenntnis gleichwertig. Wir erkennen nicht nur Dinge [...], sondern wir erkennen ein Ding oft auch durch etwas anderes [...]".[16] Eine fiktive architektonische Praxis entlarvt damit den eigentlichen Charakter der Architektur: Man kann nur spekulieren, indem man sich der Wahrheit entzieht.[17] Ein Paradox, das Gerald Murnane nicht treffender hätte beschreiben können: „Verstehen wollen, wie das sogenannte Tatsächliche und das sogenannte Mögliche (das, was man getan hat und das, wovon man nur geträumt hat) in der Art von Text, die wir True Fiction nennen, schließlich ununterscheidbar werden".[18]

(UN-)WISSEN UND FIKTION Aus streng wissenschaftlicher Sicht ist der Begriff Fiktion oft mit einer Konnotation des Unseriösen verbunden. Das Selbstverständnis vieler Wissenschaftsbereiche beruht auf der Annahme, dass Wissenschaft eigentlich das Gegenteil von Spekulation ist – eine Annahme, die hier nicht weiter diskutiert werden soll.[19] Doch das, was Architekt:innen tun, ist in den meisten Fällen irgendwie auf ‚die Zukunft' bezogen und damit fast immer spekulativ. Vilém Flussers ‚Philosophische Fiktion' macht deutlich, dass wir, um überhaupt über die Welt nachdenken zu können, sie erfinden oder mithilfe verschiedener Fiktionen zu rekonstruieren versuchen müssen. Auch die Wissenschaft und die Architektur sind in diesem Komplex angesiedelt.[20]

229

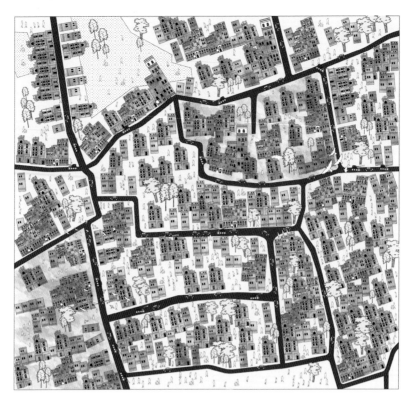

3 | Miniatures of the urban fabric Sanaa 2021

forms of knowledge emerge, which feed especially off the experience in the architectural creation process ('architects') and in the usage, appropriation and experience process ('recipients') and the dialogue between both.[23] The starting point of the project 'Old City, New Futures' is to not only reflect on this and transfer it into a discourse but also to actively fill it with life through practice-oriented debates in architectural research. The project itself is embedded in a collaborative, practice-oriented process that aims to study local and regional perspectives with a view to the correlation between history, the present and the future in inhabited space. As a materialised metaphor, the architectural drawings symbolise the observation that the self-image of a society is both negotiated by means of symbolic spaces and performatively expressed in symbolic spaces. It is therefore an attempt to develop an understanding of places as places of knowledge and spaces as spaces of negotiation.[24]

COLLECTIVE MIND AND MEMORIES   A series of 'collages' deals with a wide spectrum of events in Sanaa, which has found it difficult to recover from one disaster after another. They thematise, for example, that the buildings of the old town architecture are gradually disappearing due to disasters such as air raids, civil wars and floods (fig. 1). The urban fabric and the 'spirit' of the city are influenced by the events experienced over the course of time and take their place in collective memory. Evidently, the architecture of a city cannot be reduced just to buildings. Instead, the people in the city,

Parallelen finden sich in dem von Donna Haraway entwickelten ‚SF'-Ansatz.[21] Demnach sei das Denken wie ein Fadenspiel konstituiert, das Fiktion mit Fakten verbindet, neue Geschichten mit offenen Enden erfindet, die weiter verbunden werden können. Die spekulative Architektur verfügt über ein methodisches Instrumentarium, mit dem alternative Modelle und Wissensformen erforscht und potenziell legitimiert werden können, indem Welten geschaffen werden, die nicht oder noch nicht auf gesellschaftlich normierten Wahrheiten beruhen; eine Form des Ausprobierens, Skizzierens, Prototypisierens, Erforschens und Kommunizierens von Ideen, die es uns ermöglicht, „eine Brücke zwischen Vorstellungskraft und Materialisierung zu schlagen, indem wir Dinge modellieren, herstellen und Geschichten mithilfe von Objekten erzählen, die nun in einem sehr realen Sinne tatsächliche Gesprächsgegenstände sind".[22] SF steht in diesem Zusammenhang sowohl für Science Fiction als auch für Science Fact, für spekulativen Feminismus oder für Fadenspiele, die verschiedene Elemente als Punkte lose miteinander verbinden.

MATERIALISIERTE METAPHERN   Der Begriff Forschung erscheint im Zusammenhang mit Architektur streckenweise diffus. Es stellt sich die Frage, welche originären Methoden der Wissensgenerierung in den architektonischen Teildisziplinen – und vor allem: aus ihnen heraus – entwickelt und angewendet werden können. Dies wird nicht unbedingt dadurch erleichtert, dass wir dort in Bereichen arbeiten, in denen das Subjektive mit dem Objektiven, das Implizite mit dem Expliziten und das Spekulative mit evidenz- und faktenbasiertem, ‚wissenschaftlich validiertem' Wissen verschmolzen wird. Dennoch entstehen gerade an dieser Schnittstelle möglicherweise neue, hybride Wissensformen, die sich vor allem aus der Erfahrung im architektonischen Entstehungsprozess (‚Architekt:innen') und im Nutzungs-, Aneignungs- und Erfahrungsprozess (‚Rezipient:innen') sowie aus dem Dialog zwischen beiden speisen.[23] Dies nicht nur zu reflektieren und in einen Diskurs zu überführen, sondern ihn durch praxisorientierte Debatten in der Architekturforschung aktiv mit Leben zu füllen, ist der Ausgangspunkt des Projekts ‚Old City, new Futures'. Das Projekt selbst ist eingebettet in einen kollaborativen, praxisorientierten Prozess, der darauf abzielt, lokale und regionale Perspektiven mit Blick auf den Zusammenhang von Geschichte, Gegenwart und Zukunft des gelebten Raums zu untersuchen. Als materialisierte Metapher symbolisieren die architektonischen Zeichnungen die Beobachtung, dass das Selbstbild einer Gesellschaft sowohl mittels symbolischer Räume verhandelt als auch in symbolischen Räumen performativ zur Geltung kommt. Es handelt sich also um einen Versuch, ein Verständnis von Orten als Orten des Wissens und von Räumen als Räumen der Verhandlung zu entwickeln.[24]

KOLLEKTIVES GEDÄCHTNIS   Eine Serie von ‚Collagen' befasst sich mit einem breiten Spektrum an Ereignissen in Sanaa, das sich von aufeinanderfolgenden Katastrophen mitunter nur schwer erholen konnte. Thematisiert wird unter anderem, dass die Gebäude der Altstadtarchitektur durch Katastrophen wie Luftangriffe, Bürgerkriege

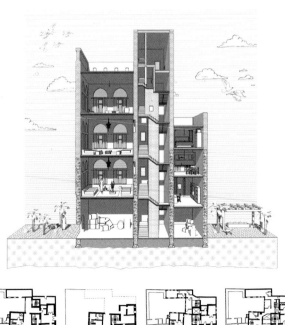

4a | Place and identity: support and sustain vs. change and transform Traditional house section with spaces and materials

the socio-cultural dynamics, the vegetation, the animals and the climate together form the texture and the spirit of the city.[25] These characteristics are also included in the image series and worked on to show how closely they are connected and, in some cases, reinforce each other. At the centre of a chronological table there is a collage by means of which the history of Sanaa is told according to certain key moments. The strategically important location of the city, especially for trade, is also expressed by the characteristic architecture that has developed in accordance with the particularities of the region. After a period of growth, the city is experiencing decline due to various events that have occurred over time (fig. 2). Furthermore, a series of miniatures tells the story of Sanaa's urban fabric, which reflects the city-specific structure, with its multi-storey residences, material-related characteristics such as façade types, the use of bricks, clay and stone, as well as a specific local colour aesthetic. Catastrophic events such as floods and their effect on population growth are also taken up. Positive and negative incidents are manifested equally in the collective memory of the city and therefore also in the miniatures (fig. 3). As the art historian Tolga Degerlier establishes, cities do not only exist primarily for people, but people keep these cities alive.[26] In everyday life in the city of Sanaa, this collective effect contributes to creating and preserving memories, which manifest not least in the (urban and social) architecture. The identity of a place is therefore formed through the associated, furthered and maintained memories.[27] Both influence each other mutually

4b | Place and identity: support and sustain vs. change and transform Traditional house plan typology example

und Überschwemmungen nach und nach verschwinden (Abb. 1). Das Stadtgefüge und der ‚Geist' der Stadt werden durch die im Laufe der Zeit erlebten Ereignisse beeinflusst und nehmen ihren Platz im kollektiven Gedächtnis ein. Offensichtlich lässt sich die Architektur einer Stadt nicht nur auf Gebäude reduzieren. Vielmehr bilden die Menschen in der Stadt, die soziokulturelle Dynamik, die Vegetation, die Tiere und das Klima zusammen die Textur und den Geist der Stadt.[25] Diese Merkmale werden ebenfalls in die Bildserie aufgenommen und verarbeitet, um zu verdeutlichen, wie sehr sie miteinander in Verbindung stehen und sich teils gegenseitig verstärken. Im Zentrum einer Zeittafel steht eine Collage, anhand derer die Geschichte von Sanaa entlang bestimmter Bruchstellen erzählt wird. Die strategisch wichtige Lage der Stadt, insbesondere für den Handel, drückt sich auch durch die charakteristische Architektur aus, die sich entsprechend den Merkmalen der Region entwickelt hat. Nach einer Periode des Wachstums erlebt die Stadt einen Niedergang aufgrund verschiedener Ereignisse, die im Laufe der Zeit stattgefunden haben (Abb. 2). Darüber hinaus erzählt eine Reihe an Miniaturen die Geschichte des städtischen Gefüges Sanaas, in denen die stadtspezifische Struktur, mit ihren mehrstöckigen Wohnungen, materialbezogenen Merkmalen wie Fassadentypen, die Verwendung von Ziegeln, Lehm und Stein sowie eine ortsspezifische Farbästhetik, verarbeitet wird. Auch katastrophale Gegebenheiten wie Überschwemmungen und deren Auswirkungen auf die Bevölkerungszunahme werden dabei aufgegriffen. Positive wie negative Ereignisse manifestieren sich

5 | Past, present and future: Evolution of architectural structures in Sanaa over time 2022

and help to support and preserve society and culture, as well as to change and transform them (fig. 4). Further works of this project are concerned with the development of architectural structures (fig. 5), the handling of the collective spirit and memories (fig. 6) and the existence of 'physical things' (fig. 7).

DECONSTRUCTIVE AND PROJECTIVE (POWER OF) IMAGINATION

Architecture, even in its early form – the sketch, the image, the model – negotiates society. It thereby creates an independent knowledge genre that can influence this society to a greater or lesser degree. Complementarily to science, it thereby enables access to knowledge that is conveyed not only through facts but for example also through speculation, provocation, association or aesthetic reflection. Its capability for epistemic speculation is one of the fields that has not yet been adequately investigated.[28] The research and experimentation with various approaches to temporal implications of the 'spectral' essence of a city and its effects through the medium of space is a very promising field for providing a contribution to this. Speculative practice both in research and in architecture can be roughly divided into two types: deconstructive and projective imagination.[29] The former could be referred to as a practice that deconstructs real contexts and reconfigures them. The latter imagines an alternative reality and produces knowledge through the aesthetic

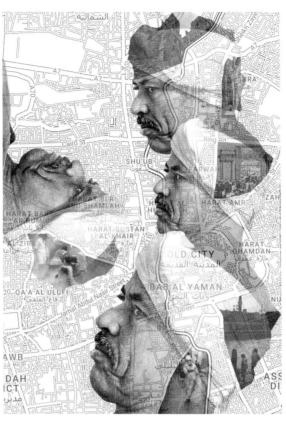

6 | Collective mind and memories: Plan, structure and events belonging to Sanaa are permanently present 2022

gleichermaßen im kollektiven Gedächtnis der Stadt, und somit auch in den Miniaturen (Abb. 3). Wie der Kunsthistoriker Tolga Degerlier feststellt, existieren Städte nicht nur vorrangig für Menschen, sondern Menschen halten diese Städte am Leben.[26] Im täglichen Leben in der Stadt Sanaa trägt diese kollektive Wirksamkeit dazu bei, Erinnerung zu schaffen und zu bewahren, die sich nicht zuletzt in der (städtischen wie gesellschaftlichen) Architektur manifestiert. Die Identität eines Ortes wird somit durch die damit verbundenen, weitergetragenen und aufrechterhaltenen Erinnerungen gebildet.[27] Beides beeinflusst sich gegenseitig und trägt dazu bei, Gesellschaft und Kultur zu stützen und zu erhalten bzw. zu verändern und zu transformieren (Abb. 4). Weitere Arbeiten dieses Projekts befassen sich mit der Entwicklung architektonischer Strukturen (Abb. 5), dem Umgang mit kollektivem Geist und Erinnerungen (Abb. 6) und der Existenz ‚psychischer Dinge' (Abb. 7).

DEKONSTRUKTIVE UND PROJEKTIVE VORSTELLUNGSKRAFT
Architektur, selbst in ihrer frühen Form – der Skizze, dem Bild, dem Modell –, verhandelt Gesellschaft. Dabei schafft sie eine eigenständige Wissensgattung, die diese Gesellschaft mehr oder weniger stark beeinflussen kann. Komplementär zur Wissenschaft ermöglicht sie damit einen Zugang zu Wissen, das nicht nur durch Fakten, sondern beispielsweise auch durch Spekulation, Provokation, Assoziation oder ästhetische Reflexion vermittelt wird.

235

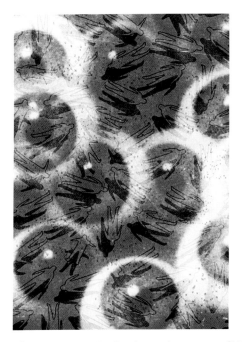

7 | 'Recognising psychic things from the expressive movements .... (Heider 2021)', 2022

operation of changing reality.[30] Critical-speculative, architectural practice meets the speculative forms of philosophical world development here. One might think of Slavoj Žižek's Lacanian "Philosophy of the real as absent, non-existent" and what Mark Llewllyn calls the "impact this has on our rereading and re-visioning of the past through fiction, itself in some ways a non-real construct".[31] "The past is forever a reflection that our individual human future is not limitless, and in that sense ensures that our return to history and our belief in something beyond the here and now are indivisibly linked within the imagination."[32]

RÉSUMÉ   For architectural research (but also beyond it), there are remarkable overlaps of an idea of the spectral with aspects of the temporal and spatial, which can be traced with regard to the existence and development of present-day cities and which we refer to in this project as epistemic images.[33] Forms of visualisation like in the project "Old City, ..." take on a special role in knowledge production in an architectural context. The questions of which visualisations produce new knowledge, which reproduce old knowledge and which epistemic power is generated from the associated images and things are significant for discourse within and beyond architecture research.[34] Because one can gain insights not only from realistic and depicting but also from speculative images by understanding them in a "specific way as true".[35] In doing so, they can help to identify and understand certain facts and contexts within the realm of the ghost and the phantom – or at least to imagine them.

Ihre Fähigkeit zur epistemischen Spekulation ist eines der noch nicht ausreichend erforschten Felder.[28] Die Erforschung und das Experimentieren mit verschiedenen Ansätzen zu zeitlichen Implikationen der ‚geisterhaften' Beschaffenheit einer Stadt und ihrer Auswirkungen durch das Medium des Raums ist ein vielversprechendes Feld, um einen Beitrag dazu zu leisten.

Die spekulative Praxis sowohl in der Forschung als auch in der Architektur lässt sich dabei grob in zwei Typen einteilen: dekonstruktive und projektive Imagination.[29] Erstere könnte man als eine Praxis bezeichnen, die reale Zusammenhänge demontiert und neu konfiguriert. Letztere imaginiert eine alternative Realität und produziert Wissen durch die ästhetische Operation der Realitätsveränderung.[30] Die kritisch-spekulative, architektonische Praxis trifft hier auf die spekulativen Formen der philosophischen Weltentwicklung. Man könnte an Slavoj Žižeks Lacan'sche „Philosophie des Realen als abwesend, nicht existent" denken und an das, was Mark Llewllyn als die Auswirkungen bezeichnet, die dies auf unser Wiederlesen und die Neupräsentation der Vergangenheit durch Fiktion hat, die selbst in gewisser Weise ein nicht reales Konstrukt sei.[31] Die Vergangenheit, nach Llewlyn, ist immer auch eine Reflexion darüber, dass unsere individuelle menschliche Zukunft nicht grenzenlos ist, und stellt in diesem Sinne sicher, dass unsere Rückkehr zur Geschichte und unser Glaube an etwas jenseits des Hier und Jetzt in der Imagination untrennbar miteinander verbunden sind.[32]

RESÜMEE   Für die Architekturforschung (aber auch darüber hinaus) zeichnen sich bemerkenswerte Überschneidungen einer Idee des Geisterhaften mit Aspekten des Zeitlichen und des Räumlichen ab, die sich im Hinblick auf die Existenz und Entwicklung heutiger Städte verfolgen lassen und die wir in diesem Projekt als epistemische Bilder bezeichnen.[33] Formen der Visualisierung wie im Projekt ‚Old City, ...' nehmen eine besondere Rolle bei der Wissensproduktion im architektonischen Kontext ein. Die Fragen, welche Visualisierungen neues Wissen produzieren, welche altes Wissen reproduzieren und welche epistemische Kraft von den damit verbundenen Bildern und Dingen ausgeht, sind für den Diskurs diesseits und jenseits der Architekturforschung von Bedeutung.[34] Denn nicht nur aus realistischen, abbildenden, sondern auch aus spekulativen Bildern lassen sich Erkenntnisse gewinnen, indem man sie in einer „spezifischen Weise als wahr" versteht.[35] Dabei können sie helfen, bestimmte Sachverhalte und Zusammenhänge im Bereich des Gespenstischen und des Phantomhaften zu erkennen und zu verstehen – zumindest aber: zu imaginieren.

* Old city, new futures is part of the three-year research project ‚Speculative space' funded by the City of Hamburg, located at the Center for Design Research at HAW Hamburg http://speclog.xyz. I would like to thank my project partner Emine Yorganci for the fruitful collaboration on the Sanaa studies, especially with regard to the visual material. | Old city, new futures ist Teil des von der Stadt Hamburg geförderten dreijährigen Forschungsprojekts ‚Speculative Space', angesiedelt am Zentrum für Designforschung der HAW Hamburg http://speclog.xyz. Ich danke meiner Projektpartnerin Emine Yorganci für die fruchtbare Zusammenarbeit im Rahmen der Sanaa-Studien, insbesondere im Hinblick auf das Bildmaterial.

1 Cf. | Vgl. Andres Janser/Tom Bieling, Die Welt als Modell: Über Modelle als epistemische Praxis. DESIGNABILITIES Design Research Journal, 07 (2016), on: | auf: https://designabilities.files.wordpress.com/2016/07/dsgnblts_andresjanser_u_tombieling_dieweltalsmodell_.pdf, 20.9.2022 **2** Cf. | Vgl. Marion Godau/Tom Bieling, Undergraduate research in design, in: Harald Mieg et al. (eds.), Cambridge handbook on undergraduate research, Cambridge, UK: Cambridge University Press 2021 **3** Melanie Franke/Alain Gloor, Kunst & Wissen. Narrative Strategien als epistemologische Mittel in den ästhetischen Praktiken der Gegenwartskunst. in: Flavia Caviezel/Beate Florenz/Melanie Franke/Jörg Wiesel (eds.), Forschungsskizzen. Einblicke in Forschungspraktiken der Hochschule für Gestaltung und Kunst FHNW, Köln: Lehmanns Media 2013, 21–29 **4** Cf. | Vgl. Margitta Buchert (ed.), Produkte | Products – Design and Research in Architecture and Landscape. Reader of the 11th Symposium and PhD Peer Review on Design and Research in Architecture and Landscape (online), 21.–23. April 2022, organized at a_ku | Fakultät für Architektur und Landschaft, Leibniz Universität Hannover 2022 **5** htpps://speclog.xyz, 23.9.2022 **6** Cf. | Vgl. Wael Al-Ahnomi, The old city of Sana'a: A living history under threat – Sana'a Center for Strategic Studies, on: | auf: https://sanaacenter.org/publications/main-publications/14892, 14.11.2021; Ali Mohammed Amer, Providing educational needs to the old city of Sana'a according to the concept of sustainable conservation. Journal of the Arab American University, 2(2016) 2; Michele Lamprakos, Building a World Heritage city. Sana'a, Yemen. Heritage, culture and identity. London/New York: Routledge/Taylor & Francis 2015, 101; Robert Lewcock, The Old City of Sana'a, in: Ahmet Evin (ed.), Development and urban metamorphosis, Volume 1, Yemen at the Cross-Roads, Singapore: Concept Media/Aga Khan Award for Architecture 1983, 71–80; Mohammed Abdulaziz Saad Yusr, The cultural heritage of old Sana'a. Sana'a: Sana'a University 2013, 56–57 **7** Yüksel Burçin Nur, Temporality in architecture. Hagia Sophia, Yıldız Technical University/Graduate School of Science and Engineering/Architecture Main Science/Architectural Design Science 2017 **8** Cf. | Vgl. Maria del Pilar Blanco/Esther Peeren (eds.), Popular ghosts. The haunted spaces of everyday culture, in: Journal of the Fantastic in the Arts Vol. 22, 3(2011), 418–421 **9** Ibid. **10** Maria del Pilar Blanco/Esther Peeren (eds.), The Spectralities Reader: Ghosts and haunting in contemporary Cultural Theory, London: Bloomsbury, 2013 **11** Cf. | Vgl. John Pile, 12 spectral cities: Where the repressed returns, in: Jean Hillier/Emma Rooksby (eds.), Habitus: A sense of place, Milton Park, UK: Routledge/Taylor & Francis 2005; Hanne Loreck, Das Seltsame und Geister (in) der Kunst und Wissenschaft. Lehrveranstaltung, Summer Semester 2021, HFBK Hochschule für bildende Künste Hamburg 2021 **12** Ibid. **13** Maria del Pilar Blanco/Esther Peeren (eds.) (2013), op. cit. (note | Anm. 9), 1–3 **14** Avery F. Gordon, Ghostly matters: Haunting and the Sociological Imagination, Minneapolis: University of Minnesota Press, 2008; cf. | vgl. Caroline Herbert, National Hauntings: Specters of Socialism in Shree 4202 and Deewar, in: Maria del Pilar Blanco/Esther Peeren (eds.), (2010), op. cit. (note |Anm. 8), 79 **15** Cf. | Vgl. Julian Wolfreys, Victorian hauntings. Spectrality, gothic, the uncanny and literature, London: Red Globe 2001 **16** Fritz Heider, Ding und Medium,

Berlin: Kadmos 1921, Translation | Übersetzung: Tom Bieling   **17** Cf. | Vgl. Craig Bremner, A fictional theory of design[ing], in: Paul A. Rodgers/Craig Bremner (eds.), 118 Theories of designing, Wilmington et al.: Vernon 2021, 235   **18** Cf. | Vgl. Gerald Murnane, A Million Windows. Sydney: Giramondo 2014, 140   **19** Cf. | Vgl. Tom Bieling (2022), Das Zeug zur Erkenntnis. Forschung durch Spekulatives Design, in: Konstellationen. Wissensansprüche zwischen Kunst, Philosophie und Politik, Tübingen (In press | In Druck)   **20** Cf. | Vgl. Tom Bieling, Experiment und Versprechen. Über die Entgrenzung des Denkens, in: Flusser Studies 33(2022) on: | auf: https://www.flusserstudies.net/sites/www. flusserstudies.net/files/media/attachments/bieling-experiment-versprechen.pdf, 20.9.2022   **21** Cf. | Vgl. Donna Haraway, Staying with the trouble. Making Kin in the Chthulucene. Experimental futures, Durham, NC: Duke University Press 2016   **22** Cf. | Vgl. ibid., 250   **23** Cf. | Vgl. Tom Bieling, Fact and fiction. Design as a search for reality on the circuit of lies, in: Flusser Studies 29(2020), on: | auf: https://www.flusserstudies.net/sites/www.flusserstudies.net/files/ media/attachments/bieling-fact-fiction.pdf, 20.9.2022   **24** Cf. | Vgl. Tom Bieling/Frieder Bohaumilitzky/Torben Körschkes/Anke Haarmann, Design of unrest. Right-wing metapolitics – paralogy – knowledge spaces – chaos. Attending (to) futures. Film 2021; ids., Designing Unrest, in: INTERACTIONS – Design and Democracy, Nov/Dez 2021, New York, NY: ACM 2021; ids., Design of unrest: Right-wing metapolitics – paralogy – knowledge spaces – chaos, in: ATTENDING [TO] FUTURES – Matters of Politics in Design, Education, Research, Practice, Hamburg: Adocs 2022   **25** Degerlier, Tolga (2021): Sehirlerin Mimarisi: San'a (Architektur der Städte / Architecture of Cities: Sana'a) on |auf: https://medium.com/ t%C3%BCrkiye/%C5%9Fehirlerin-mimarisi-sana-68e475f18a2f, 21.9.2022   **26** Ibid.   **27** Hatice Ayataç, Culture, space and memory working group programme, on: | auf: https://kentarastirmalari.org/culture-space-and-memory/, 1.3.2022   **28** Anke Haarmann, Epistemische Spekulation, 2020, on: | auf: http://speclog.xyz/posts/epistemische-spekulation, 21.11.2021   **29** Anke Haarmann (2018), Spekulative Imagination. Learning from design, Kongress: „Das ist Ästhetik!" X. Kongress der Deutschen Gesellschaft für Ästhetik (Lecture | Vortrag 17.2.2018) Offenbach a. M.: Hochschule für Gestaltung   **30** Ibid.   **31** Cf. | Vgl. Slavoj Žižek, Troubles with the Real: Lacan as a viewer of alien. How to read Lacan, New York, NY: W. W. Norton & Company 2007, 66   **32** Mark Llewellyn, Spectrality, s(p)ecularity, and textuality. Or, some reflections in the glass, in: Rosario Arias/Patricia Pulham (eds.), Haunting and spectrality in Neo-Victorian fiction, Basingstoke: Palgrave MacMillan 2009, 23–43   **33** Cf. | Vgl. Alexander Marr/Christopher P. Heuer, The uncertainty of epistemic images, 2020, in: 21: Inquiries into art, history, and the visual. Beiträge zur Kunstgeschichte und visuellen Kultur, 2(2020), 251-255; Birgit Schneider/Horst Bredekamp/Vera Dünkel (eds.), Das Technische Bild: Kompendium zu einer Stilgeschichte wissenschaftlicher Bilde, Berlin: De Gruyter/Akademie 2012   **34** Cf. on ,images' | Vgl. zu ,Bilder': Horst Bredekamp/Gabriele Werner, Bildwelten des Wissens: Bilder in Prozessen, Berlin: De Gruyter/Akademie 2003, passim; Olaf Breidbach, Bilder des Wissens. Zur Kulturgeschichte der wissenschaftlichen Wahrnehmung, Paderborn: Wilhelm Fink 2005; Nora S. Vaage/Rasmus T. Slaattelid/Trine Krigsvoll Haagensen/Samantha L. Smith (eds.), Images of knowledge. The epistemic lives of pictures and visualisations, Lausanne: PL Academic Research 2016, passim; and on 'things' | und zu ,Dingen'Hans-Jörg Rheinberger, Toward a history of epistemic things, Stanford: Stanford University Press 1997, passim   **35** Cf. | Vgl. Tom Bieling, Fact and Fiction. Design as a search for reality on the circuit of lies, in: Flusser studies 29(2020), on: | auf: http://www.flusserstudies.net/sites/www.flusserstudies.net/files/media/attachments/bieling-fact-fiction.pdf, 11.8.2020; Rolf F. Nohr, Nützliche Bilder. Bild, Diskurs, Evidenz, Münster: Lit Verlag 2014, 15

"And someplace lions still walk, and know, as long as they are glorious,

of no powerlessness."

„Und irgendwo gehn Löwen noch, und wissen, solang sie herrlich sind,

von keiner Ohnmacht."

Rainer Maria Rilke

APPENDIX

BIOGRAFIEN BIOGRAPHIES

MARGITTA BUCHERT ist Professorin für ‚Architektur und Kunst 20. und 21. Jahrhundert'
an der Fakultät für Architektur und Landschaft der Leibniz Universität Hannover. Ihre Lehrinhalte
fokussieren Architekturtheorie, Entwurfstheorie, Grundlagen der Gestaltung sowie Spannweiten
der Moderne. Forschungsschwerpunkte bilden ‚Reflexives Entwerfen', ‚Urbane Architektur' sowie
Ästhetik und Kontextualität von Architektur, Kunst, Stadt und Natur. Als eingeladene Dozentin
und Expertin ist sie für verschiedene nationale und internationale Institutionen tätig. Sie kura-
tiert die jährlichen Symposien ‚Design and Research in Architecture and Landscape' (DARA) und
ist akademische Partnerin im innovativen, internationalen EU-geförderten Forschungsnetzwerk
‚Communities of Tacit Knowledge – TACK', initiiert von zehn führenden akademischen Instituti-
onen in Europa. | Margitta Buchert is professor in 'Architecture and Art 20th/21st Centuries' at
the Faculty of Architecture and Landscape Sciences of Leibniz University Hannover. Her teaching
is focused on architectural theory, design theory, design principles, as well as wingspans of
modernity. The primary fields of her research are 'Reflexive Design', 'Urban Architecture' along
with the aesthetics and contextuality of architecture, arts, cities, and nature. As an invited
lecturer and expert, she works for various national and international institutions. She curates
the annual symposia on 'Design and Research in Architecture and Landscape' (DARA) and is
academic partner in the innovative, international, EU-funded research network 'Communities
of Tacit Knowledge – TACK', initiated by ten leading academic institutions in Europe. Aus-
gewählte Publikationen | Publications include: Landschaftlichkeit als Architekturidee. Lands-
cape-ness as Architectural Idea, Berlin: Jovis 2022; (ed.), Intentionen Reflexiven Entwerfens.
Entwerfen und Forschen in Architektur und Landschaft. Intentions of Reflexive Design. Design
and Research in Architecture and Landscape, Berlin: Jovis 2021; (ed.), Entwerfen gestalten.
Medien der Architekturkonzeption. Shaping design. Media of architectural conception, Berlin:
Jovis 2020; (ed.), Prozesse Reflexiven Entwerfens. Entwerfen und Forschen in Architektur und
Landschaft. Processes of Reflexive Design. Design and research in architecture and landscape,
Berlin: Jovis 2018; Preservation as an origin, in: Maurizio Carta/Sarah Hartmann/Jörg Schröder
(eds.), Creative heritage, Berlin: Jovis 2018, 34–35; Bigness and porosity, in: Sophie Wolfrum
et al. (ed.), Porous city. From metaphor to urban agenda, Berlin u.a.: Birkhäuser 2018, 84–88 243

TOM BIELING ist Professor für Designtheorie an der HfG Offenbach und lehrt Design-wissenschaft an der HAWK Hildesheim. Am Zentrum für Designforschung der HAW Hamburg (2019–2022) vertrat er die Professur für Designtheorie und -forschung. Zuvor Gastprofes-suren an der Universität zu Trient und der GUC Cairo sowie verschiedene Lehraufträge für Designtheorie und -forschung. Am Design Research Lab der Berliner Universität der Künste (2010–2019) leitete er unter anderem das Forschungscluster ‚Social Design'. Zuvor war er wissenschaftlicher Mitarbeiter an den T-Labs / TU Berlin (2007–2010). Er ist Mitherausgeber der Buchreihe ‚Design Meanings' (Mimesis), sowie der BIRD-Reihe (Birkhäuser / De Gruyter), Teil des Board of International Research in Design und Initiator von designforschung.org (seit 2008). Er ist Mitbegründer des Design Research Networks und der Initiative ‚Design promoviert' sowie Mitglied im Wissenschaftlichen Beirat des Instituts Mensch, Ethik und Wissenschaft. | Tom Bieling is professor of design theory at HfG Offenbach University of Art and Design and teaches design studies at HAWK Hildesheim. At the Centre for Design Research at HAW Hamburg (2019–2022), he was professor of 'Design theory and research', previously guest professor at the University of Trento and GUC Cairo and held various teaching positions for design theory and research. At the Design Research Lab of Berlin University of the Arts (2010–2019), he headed the research cluster Social Design, among others. Previously research assistant at T-Labs / TU Berlin (2007–2010). He is co-editor of the book series Design Meanings (Mimesis) and the BIRD series (Birkhäuser / De Gruyter), member of the Board of International Research in Design and initiator of designforschung.org (since 2008). He is co-founder of the Design Research Network and the initiative 'Design promoviert' (PhD in design), as well as a member of the Scientific Advisory Board of the institute Mensch, Ethik und Wissenschaft (Man, ethics, science). Publika-tionen | Publications: Inklusion als Entwurf, Basel: Birkhäuser 2019, Design (&) activism, Mime-sis International 2019, Gender (&) design, Mimesis International 2020. www.tombieling.com

ANDREA CANCLINI ist Dozent an der School of Architecture der Lancaster University und ehemaliger Dozent an der Fakultät für Architektur des Politecnico di Milano für ‚Theorie des zeitgenössischen architektonischen Design' und im ‚Design Studio' sowie Gastprofessor an der Beirut Arab University. Er nahm an mehreren internationalen Konferenzen teil, darunter an der PhD School am Politecnico di Milano, am Courtauld Institute of Art an der University of London, am Istituto Universitario di Architettura di Venezia, an der Katholieke Universiteit Leuven in Brüssel, an der AHRA Conference in der Loughborough University, der Jade Universität

und der ETSAM Madrid. Zudem veröffentlichte er Artikel in von Scopus indizierten Zeitschriften wie ‚The Plan Journal' und ‚aut aut' sowie Buchkapitel und begutachtete Konferenzberichte in Italien, Portugal, der Türkei, China, England, dem Libanon, Schottland und Belgien über sein Hauptforschungsthema: die kulturellen Grundlagen der modernen und zeitgenössischen Architekturkritik. Zu diesen Forschungen gehört auch seine Doktorarbeit am Politecnico di Torino, die sich mit dem Wesen und der Rolle der French Theory im amerikanischen Architekturdiskurs der 1970er Jahre beschäftigt. | Andrea Canclini is lecturing at the School of Architecture at Lancaster University and a former lecturer at the Faculty of Architecture of the Politecnico di Milano, teaching 'Theory in contemporary architectural design' and 'Design studio', and visiting professor at the Beirut Arab University. He participated in several international conferences at, among others, the PhD School in Politecnico di Milano, The Courtauld Institute of Art at the University of London, the Istituto Universitario di Architettura di Venezia, the Katholieke Universiteit Leuven in Brussels, the AHRA Conference in Loughborough University, the Jade Universität, the ETSAM Madrid, and published articles in Scopus-indexed journals such as 'The Plan Journal' and 'aut aut', as well as book chapters and peer-reviewed conference proceedings in Italy, Portugal, Turkey, China, England, Lebanon, Scotland, Belgium about his main research topics: the cultural basis of modern and contemporary architectural criticism. His research includes his PhD dissertation at the Politecnico di Torino, which focused on the nature and the role of the French Theory on American architectural discourse during the Seventies.

DIANA GOUVEIA AMARAL ist Architektin, Stadtplanerin und Doktorandin an der Fakultät für Architektur, Kunst und Design der Universität von Minho, Portugal. Seit 2020 ist sie Mitglied der Forschungsgruppe Lab2PT (Laboratory of Landscape, Heritage and Territory) und studiert im internationalen Master of Architecture an der Katholieke Universiteit Leuven in Belgien. Sie verbindet soziale und partizipatorische Projekte unterschiedlicher Größenordnung und Herangehensweisen, wie die Sanierung der von Bränden zerstörten Häuser in Pedrógão, Portugal (2018), oder das staatlich finanzierte Projekt für Architektur mit Kindern ‚Palácio da Imaginação' (2022). Bis 2019 entwickelte sie Stadt- und Mobilitätspläne der Stadt Lissabon, in Zusammenarbeit mit Ateliermob. Von 2019 bis 2021 arbeitete sie bei Bysteel FS im Bereich Fassadentechnik bei internationalen Projekten wie von Richard Rogers. Ihre Doktorarbeit ist eine Begegnung zwischen dem technologischen Ansatz der Fassade und dem städtischen Maßstab: ‚Rethinking collective spaces through the facade element: From formal elements to informality'

(Kollektive Räume durch das Element der Fassade neu denken: Von formalen Elementen zur Informalität) an der U. Minho und der KU Leuven und unterstützt durch nationale Mittel des FCT/PT. Seit 2021 ist sie Mitglied des Promovierendenkollegs der Universität von Minho. | Diana Gouveia Amaral is an architect, urban planner and PhD student at the Faculty of Architecture, Art and Design of the University of Minho, Portugal. She has been a member of the research group Lab2PT (Laboratory of Landscape, Heritage and Territory) since 2020, and is studying in the international Master of Architecture programme at the Katholieke Universiteit Leuven in Belgium. She combines social and participatory projects of different scales and approaches, such as the rehabilitation of houses destroyed by fires in Pedrógão, Portugal (2018) or the state-funded project for architecture with children 'Palácio da Imaginação' (2022). Until 2019, she developed urban and mobility plans for the city of Lisbon, in collaboration with Ateliermob. From 2019 to 2021, she worked at Bysteel FS in façade engineering on international projects by architects such as Richard Rogers. Her PhD thesis is an encounter between the technological approach of the façade and the urban scale: 'Rethinking collective spaces through the façade element: From formal elements to informality' at U. Minho and KU Leuven and supported by national funds from FCT/PT. Since 2021, she has been a member of the Doctoral College of the University of Minho.

VALERIE HOBERG studierte Architektur und Städtebau an der Leibniz Universität Hannover sowie der ENSA Paris Malaquais. Während des Studiums Mitarbeit in unterschiedlichen Architekturbüros und 2014 bis 2019 Entwurfs- und Wettbewerbsarchitektin in Bremen. Seit 2018 freischaffende Illustratorin. Seit 2019 wissenschaftliche Mitarbeiterin an der Abteilung a_ku Architektur und Kunst 20./21. Jahrhundert, Prof. Dr. Margitta Buchert, IGT, FAL, Leibniz Universität Hannover und Architektin und Städtebauerin in der Stadtentwicklung in Bremen. Sie promoviert bei Prof. Dr. Margitta Buchert zum Thema ‚Künstlerische Reflexionen in der Architektur. Eduardo Chillida und Aires Mateus, Ensamble Studio, Smiljan Radic. | Valerie Hoberg studied architecture and urban planning at Leibniz University Hannover and ENSA Paris Malaquais. During her studies, she worked in various architecture offices, and from 2014 to 2019, she was design and competition architect in Bremen. Since 2018, she has worked as a freelance illustrator. Since 2019, assistant researcher and lecturer at the department Architecture and Art 20./21. Century, Prof. Dr. Margitta Buchert, IGTA, Faculty of Architecture and Landscape Sciences, Leibniz University Hannover and worked as an architect and urban planner for the city of Bremen. She is doing her PhD on the subject of 'Art in Architecture. Eduardo Chillida and Aires Mateus, Ensamble Studio,

Smiljan Radic', supervised by Prof. Dr. Margitta Buchert. Publikationen | Publications: Entfremdende Interpretationen. Estranging interpretations, in: Margitta Buchert (ed.), Intentionen Reflexiven Entwerfens. Intentions of Reflexive Design. Entwerfen und Forschen in Architektur und Landschaft. Design and research in architecture and landscape, Berlin: jovis 2021, 122–137; Handzeichnung. Hand drawing, in: Margitta Buchert (ed.), Entwerfen gestalten. Shaping design. Medien der Architekturkonzeption. Media of architectural conception, Berlin: jovis 2020, 38–53; Fragen, nicht Antworten. Die Kunst und der Raum von Martin Heidegger, in: Margitta Buchert (ed.): Das besondere Buch. Architektur Theorie Praxis, Hannover: LUH 2019, 55–64

S U S A N J E B R I N I ist Architektin, Bühnenbildnerin, Mezzosopranistin und studierte Architektur an der Leibniz Universität Hannover sowie Opern- und Konzertgesang bei Prof. Charlotte Lehmann. Parallel arbeitete sie bereits als Bühnen- und Kostümbildnerin an der Staatsoper Hannover. Derzeit promoviert sie bei Prof. Dr. Margitta Buchert zum Thema Raum und Musik: ‚Studien zu einer ganzheitlichen Raumwahrnehmung'. Sie entwickelt Raumkonzepte und Konzertformate, die sich insbesondere mit dem Rezeptionsverhalten von Raum- und Musikwahrnehmung auseinandersetzen. Eine ihrer Produktionen wurde mit dem Kulturpreis pro visio prämiert. Mit ihrem Ensemble trio.s gewann sie 1. Preise beim Wettbewerb #LIEDINNOVATION Rhonefestival Schweiz, beim IOAC Trossingen sowie beim Festival ‚Klassik in der Altstadt' und war Stipendiatin der Yehudi Menuhin Stiftung LiveMusicNow e.V. Hannover. Engagements als Sängerin: u.a. Ruhrtriennale, Podium Festival Esslingen, Oper Frankfurt, Semperoper, Staatsoper Hamburg, Staatsoper Hannover, Nationaltheater Mannheim, Euro Classic Festival Zweibrücken, ChorWerkRuhr und Solistenensemble Spinario, Radialsystem Berlin, West-Östlicher Divan Salzburg, MdM Salzburg, Beethovenfest (Bundeskunsthalle Bonn in Zusammenarbeit mit dem Freyer Ensemble Berlin). | Susan Jebrini is an architect, scenographer, mezzo-soprano and studied architecture at Leibniz University Hannover as well as voice and opera with Prof. Charlotte Lehmann. During her studies, she worked as a stage and costume designer at the Hanover State Opera. She is currently pursuing a PhD with Prof. Dr. Margitta Buchert on the subject of space and music: 'Studies on a holistic perception of space'. She develops spatial concepts and concert formats that focus on the reception of space and music perception. One of her productions was awarded the pro visio cultural prize. With her ensemble trio.s she won 1st prizes at the competition #LIEDINNOVATION Rhonefestival Switzerland, at the IOAC Trossingen as well as at the festival 'Klassik in der Altstadt' and was a scholarship holder of the Yehudi Menuhin

Foundation LiveMusicNow e.V. Hannover. Engagements as a singer: Ruhrtriennale, Podium Festival Esslingen, Oper Frankfurt, Semperoper, Staatsoper Hamburg, Staatsoper Hannover, Nationaltheater Mannheim, Euro Classic Festival Zweibrücken, ChorWerkRuhr and Solistenensemble Spinario, Radialsystem Berlin, West-Östlicher Divan Salzburg, MdM Salzburg, Beethovenfest (Bundeskunsthalle Bonn in collaboration with the Freyer Ensemble Berlin), among others.

A N D R E A S   L E C H N E R ist assoziierter Professor an der Architekturfakultät der TU Graz und führt sein eigenes Architekturbüro. Er studierte an der TU Graz und arbeitete nach mehreren Studienaufenthalten in Los Angeles in Büros in Berlin, Tokio und Wien. An der TU Graz war er von 2009 bis 2011 Universitätsassistent und promovierte 2009 mit einer Arbeit zu den Geschäftsbauten von Luxuskonzernen auf der Tokioter Omotesando-dori. Er war Gastforscher an der Università IUAV di Venezia und der Royal Danish Academy of Fine Arts in Kopenhagen sowie Vortragender bzw. Gastprofessor in Kopenhagen, Genua, Hamburg, Innsbruck und Istanbul. Er gewann den ersten Preis bei Europan 10 am Standort Graz und nahm an der zweiten Istanbul Design Biennial 2014 und der 15. Architekturbiennale 2016 in Venedig teil. Seine Habilitation wurde 2018 als ‚Entwurf einer architektonischen Gebäudelehre' publiziert und ausgezeichnet. Die zweite überarbeite deutsche Auflage wurde 2021 gemeinsam mit der ersten englischen Auflage unter dem Titel ‚Design thinking - Blueprint for an architecture of typology' veröffentlicht. Als wissenschaftlicher Autor und Gutachter ist er auch Mitherausgeber des zweisprachigen Architekturmagazins GAM und leitet ein dreijähriges, von der österreichischen FFG gefördertes Forschungsprojekt zu ‚Counterintuitive typologies'. Er ist Mitglied der Grazer Altstadt-Sachverständigenkommission und der Kammer der Architekten und Ingenieurkonsulenten. | Andreas Lechner is associate professor at the Institute of Design and Building Typology at Graz University of Technology and founded his architecture design and research studio in 2009. He studied at TU Graz and, after formative study stays in Los Angeles, worked as an architect at offices in Berlin, Tokyo and Vienna. At TU Graz, he was assistant professor from 2007 to 2011 and obtained a doctorate in 2009. He was a visiting researcher at the Università Iuav di Venezia and the Royal Danish Academy of Fine Arts in Copenhagen and held lectures and visiting professorships in Copenhagen, Genoa, Hamburg, Istanbul and Innsbruck. He won first prize at Europan 10 and participated in the second Istanbul Design Biennial 2014 and the 15th Venice Architecture Biennale 2016. His habilitation thesis was published

as awards-winning 'Entwurf einer architektonischen Gebäudelehre' (Draft of an architectural building theory, 2018). The second and revised German edition is published together with its English version titled 'Design thinking – Blueprint for an architecture of typology' (2021). As scholarly author and reviewer, he is also co-editor of the bilingual peer-reviewed GAM Architecture Magazine and is leading a three-year 'Counterintuitive building types' research project funded by the Austrian Research Promotion Agency. He is a member of the Expert Commission on the Historic Center of Graz and of the Austrian Federal Chamber of Architects and Engineers.

GENNARO POSTIGLIONE ist Professor für Innenarchitektur am Politecnico di Milano, Abteilung DAStU. Seine Forschung fokussiert die Gestaltung von Innenräumen an der Schnittstelle zwischen Menschen, Orten und Praktiken, zwischen Architektur, Ethnografie und materieller Kultur. Dies zeigt sich auch in seiner Forschungstätigkeit, die sich auf die adaptive Wiederverwendung von weniger bedeutendem und vernachlässigtem Kulturerbe konzentriert und ein klares Interesse an der Architektur und ihrer Aufgabe zeigt, auf die Bedürfnisse der Menschen zu reagieren und gleichzeitig über die eigenen Grundsätze der Disziplin zu reflektieren. Dies gilt auch für seine aktuelle Forschungsarbeit ‚Typology affordances in architecture' (mit Andreas Lechner, TU Graz), in der er die Gleichwertigkeit zwischen Idee und Ideal der Familie und den Haustypologien und gleichzeitig das Paradigma des Funktionalismus in der Architektur hinterfragt. Er ist Mitglied des Redaktionsbeirats der Zeitschrift ‚AREA', des Peer Review-Journals 'Amps' und des Beirats des Peer-Review-Journals ‚Interiors'. Er war PI in mehreren nationalen und europäischen Forschungsprojekten wie ‚AWLM – The Atlantic Wall Linear Museum' (2005–2006), MeLA – Museum and Libraries in the Age of Migrations (2011–2015), ‚ReCall - European Conflict Archaeological Landscape Reappropriation' (2012–2014), ‚TT – Transatlantic Transfer: the Italian presence in post-war America' (2020–2023). | Gennaro Postiglione is professor of interior architecture at Politecnico di Milano, DAStU Department. His research focuses on interiors culture at the interface of people, places and practices, crossing architecture, ethnography and material culture. This also nourishes his research by design activity focused on the adaptive reuse of minor and neglected heritage, showing a clear interest in architecture and its task of responding to people's needs while reflecting on the discipline's own principles. This is also the case for his current research on 'Typology affordances in architecture' (with Andreas Lechner, TU Graz), questioning the equivalence between

the idea(l) of family and the house typologies and, at the same time, the paradigm of functionalism in architecture. He is a member of the editorial board of the 'AREA' magazine, the peer-reviewed journal 'Amps', and is a member of the advisory board of the peer-reviewed journal 'Interiors'. He has been PI in several national and European research projects such as AWLM – The Atlantic Wall Linear Museum (2005–06), MeLA – Museum and Libraries in the Age of Migrations (2011–15), ReCall – European Conflict Archaeological Landscape Reappropriation (2012–14), TT – Transatlantic Transfer: the Italian presence in Post-war America (2020–23).

MARTIN PROMINSKI ist Professor für ,Entwerfen urbaner Landschaften' an der Leibniz Universität Hannover. 2004 Promotion ,Landschaft entwerfen', bei Prof. Loidl, TU Berlin. Von 2003 bis 2008 Juniorprofessur ,Theorie aktueller Landschaftsarchitektur' an der Leibniz Universität Hannover. Mitgründer des Journal of Landscape Architecture und bis 2010 dessen Herausgeber. Mitglied im STUDIO URBANE LANDSCHAFTEN, einer interdisziplinären Plattform für Forschung, Praxis und Lehre. Mitgründer der ,Sino-German Cooperation Group on Urbanization and Locality Research' mit Prof. Fang Wang, Universität Peking. Mitgründer von mesh Landschaftsarchitekten, Hannover/Tokyo 2018. Seine Forschungsthemen sind biodiversitätsfördernde Entwurfsstrategien, Potenziale entwerfender Forschung sowie neue Konzepte von Natur und Entwerfen im Anthropozän. Ausgewählte Publikationen: Design research for urban landscapes: Theories and methods, Hrsg. mit Hille von Seggern, 2019; Water-related urbanization and locality: Protecting, planning and designing urban water environments in a sustainable way, Hrsg. mit Fang Wang, 2020; River. Space. Design., mit Antje Stokman et al., 2017. | Martin Prominski is professor in 'Designing urban landscapes' at Leibniz University Hannover. PhD 'Landschaft Entwerfen, (Designing landscape) with Prof. Loidl at TU Berlin in 2004. 2003–2008 junior professor of 'Theory of contemporary landscape architecture' at Leibniz University Hannover. Co-founder of the Journal of Landscape Architecture (JoLA) in 2006 and editor until 2010. Member of the STUDIO URBANE LANDSCHAFTEN, an interdisciplinary platform for research, practice and teaching on urban landscapes. Co-founder of the

'Sino-German Cooperation Group on Urbanization and Locality Research' together with Peking University (with Prof. Fang WANG) in 2016. Co-founder of mesh landscape architects, Hannover/Tokyo in 2018. His current research focuses on design research strategies, qualification of urban landscapes and concepts of nature and culture in the anthropocene. Publications include Design research for urban landscapes, ed. with Hille von Seggern, 2019, River. space. design., with Antje Stokman et al., 2017; Water-related urbanization and locality: Protecting, planning and designing urban water environments in a sustainable way, ed. with Fang Wang, 2020.

SARAH WEHMEYER studierte Architektur an der Leibniz Universität Hannover und arbeitete in Architekturbüros in Münster, Hannover und Winterthur (CH). Nach dem Masterabschluss 2015 Zusammenarbeit mit Römeth BDA . Wagener Architekten in Hannover, mit dem BDA sowie wissenschaftliche Mitarbeiterin und Dozentin in der Abteilung a_ku (Architektur und Kunst 20./21. Jahrhundert), IGTA, Fakultät für Architektur und Landschaft, Leibniz Universität Hannover. Dissertation zum Thema 'Collage als Praktik forschenden Entwerfens' unter der Betreuung von Prof. Dr. Margitta Buchert. | Sarah Wehmeyer studied architecture at Leibniz University Hannover and worked in architectural practices in Münster, Hanover and Winterthur (CH). After the Master's degree in 2015 cooperation with Römeth BDA. Wagener Architects in Hanover BDA, as well as engagement as scientific assistant and lecturer in the department a_ku (Architecture + Art 20th/21st century), IGTA, Faculty of Architecture and Landscape Sciences, Leibniz University Hannover. Dissertation on 'Collage as practice of research-orientated design', supervised by Prof. Dr. Margitta Buchert. Veröffentlichungen | Publications: Collage-based research and design, in: TUM (ed.) Dimensions of architectural knowledge, Journal Ausgabe 1: Research perspectives in architecture, Bielefeld: transcript 2021; Collage, in: Margitta Buchert (ed.), Entwerfen gestalten. Shaping design. Medien der Architekturkonzeption. Media of architectural conception, Berlin: Jovis 2020, 202–218; Produktive Negationen entdecken. Zur Ästhetik des Hässlichen von Karl Rosenkranz, in: Margitta Buchert (ed.), Das besondere Buch. Architektur Theorie Praxis, Hannover: LUH 2019, 43–52

REFERENZEN REFERENCES

ZITATE INDEX OF CITATIONS

INTRO Alex F. Osborn, Creativity, The International Center for Creativity Studies New York, auf: https://creativity7.wixsite.com/alexosborn/quotes///23.9.2020 WISSENSRÄUME Gilles Deleuze, Foucault, Frankfurt a. M.: Suhrkamp 2013, 34 TYPEN VON TYPEN Enrico Coen, The art of genes. How organisms make themselves, Oxford 1999, 19 ZUKUNFTSENTWÜRFE Nelson Goodman, Weisen der Welterzeugung, Frankfurt a. M. 1991, 18 OUTRO Rainer Maria Rilke, Duineser Elegien, Leipzig: Insel 1923, 19 (Vierte Elegie)

ABBILDUNGEN INDEX OF ILLUSTRATIONS

BIELING 1–7 Emine Yorganci CANCLINI 1–7 © Courtesy of Hiroshi Hara + ATELIER Φ and | und Gendaikika-kushitsu Publishers, Tokyo 8–9 © Courtesy of Hiroshi Hara + ATELIER Φ 10 © Kakidai, Umeda Sky Building (Kita-ku, Osaka City, Osaka Prefecture), licensed under CC BY-SA 4.0, https://commons.wikimedia.org/wiki/File:2018_Umeda_Sky_Building.jpg 11 © Courtesy of b.mate26, https://www.instagram.com/p/Ch6tdpCup1H/, 7.9.2022 GOUVEIA 1 Soldier and laughing girl, circa 1657, Johannes Vermeer 2 Diana Araújo 3 © Photo courtesy of Philippe Ruault 4 Salomé Macedo 5–8, 10–12 Diana Gouveia Amaral 9 Diana Gouveia Amaral, Hashir Ahmad HOBERG 1, 3–9, 11–13 © Ensamble Studio 2, 10 Architecture: © Ensamble Studio, photo: Valerie Hoberg JEBRINI 1, 3, 9 © Susan Jebrini 10 © Susan Jebrini 2, 6–8, 11 © Susan Jebrini, photo | Foto: Sarah Ubrig 4–5 © Leif Thomsen LECHNER 1, 6 Andreas Lechner 2–5, 7–9 Andreas Lechner, Park Books POSTIGLIONE 1 No Copyright – United States; Rights URI: http://rightsstatements.org/page/NoC-US/1.0/, https://dome.mit.edu/handle/1721.3/21280 2, 5–9 Gennaro Postiglione 3 Courtesy of Smithson Family Collection, Foto | photo: David Casino 4 © Courtesy of OASE Journal 10 © Courtesy of Per Olaf Fjeld PROMINSKI 1 Martin Prominski/Felix Brennecke 2 Eva Liebig/Dag-Ole Ziebell 3 David Kreis 4 Martin Prominski WEHMEYER 1 © Bas Princen 2 © Courtesy of Iwan Baan 3, 6–8 Sarah Wehmeyer 4 © Courtesy of OMA 5 © 2022 Rem Koolhaas 9, 12 © Courtesy of OFFICE 10 © Courtesy of Dogma 11 © Courtesy of Tatiana Bilbao Estudio

IMPRESSUM

© 2023 by jovis Verlag GmbH

Das Urheberrecht für die Texte liegt bei den Autor:innen.

Text by kind permission of the authors.

Das Urheberrecht für die Abbildungen liegt bei den Fotograf:innen / Inhaber:innen
der Bildrechte. Die Urheberrechte sind sorgfältig und nach bestem Wissen wiedergegeben;
bitte informieren Sie uns im Fall eines Bildrechteanspruchs.

Copyright for all images resides with the photographers/holders of the picture rights.

The sources and owners of rights are given to the best of our knowledge;
please inform us of any we may have omitted.

Alle Rechte vorbehalten. All rights reserved.

Herausgeberin Editor: Margitta Buchert,
Architektur und Kunst 20./21. Jahrhundert Architecture and Art 20th/21st Centuries,
Leibniz Universität Hannover Leibniz University Hannover,
www.igt-arch.uni-hannover.de/a_ku

Übersetzungen Translations: Lynne Kolar-Thompson, Valerie Hoberg
Gestaltung Design: Margitta Buchert, Julius Krüger
Satz Setting: Julius Krüger, Berlin
Korrektorat Proofreading: Miriam Seifert-Waibel, Bianca Murphy, Valerie Hoberg
Lithografie Lithography: Bild1Druck, Berlin
Druck und Bindung Printing and Binding: GRASPO CZ, a.s., Zlín

Bibliografische Information der Deutschen Bibliothek

Bibliographic information published by Deutsche Nationalbibliothek:

Die Deutsche Nationalbibliothek verzeichnet diese Publikation
in der Deutschen Nationalbibliografie; detaillierte bibliografische
Daten sind im Internet über http://dnb.ddb.de abrufbar.

The Deutsche Nationalbibliothek lists this publication in Deutsche Nationalbibliografie;
detailed bibliographic data are available on the Internet at http//dnb.d-nb.de.

jovis Verlag
Lützowstraße 33
10785 Berlin
www.jovis.de

ISBN 978-3-86859-749-3 (Softcover)
ISBN 978-3-86859-834-6 (PDF)